THE MAKERS OF CHRISTENDOM

General Editor: CHRISTOPHER DAWSON

THE ANGLO-SAXON MISSIONARIES
IN GERMANY

THE MAKERS OF CHRISTENDOM

General Editor: CHRISTOPHER DAWSON

The Anglo-Saxon Missionaries in Germany

Being the Lives of SS. Willibrord, Boniface,
Sturm, Leoba and Lebuin, together with
the Hodoeporicon *of St. Willibald*
and a selection from the corres-
pondence of St. Boniface

19860

TRANSLATED AND EDITED

by

C. H. TALBOT

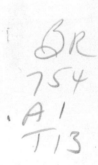

SHEED AND WARD

NEW YORK · 1954

CONTENTS

GENERAL INTRODUCTION

THE TEXTS gathered together in the present volume provide a cross-section of the religious life of the eighth century difficult to parallel elsewhere. Two biographies of the archbishops who initiated the missionary enterprise on the Continent show how their labours transformed the face of Europe within the space of a single generation, whilst the life of one of their disciples illustrates how their work was continued. The correspondence of St. Boniface brings into closer focus the kind of difficulties they encountered and introduces us into the homely atmosphere of their friends, relatives and well-wishers. Two further biographies, one of the abbot of the first monastery to be founded in Germany, the other of the abbess Leoba, give an illuminating picture of the beginnings of monastic life amidst barbarian surroundings and throw light on the characters and attainments of the men and women who embarked on this hazardous adventure. Finally, the description of Willibald's travels through Italy, the Greek archipelago and the Holy Land show the devotion, allied to a spirit of adventure, which animated these early pilgrims and missionaries. Bishops, priests, monks, nuns and simple clerics flit through these pages and tell us their unvarnished tale, which, slight though it may be in certain cases, deeply impresses by contrast with the grim background against which it unfolds.

When the Anglo-Saxon missionaries first set foot on the Continent the series of crises which had riven the Frankish kingdoms for so long had reached their climax, and one family, the Carolings, was in the ascendant. The vast Merovingian kingdom, which comprised nearly all modern France and most of the German countries (with the exception of the modern Netherlands and north-west Germany), had been torn apart by warring factions amongst the aristocracy; and in the farther eastern territories, like Bavaria and Thuringia, the rulers had become almost independent.

The decisive battle of Tertry in 687 gave the preponderance of power to the more German parts of the kingdom; and during the next four generations, from Pepin II to Charles the Great, a great period of reconstruction was to follow, with a strong central government re-establishing the frontiers and incorporating into one kingdom all the loose units of the independent tribes.

The Church in these lands had suffered greatly during the years of struggle. The influence of the Papacy had always been very small because the king exercised complete control over the choice and installation of bishops, but with the decay of royal power the tendency of the Church to become territorial became intensified and bishoprics were in danger of becoming the proprietary apanages of aristocratic families. Bishops, who for the most part belonged to these families, became involved in political struggles, and their installation or expulsion was decided on purely secular considerations. As a result, ecclesiastical organization broke down, ecclesiastical provinces ceased to exist and Church discipline could not be enforced. The education of the clergy fell into complete neglect, and the instruction of the people suffered.

Owing to the superficial nature of the conversion of the Franks, many of whom had accepted Christianity from a feeling of loyalty to their chiefs, paganism lingered on: and whilst practising an attenuated and sometimes perverted type of Christianity, they persisted in their cult of the old gods. The real work of instruction, therefore, still remained to be done. The missionary efforts of the Frankish Church were small, unsustained, and too fitful to cope with the enormous difficulties to be faced. The Irish, under Columbanus, were earlier in the field and at first enjoyed unprecedented success. From Luxeuil, where their monastery was situated, they spread their influence far and wide, but their singular views on the observance of Easter and the form of the tonsure, their independence of local bishops and Columbanus's outspoken denunciations of the morals at court, made their position untenable and they were forced to depart. Round the lake of Constance, where the Abbey of St. Gall still stands as a reminder of their activities, and at Bobbio, in northern Italy, where their learning shone with undimmed lustre throughout the Middle Ages, their labours were of a more enduring character; but, on the whole, their practice of consecrating bishops with no fixed responsibilities, no jurisdiction, no ties and no superiors, except the abbot of the monastery to which they were attached, was not conducive to the establishment of Christianity on a lasting basis amongst the pagan population. Lofty ascetic ideals and burning missionary zeal were not enough. Too much depended upon the personal character of the preacher, so that when the first enthusiasm had spent its force the itinerant missionary too often left his converts to fend for themselves. To organize their groups of people into parishes, to establish bishoprics, to enlist the support of courts and kings, so that high and low, rulers and subjects, could be knit into compact Christian units, did not enter into their scheme of evangelization. Even the monasteries which had accepted the Rule of Columbanus and in which a number of Irish monks could always be found gradually lost their early character: the discipline was too severe; the application of the rule was left too much to the whim of the superior, and the spirit of intransigence, which was so marked a feature of the Irish missionaries, repelled those whom a kindlier attitude might have attracted. As a result, the Benedictine Rule, which was more adaptable, more " discreet " in the demands it made upon its subjects, was first introduced to modify the excessive asceticism of the Celtic monks and soon succeeded in eliminating it altogether. Thus by the time the Anglo-Saxon missionaries arrived on the scene the work of conversion in most parts had to be begun afresh. The memory of the early Irish saints was still alive, but the fruits of their labours had either disappeared or been interwoven with pagan practices and superstitions.

At the same time as Columbanus was reviving monasticism among the Franks St. Augustine was preaching the faith in England. Though the success of his mission was local (for the north of England was evangelized by the Irish from Iona), the results were far-reaching and permanent, for the Church in southern England was founded, not by wandering preachers whipping up a feverish enthusiasm among a heathen population but by diplomats, lawyers and architects, who wove Christianity into the framework of the State, and in so doing, strengthened it and gave it a chance of development. Augustine's work was political as well as religious; and by establishing a hierarchy subject to Rome, organizing systematic administration, and inculcating a respect for written law, he ensured that his work would endure even when he and his companions were no longer there. Pope Gregory, who had sent him, planned and supported the whole enterprise with admirable statesmanship. On all questions that did not involve faith or morals he insisted that the process of conversion should be carried on and facilitated by a spirit of compromise. Heathen temples which had long been centres of public worship were to be adapted and consecrated to Christian uses; pagan festivals were to be arranged to coincide with Christian feast days; and any ritual, whether Roman, Gallican or Irish, was to be adopted, if it appealed to English taste and custom. In this way conversion to the Christian faith did not involve a disruption of the English settled mode of life; it was less likely to lead to violent reactions and to a complete reversion to the past as soon as the early fervour had cooled down. On the other hand, there was to be strict discipline among the clergy. Each man was required to stay and work in the place to which he was appointed, and the tradition of wandering preachers was brought to an end. The country was to be organized into permanent provinces, dioceses and parishes; bishops and priests were to be bound to particular districts, and within this framework national unity and local self-government could equally take root. This well-devised and far-sighted plan was to have consequences that reach down to our own day.

Its immediate results were, by comparison, insignificant, and it was not till much later in the century that the full flowering of the scheme could be observed. When the Synod of Whitby met in 663 for the ostensible purpose of composing the differences between the Celtic and Roman methods of dating Easter the debate really resolved itself into the question of which concept of the Church was to prevail: whether it should be monastic, segregated from the world, loosely bound together by personalities of outstanding sanctity and scholarship, or whether it should be a highly organized society with the Pope as its central authority, using its diplomatic resources to bind the secular rulers to its religious purposes, and firmly united in one discipline by able lawgivers and administrators. Both conceptions were necessary for the healthy continuance of the Church; but it was the Roman view, upheld by St. Wilfrid of York and his party, which prevailed. Thenceforward statesmanship, organization, discipline were to be the keynotes in the conduct of ecclesiastical affairs. The immediate result was a generation of scholars, saints and prelates, through whose labours the face of England, and later the face of Europe, was to be completely transformed.

Wilfrid's most important achievement was the impetus and support he gave to the foundation of monasteries following the Benedictine Rule. The organization of the country on the parish system, which formed the backbone of the Church, could not long endure without monasteries as centres of learning, where the clergy could be trained and educated. Wilfrid's activities in this field were decisive, for he not only incorporated them into the general plan of ecclesiastical organization but imbued them with his own ideas of international relations.

One of the most interesting features of the conversion of the northern peoples is that the Anglo-Saxon missionaries were drawn for the most part from these monastic houses. Though missionary work was not an essential part of the Benedictine Rule, the sending of Augustine from his monastery on the Celian Hill to the conversion of England had consecrated it on the highest authority. Among the Irish monks, the *peregrinatio pro Christo*, voluntary exile for the purpose of spreading the Gospel, had always been an accepted principle of the monastic vocation, and the blending of the two traditions, Roman and Irish, had, no doubt, a great deal to do with the impulse which led so many monks and nuns to seek their salvation in apostolic work among the pagans of the Continent. But the methods of evangelization were different and bore the stamp of the newer ideas of order and discipline which formed the basis of ecclesiastical policy in England.

A steady and vigorous growth had characterized Anglo-Saxon monasticism, and the first half of the eighth century saw it reach the highest point of its development and influence. Bede's description of life in the monasteries, with their regular but simple liturgical psalmody, alternating with reading and study, domestic work, the practice of the arts and crafts and even heavy agricultural labour, gives us a fair idea of the discipline, the sense of order, the appreciation of tradition and the feeling of stability that prevailed there. Hand in hand with this went a passion for learning, fostered by Benet Biscop in the north and by Aldhelm of Malmesbury in the south, which was to make England supreme in the field of scholarship. Though the scope of studies was not large—grammar, verse, the Scriptures and canon law—the enthusiasm and the spirit of emulation was such that gradually the standard of scholarship was raised and the search for new texts and the consequent multiplication of books grew with surprising rapidity. The finest fruits of Eastern and Latin scholarship brought by Theodore to Canterbury and by Benet Biscop to Wearmouth and Jarrow were copied and exchanged, and monasteries vied with one another in building up and enriching their libraries.

The prominent part played by women in this intellectual renaissance is remarkable. We learn from the biography of St. Boniface that nuns as well as monks attended his lectures, whilst those who were prevented by distance from receiving his direct instruction took what might be called a correspondence course and " conned the Scriptures daily page by page ". Their literary attainments were considerable, comparing favourably with those of the men, if we except Bede and others of the same rank; and the biography of Leoba tells us that she was so deeply versed in the Scriptures, the writings of the Fathers and canon law that she was consulted by abbots, bishops and kings. It is no coincidence that of all the companions who surrounded Willibald in his bishopric of Eichstatt it was a nun who undertook the task of recording for posterity the description of his journeys and the founding of his diocese. The degree of freedom and independence which these nuns enjoyed, the influence they were able to exert and the confidence they inspired in such men as Boniface, Lull and Willibald, is no small tribute to the strength of the monastic tradition in which they were trained. Never, perhaps, has there been an age in which religious women exercised such great power, for it is extremely doubtful if even Boniface without their help would have enjoyed the measure of success in every field which attended his labours.

If we are to judge by some of his letters and by the names which appear in the fly-leaves and margins of manuscripts we must conclude that the production of books, on which he largely depended for personal study and for the training of others, was their particular province. Certain it is that they played an important rôle in the education and the conversion of the heathen, and Saint Boniface's request that Leoba should lie beside him in his tomb is at once a symbol of it and a proof.

The astonishing results that followed the Anglo-Saxon missionary enterprise must have made it quite clear that organization, discipline, corporate effort and a certain degree of stability, the methods advocated by Wilfrid's Roman party, were the indispensable requisites for lasting success in establishing the faith among the pagan tribes of the North, and therefore as soon as Boniface found the right man and a suitable place he began to arrange for the introduction of monastic life into Germany. As in his native country the fostering of monastic vocations followed upon the organization of dioceses and parishes, so also in Germany it was to follow on the establishment of the hierarchy and the settling of priests in the country districts. Not only would the presence of such a centre of spiritual and intellectual life be a steadying influence on the vacillating and warlike barbarians, but it would serve also as a nursery and training ground for future missionaries. The steady stream of recruits coming from England, " the monks, clerics, scholars and writers ", who had shared in his labours, could not be relied upon to continue after his death. The future stability of his work and the gradual spreading of monastic life to all the parts of his vast missionary territory could be ensured only by fostering vocations among the natives. It is significant that his first step in this project was to send Sturm and Leoba to Rome and Monte Cassino to learn there the customs and traditions which prevailed in the Benedictine houses. The consequent foundation of the Abbey of Fulda resulted in a complete transformation of cultural conditions in Germany, and the spreading of its sphere of influence was as remarkable as it was extensive. From its school came forth a long line of scholars, of whom Rhabanus Maurus was the first, and to its training may be traced Walafrid Strabo and the school of Reichenau, Lupus and the school of Ferrières, Heiric, Remi and the school of Rheims, and many others. That such far-reaching consequences were due to a small band of Anglo-Saxon monks is a remarkable testimony to the vigour of the root from which it all stemmed.

The changes brought about by Willibrord, Boniface and their companions on the Continent were not solely of a cultural nature. They extended also to ecclesiastical organization and to canon law. By introducing the discipline that prevailed in their native country to the new converted provinces and then extending it to the entire Frankish kingdom, they ensured that the central authority of Rome should be everywhere paramount.

The system of ecclesiastical provinces, in which all the bishops should be subject to an archbishop appointed by the Holy See, the custom of receiving the pallium before exercising archiepiscopal jurisdiction, the appointment of *chorepiscopi*, or coadjutor bishops, to assist in the work of administering an unwieldy province—all these and other practices, later to be taken as normal, were introduced to the Continent by the Anglo-Saxon missionaries. Equally important was the principle of attaching clergy to clearly defined districts and forbidding them to leave without permission, whilst the monasteries and their schools were an essential instrument in the transition from the primitive conception of the Church as a network of communities of " saints " to the medieval conception of the Church as an institution for preaching and ministering to the people in every land. The policy of carrying out ecclesiastical reform on a large scale with the support of the secular power, the first known instance in the West of the bringing together of the imperial and papal power, was also the direct result of their intervention.

But the most momentous achievement was the instilling into the Frankish and German churchmen of a lively attachment to Rome and a firm belief in the unity of the universal Church. The idea of a territorial Church, which had held sway in the Frankish kingdoms for so long and which seemed likely to grow in Germany under the influence of the Irish, was decisively suppressed. The separation of Church and State and the recognition of the supremacy of each within its own sphere, which has largely conditioned the civilization of western Europe, was brought about at this time, and the freedom of worship, freedom to teach and the right to economic independence, can be traced through the Anglo-Saxon missionaries to the policy of Theodore of Canterbury and ultimately of Gregory the Great. The great turning-point, therefore, in the history of the West goes back to the conversion of England.

These, then, are some of the points of interest raised by the documents translated in this book. The writers, occasionally, may be naïve, at other times exasperatingly silent or ambiguous, but what they have to tell us is of the highest importance and fraught with far-reaching consequences for the history of the Western Church.

What is the historical value of these accounts? To a modern reader many of them may seem to be lacking in solid historical facts. This is, to a certain extent, true; but we must bear in mind that the Middle Ages was heir to the classical tradition, in which the boundary-line between fact and fiction was narrow. The historian was something between a rhetorician and a poet, consequently there was a perpetual confusion between history and legend. For the Middle Ages, history was what one told you, what you read in books. As a result, hagiographers were concerned not so much with the sifting of evidence as with the taste of their readers and the production of " elegant literary compositions ". For the most part such writings were meant to edify rather than instruct; and as they were read out at liturgical services or in the monastic refectory, the insistence on miracles, sometimes of a trivial nature, is apt to be disconcerting. The space allotted to them is certainly disproportionate compared to the space allowed for other details. These faults, common to all hagiographical writings, should not, however, blind the reader to the solid substratum of truth that lies beneath these embellishments: the sympathetic eye will discern the honest attempts of the authors in this book to record historical facts and to base their accounts on the testimony of eye-witnesses or on the notes of those who came into close contact with their heroes. In the case of the nun of Heidenheim, who wrote down the travels of Willibald, we can even detect in the change of the pronouns from " they " to " we " the authentic words of Willibald himself. The correspondence of St. Boniface naturally escapes this criticism. Here we see depicted in stark reality all the difficulties that beset the missionary in his day-to-day struggle with the powers of evil: worldly bishops, dissolute priests, pagan superstition, problems of doctrine, questions of discipline, political rivalries. The penitentials of Columbanus and Theodore take on a new significance in the light of Boniface's reports. Without elaboration or exaggeration, with no hint of weariness or self-pity, he records conditions as they affected the progress of his work, conscious only of his obligation to fulfil the promises made at his consecration over the tomb of St. Peter and of his determination to remain a loyal servant of the Holy See. These letters, factual, unaffected and utterly sincere, supply the means not only of controlling the statements made by the writers of the biographies, but also of bringing into clear relief the vague and non-committal phrases in which they tell their tale. We begin to realize that their simplicity and ingenuousness conceal heroism of a high order, all the more admirable because of its utter selflessness. The gigantic task of bringing hordes of fierce heathens to accept the faith was to them merely a task of ordinary dimensions, accomplished by dogged perseverance and hardly worthy of being described in detail. What was achieved appeared to them of less consequence than the sanctity of the person who achieved it. That is one of the reasons, perhaps, why we are given so few details of the problems they had to face and so many stories of the miracles they performed. This atmosphere of reserve, therefore, which surrounds their work of evangelization gives an added weight to what they have to tell us. It is a guarantee of their essential veracity. It matters little if some of the miracles have been transferred from one saint's life to another, or if some of the virtues with which they are credited sound as if they had been taken bodily from a list in a catechism. This is proof of admiration rather than of imagination.

What is surprising, considering the stature of the saints here portrayed and the importance of the work they accomplished, is the comparative neglect into which they have fallen. People who can talk eloquently about Spanish, French or Italian saints and can enthuse about post-tridentine personalities or present-day *beati* are quite dumb when confronted with Leoba or Lebuin. The names of Willibrord and Boniface are perhaps more familiar, because " they sound so amusing "; but of the characters that lie behind these names and of their significance for the growth of Christendom they are woefully ignorant. The reason lies, maybe, in the fact that their activities were concerned with countries not our own, and their history belongs more essentially to the lands of which they were the apostles. Besides, they lived a long time ago, and the problems they had to face seem so far distant from the conditions in which we live to-day.

A more reasonable explanation seems to be that in certain quarters a lack of attention has been deliberately fostered; for whereas the lives of the Irish and Frankish saints of the same period may be made to yield arguments (of dubious validity) to prove their independence of and antagonism to the Church of Rome, the words and actions of the Anglo-Saxon missionaries are incontestable proof that this country, from the first moment of its conversion, was bound by strong and indissoluble ties to the Holy See. That was their reputation at the time among the other Christian peoples of Europe, that was the source of their greatness and their strength, and that proved to be the root cause of their overwhelming impact on the heathen population of the West. It will be no small gain if this truth, so long kept out of view, becomes better known through the perusal of the pages that follow.

BIBLIOGRAPHY

The Life of Willibrord, written by Alcuin, was first published by Surius in his collection *De Probatis Sanctorum Historiis* (Cologne, 1575), vol. vi, pp. 127–37. The critical edition was prepared by W. Wattenbach, *Monumenta Alcuiniana*, in the series *Bibliotheca Rerum Germanicarum*, edited by Ph. Jaffé. It appeared in Berlin in 1873 as the sixth volume of the collection (pp. 39–61), but was superseded by W. Levison's text in *Scriptores Rerum Merovingicarum*, vii, pp. 81–141. An English translation was made by A. Grieve, *Willibrord, Missionary in the Netherlands* (London, 1923), in the collection *Lives of Early and Medieval Missionaries*, published by the S.P.C.K.

The first edition of the Life of St. Boniface by Willibald was made by Henricus Canisius, *Sancti Willibaldi Eichstadiani Liber de Vita S. Bonifacii Martyris, Germanorum Apostoli*, etc., at Ingoldstadt in 1603. The critical edition was prepared by W. Levison, *Viti Bonifatii auctore Willibaldo*, for *Scriptores Rerum Germanicarum* (Hanover, 1905), pp. 1–57. An English translation, *The Life of Saint Boniface by Willibald* was made by George Washington Robinson in 1916 and published at Cambridge, U.S.A. The best edition of the correspondence is that of M. Tangl, *Die Briefe des heiligen Bonifatius* (1916). Several translations have appeared: *The English Correspondence of Saint Boniface*, by Edward Kylie (London, 1911); *Letters of Saint Boniface to the Popes and Others*, by George Washington Robinson, in *Papers of the American Society of Church History* (1923), second series, vii, pp. 157–86; *The Letters of Saint Boniface*, by Ephraim Emerton (New York, 1940), in the series, *Records of Civilization*, vol. 31.

The *Hodoeporicon* first appeared in Dom Mabillon's *Acta Sanctorum Ordinis Sancti Benedicti*, vol. iii, 2, pp. 367 seq. The best edition is that of Holder-Egger in *Monumenta Germaniae Historica Scriptores*, vol. xv, 1, pp. 80–117. An English translation was made by Canon W. R. Brownlow for the *Palestine Pilgrims Text Society* (London, 1895).

The first edition of the Life of St. Sturm came from the hands of Chr. Browerus, *Vita Sancti Sturmi Primi Abbatis Fuldensis*, in *Sidera Germaniae* (Mainz, 1616), pp. 5–24. The critical edition is found in *Monumenta Germaniae Historica, Scriptores*, vol. ii, pp. 366–77. This is, as far as I am aware, the first English translation.

The Life of St. Leoba was first published by Surius, *De Probatis Sanctorum Historiis* (Cologne, 1574), vol. v, pp. 396–406. The best edition, upon which this translation is based, is found in *Monumenta Germaniae Historica, Scriptores*, ed. Waitz (Hanover, 1887), vol. xv, 1, pp. 127–31. There has been no previous complete translation into English of this biography, though Serenus Cressy (*Church History of Brittany*, bk. xxiv, 4) translated much of it.

The Life of St. Lebuin was first published by Surius, vol. vi, pp. 277–86, but this was the text written by Hucbald of St. Amand. A translation of this appeared in Serenus Cressy's *Church History of Brittany*, vol. xxiv, 7. The present text is, however, based on the *Vita Lebuini Antiqua*, edited by A. Hofmeister, *Monumenta Germaniae Historica, Scriptores* (1926–34), vol. xxx, 2, pp. 789–95.

THE LIFE OF ST. WILLIBRORD
BY ALCUIN

The earliest Life of Willibrord, written, as Theofrid, Abbot of Echternach (1083–1100), tells us, by an unlearned Scot (i.e. an Irishman) in a rough and unpolished style, has disappeared, though its contents may be reconstructed from the biography composed by Alcuin, who probably used it as his source.

Alcuin, the author of the present Life, was born in York in 735 and became the master of the school there in 778. Four years later he was appointed head of Charlemagne's school at Aix-la-Chapelle and became a leading member of that select circle who supported the emperor in his efforts to re-educate Europe. In 796 he was removed to Tours and died in 804.

His Life of Willibrord was written at the request of Beornrade, Abbot of Echternach and Archbishop of Sens. As a relative of Willibrord and legal possessor of the Monastery of St. Andrew, founded by Willibrord's father, Wilgils, on a headland overlooking the mouth of the Humber, Alcuin must have undertaken the work as a kind of tribute to his family connections. It is not a particularly impressive piece of writing, sometimes ungrammatical and at all times turgid and rhetorical, but as it was meant to be read at public worship its lack of historical detail and its insistence on Willibrord's miracles may perhaps be excused. He wrote another version in hexameter verse for students at the monastic schools, without, however, adding anything to the material offered here.

Theofrid, mentioned above, also wrote a prose and metrical Life of Willibrord, basing it on Alcuin's material with additions from Bede, the lives of other saints and the Echternach charters. A third Life, written by a presbyter called Echebert, repeats Alcuin's Life, with certain modifications at the beginning and the end.

THE LIFE OF ST. WILLIBRORD
BY ALCUIN

THERE was in the island of Britain, in the province of Northumbria, a certain householder of Saxon descent, whose name was Wilgils, living a devout Christian life together with his wife and family. This fact was later borne out by miraculous events, for after he had given up his worldly career he devoted himself to the monastic life. Not long afterwards, as his zeal for the spiritual life increased, he entered with even more intense fervour on the austere life of a solitary, dwelling in the headlands that are bounded by the North Sea and the river Humber. In a little chapel there, dedicated to St. Andrew, the Apostle of Christ, he served God for many years in fasting, prayer and watching, with the result that he became celebrated for his miracles, and his name was in everyone's mouth. People flocked to him in great numbers, and when they did so he never failed to instruct them with sound advice and the Word of God.

He was held in such high esteem by the king and the nobles of that nation that they made over to him, in perpetual gift, a number of small landed properties that lie near those headlands for the purpose of building there a church to God. In this church the reverend father gathered together a rather small but devout company of those who wished to serve God, and there also, after the many trials of his spiritual labours, going to his reward, his body lies at rest. His successors, who still follow the example of his holiness, are in possession of this church to the present day. It is I, the least of these in merit and the last in time, who am now in charge of this little chapel, which has come to me by lawful succession, and I am writing this account of Willibrord, the holiest of fathers and the wisest of teachers, at the request of you, Bishop Beornrade,[1] who, by the grace of God, have succeeded him in

---

[1] Beornrade, abbot of Willibrord's monastery at Echternach and later Archbishop of Sens.

the episcopate, in the line of family tradition and in the care of those sanctuaries, which, as we know, he built for the glory of God.

Now, in order to relate more fully the facts concerning Willibrord's birth, and recall the signs which show that even whilst he was in his mother's womb he was chosen by God, I shall return to the point where I began. Just as the most holy forerunner of our Lord Jesus Christ, blessed John the Baptist, was sanctified in his mother's womb and preceded Christ, as the morning star precedes the sun and, as the Gospel tells us, was born of devout parents in order to bring salvation to many, so likewise Willibrord, begotten for the salvation of many, was born of devout parents.[1] Wilgils, the venerable man of whom we have already spoken, entered upon the state of matrimony for the sole purpose of bringing into the world a child who should benefit many peoples. Thus it was that his wife, mother of holy Willibrord, beheld, at dead of night whilst she slept, a heavenly vision. It seemed to her as if she saw in the sky the new moon, which, as she watched, slowly increased until it reached the size of the full moon. Whilst she was gazing intently upon it, it fell swiftly into her mouth, and when she had swallowed it her bosom was suffused with light. Filled with fear, she awoke at once and went to recount the dream to a holy priest, who asked her whether during the night on which the vision came to her she had known her husband in the customary way. When she assented, he replied as follows: " The moon which you saw changing from small to great is the son whom you conceived on that night. He will disperse the murky darkness of error with the light of truth, and wherever he goes he will carry with him a heavenly splendour and display the full moon of his perfection. By the brightness of his fame and the beauty of his life he will attract to himself the eyes of multitudes." This interpretation of the dream was borne out by the actual course of events.

When her time was come the woman bore a son, and at his baptism his father gave him the name of Willibrord. As soon as

[1] Willibrord was born, probably, 6 November 658.

the child had reached the age of reason[1] his father gave him to the church at Ripon to be instructed by the brethren there in religious pursuits and sacred learning, so that living in a place where he could see nothing but what was virtuous and hear nothing but what was holy his tender age should be strengthened by sound training and discipline. From his earliest years divine grace enabled him to grow in intelligence and in strength of character, at least as far as was possible at such an age, so that it seemed as if in our day there had been born another Samuel, of whom it was said: " The boy grew up and advanced in favour both with God and with men."

Hence, in the monastery of Ripon, the youth who was to prove a blessing to many received the clerical tonsure[2] and made his profession as a monk, and, trained along with the other youths of that holy and sacred monastery, he was inferior to none in fervour, humility and zeal for study. In fact this highly gifted boy made such progress as the days went by that the development of his intelligence and character so outstripped his tender years that his small and delicate frame harboured the wisdom of ripe old age.

When this youth, as highly endowed with sacred learning as he was with self-control and integrity, reached the twentieth year of his age he felt an urge to pursue a more rigorous mode of life and was stirred with a desire to travel abroad. And because he had heard that schools and learning flourished in Ireland,[3] he was encouraged further by what he was told of the manner of life adopted there by certain holy men, particularly by the blessed

---

[1] This is probably the correct interpretation of the phrase " when he was weaned ". The abbot at this time was most probably St. Wilfrid, the leader of the Roman party which triumphed at the Synod of Whitby, A.D. 664. Willibrord must have served under Wilfrid until 669 when Wilfrid left to take possession of the see of York.

[2] He received the tonsure and made his monastic profession about the age of fifteen; cf. the letter of St. Boniface, Tangl, No. 26.

[3] Though the renown of the Irish schools was well deserved, it does not reflect adversely on the lack of English educational centres. St. Aldhelm of Sherborne complained at the time about students going there and asked: Were there not schools good enough in England? The real reason for going abroad seems to have been the expulsion of St. Wilfrid from the see of York in 678, which led to the voluntary exile of many monks who were in sympathy with him.

bishop Ecgbert,[1] to whom was given the title of Saint, and by Wichtberct,[2] the venerable servant and priest of God, both of whom, for love of Christ, forsook home, fatherland and family and retired to Ireland, where, cut off from the world though close to God, they lived as solitaries enjoying the blessings of heavenly contemplation. The blessed youth wished to imitate the godly life of these men and, after obtaining the consent of his abbot and brethren, hastened quickly across the sea to join the intimate circle of the said fathers, so that by contact with them he might attain the same degree of holiness and possess the same virtues, much as a bee sucks honey from the flowers and stores it up in its honey-comb. There among these masters, eminent both for sanctity and sacred learning, he who was one day to preach to many peoples was trained for twelve years, until he reached the mature age of manhood and the full age of Christ.

Accordingly, in the thirty-third year of his age the fervour of his faith had reached such an intensity that he considered it of little value to labour at his own sanctification unless he could preach the Gospel to others and bring some benefit to them. He had heard that in the northern regions of the world the harvest was great but the labourers few. Thus it was that, in fulfilment of the dream which his mother stated she had seen, Willibrord, fully aware of his own purpose but ignorant as yet of divine pre-ordination, decided to sail for those parts and, if God so willed, to bring the light of the Gospel message to those people who through unbelief had not been stirred by its warmth. So he embarked on a ship, taking with him eleven others who shared his enthusiasm for the faith. Some of these afterwards gained the martyr's crown through their constancy in preaching the Gospel, others were later to become bishops and, after their labours in the holy work of preaching, have since gone to their rest in peace.

---

[1] Ecgbert was Abbot of Rathmelsigi, probably Mellifont in Co. Louth. In 664 he had gone into voluntary exile after the Synod of Whitby, but returned to Iona in 716. He died in 729 at the age of ninety. He had long wanted to evangelize the Saxon peoples on the Continent, but was prevented from doing so by a vision.

[2] Wichtberct was a companion of Ecgbert and had spent many years in Ireland. He went on a mission to Frisia, but, having preached for two years without success, returned to Ireland.

So the man of God, accompanied by his brethren, as we have already said, set sail, and after a successful crossing they moored their ships at the mouth of the Rhine. Then, after they had taken some refreshment, they set out for the Castle of Utrecht, which lies on the bank of the river, where some years afterwards, when by divine favour the faith had increased, Willibrord placed the seat of his bishopric.[1] But as the Frisian people, among whom the fort was situated, and Radbod, their king,[2] still defiled themselves by pagan practices, the man of God thought it wiser to set out for Francia and visit Pippin,[3] the king of that country, a man of immense energy, successful in war and of high moral character. The duke received him with every mark of respect; and as he was unwilling that he and his people should lose the services of so eminent a scholar, he made over to him certain localities within the boundaries of his own realm, where he could uproot idolatrous practices, teach the newly converted people and so fulfil the command of the prophet: " Drive a new furrow and sow no longer among the briars."

After the man of God had systematically visited several localities and carried out the task of evangelization, and when the seed of life watered by the dews of heavenly grace had, through his preaching, borne abundant fruit in many hearts, the aforesaid King of the Franks, highly pleased at Willibrord's burning zeal and the extraordinary growth of the Christian faith, and having in view the still greater propagation of religion, thought it wise to send him to Rome in order that he might be consecrated bishop by Pope Sergius,[4] one of the holiest men of that time. Thus, after receiving the apostolic blessing and mandate and being filled with greater confidence as the Pope's emissary, he would return to preach the Gospel with even greater vigour, according to the

[1] Willibrord's church was built from the ruins of the old Roman camp at Fectio (Vecht).
[2] From the beginning of his reign in 697 Radbod had been antagonistic to anything that savoured of Frankish domination and had ruthlessly destroyed churches and other buildings erected by the Franks.
[3] Pippin II, mayor of the palace of Clovis II. He it was who gave the church at Antwerp, previously the scene of the labours of St. Amand and St. Eloi, to the missionaries for their shelter and support.
[4] Pope Sergius I, 687–701. Alcuin only mentions one journey to Rome, but there were two.

words of the Apostle: " How shall they preach unless they be sent? "

But when the king tried to persuade the man of God to do this he was met by a refusal. Willibrord said that he was not worthy to wield such great authority, and, after enumerating the qualities which St. Paul mentioned to Timothy, his spiritual son, as being essential for a bishop, asserted that he fell far short of such virtues. On his side, the king solemnly urged what the man of God had already humbly declined. At length, moved by the unanimous agreement of his companions, and, what is of more importance, constrained by the divine will, Willibrord acquiesced, anxious to submit to the counsel of many rather than obstinately to follow his own will. Accordingly he set out for Rome with a distinguished company, bearing gifts appropriate to the dignity of the Pope.

Four days before Willibrord arrived in Rome the Apostolic Father had a dream in which he was advised by an angel to receive him with the highest honours, because he had been chosen by God to bring the light of the Gospel to many souls: his purpose in coming to Rome was to receive the dignity of the episcopate, and nothing that he asked for was to be refused. The Apostolic Father, forewarned by this admonition, received him with great joy and showed him every courtesy. And as he discerned in him ardent faith, religious devotion and profound wisdom, he appointed a day suitable for his consecration, when all the people would be assembled together. Then he invited venerable priests to take part in the ceremony, and, in accordance with apostolic tradition and with great solemnity, he publicly consecrated him archbishop in the church of blessed Peter, Prince of the Apostles.[1] At the same time, he called him Clement and invested him with episcopal robes, conferring upon him the sacred pallium as a sign of his office, like Aaron with the ephod. Moreover, whatever he desired or asked for in the way of relics of saints[2] or liturgical vessels the Pope gave him without hesitation, and so, fortified with the

[1] Alcuin has made a mistake. The church meant is St. Cecilia in Trastevere. The day of consecration was 22 November 695.
[2] Several churches still preserve the relics brought back from Rome by Willibrord, e.g. Emmerich and Trèves.

apostolic blessing and loaded with gifts, he was sent back, duly instructed, to his work of preaching the Gospel.

Having received the blessing of the Holy See, the devoted preacher of God's Word returned with increased confidence to the King of the Franks. The king welcomed him with every mark of esteem and then despatched him, armed with his authority to preach the Gospel, more especially in the northern parts of his dominions, where, owing to the scarcity of teachers and the obduracy of the inhabitants, the light of faith shone less brightly. The more clearly the man of God saw the need of overcoming the ignorance and arresting the spiritual famine in these districts, the more vigorously he preached the Word of God. How great was the success which, through the help of divine grace, attended his labours is attested even in these days by the people whom in the cities, villages, and fortified towns he brought to a knowledge of the truth and the worship of almighty God by his holy admonitions. Other evidence is to be found in the churches which he built in each place and in the communities of monks and nuns whom he gathered together in various localities.

The man of God tried also to propagate the Gospel teaching outside the boundaries of the Frankish kingdom. He had the boldness to present himself at the court of Radbod, at that time King of the Frisians and like his subjects, a pagan. Wherever he travelled he proclaimed the Word of God without fear; but though the Frisian king received the man of God in a kind and humble spirit, his heart was hardened against the Word of Life. So when the man of God saw that his efforts were of no avail he turned his missionary course towards the fierce tribes of the Danes. At that time, so we are told, the Danish ruler was Ongendus,[1] a man more savage than any wild beast and harder than stone, who nevertheless, through divine intervention, received the herald of truth with every mark of honour. But when the latter found that the people were steeped in evil practices, abandoned to idolatry and indifferent to any hope of a better life, he chose thirty boys from among them and hastily returned with them to the chosen people of the Franks. On the journey he instructed the youths in the

[1] Ongendus has been identified with Ongentheow of Beowulf.

faith and baptized them, so that if they perished from the long sea voyage or through the ambushes of the savage dwellers of those parts he should suffer no loss in their regard. In this way he desired to anticipate the craft of the devil and to strengthen these redeemed souls by the sacraments of the Lord.

Now whilst this energetic preacher of the Word was pursuing his journey he came to a certain island on the boundary between the Frisians and the Danes, which the people of those parts call Fositeland,[1] after a god named Fosite, whom they worship and whose temples stood there. This place was held by the pagans in such great awe that none of the natives would venture to meddle with any of the cattle that fed there nor with anything else, nor dare they draw water from the spring that bubbled up there except in complete silence. On this island the man of God was driven ashore by a storm and waited for some days until the gale died down and fair weather made it possible to set sail again. He set little store by the superstitious sacredness ascribed to the spot, or by the savage cruelty of the king, who was accustomed to condemn violators of the sacred objects to the most cruel death. Willibrord baptized three persons in the fountain in the name of the Blessed Trinity and gave orders that some of the cattle should be slaughtered as food for his company. When the pagans saw this they expected that the strangers would become mad or be struck with sudden death. Noticing, however, that they suffered no harm, the pagans, terror-stricken and astounded, reported to the king what they had witnessed.

The king was roused to intense fury and had a mind to avenge on the priest of the living God the insults which had been offered to his deities. For three whole days he cast lots three times every day to find out who should die; but as the true God protected his own servants, the lots of death never fell upon Willibrord nor upon any of his company, except in the case of one of the party, who thus won the martyr's crown. The holy man was then summoned before the king and severely upbraided for having violated the king's sanctuary and offered insult to his god. With unruffled calmness the preacher of the Gospel replied: "The object

---

[1] Fositeland or Heligoland.

of your worship, O King, is not a god but a devil, and he holds you ensnared in rank falsehood in order that he may deliver your soul to eternal fire. For there is no God but one, who created heaven and earth, the seas and all that is in them; and those who worship Him in true faith will possess eternal life. As His servant I call upon you this day to renounce the empty and inveterate errors to which your forebears have given their assent and to believe in the one almighty God, our Lord Jesus Christ. Be baptized in the fountain of life and wash away all your sins, so that, forsaking all wickedness and unrighteousness, you may henceforth live as a new man in temperance, justice and holiness. If you do this you will enjoy everlasting glory with God and His saints; but if you spurn me, who set before you the way of life, be assured that with the devil whom you obey you will suffer unending punishment and the flames of hell." At this the king was astonished and replied: " It is clear to me that my threats leave you unmoved and that your words are as uncompromising as your deeds." But although he would not believe the preaching of the truth, he sent back Willibrord with all honour to Pippin, King of the Franks.

The latter was delighted at his return and begged him to persevere in his divinely appointed task of preaching the Word of God and to root out idolatrous practices and sow the good seed in one place after another. This the devoted preacher strove to carry out with characteristic energy. He traversed every part of the country, exhorting the people in cities, villages and forts where he had previously preached the Gospel to remain loyal to the faith and to their good resolutions. And as the number of the faithful increased day by day and a considerable multitude of believers came to the knowledge of God's Word, many began in their zeal for the faith to make over to the man of God their hereditary properties. These he accepted. Shortly afterwards he ordered churches to be built there, and he appointed priests and deacons to serve them, so that the new converts should have places where they could assemble on feast days and listen to wholesome instruction and where they could learn the principles of the Christian religion from those servants of God who had baptized them. Thus the man of God, favoured by divine grace, made increasing progress from day to day.

It came about, however, that Pippin, King of the Franks, died,[1] and his son Charles became head of the realm.[2] Charles brought many nations under the power of the Franks, and among these were the Frisians, whose lands were added to his dominions after the defeat of Radbod. At that time St. Willibrord was officially appointed to preach to the Frisian people, and his episcopal see was fixed at the fortress of Utrecht. Being given greater scope for the preaching of the Gospel, he now attempted to bring into the Church by baptism the people that had recently been won by the sword. He allowed no error or past ignorance to pass unnoticed and lost no time in shedding upon them the light of the Gospel, so that soon among that people the statement of the prophet was fulfilled: " In that place where it was said unto them, Ye are not my people, it shall be said unto them, Ye are the sons of the living God."

Many miracles were also wrought by divine power through His servant. Whilst the ministry of preaching the Gospel is to be preferred to the working of miracles and the showing of signs, yet, because such miracles are recorded as having been performed, I think mention of them ought not to be suppressed; and so that glory may be given to God who vouchsafed them, I will insert them into this narrative, and in this way what we know to have been achieved in former times may not be lost to future ages. Thus, when the venerable man, according to his custom, was on one of his missionary journeys he came to a village called Walichrum,[3] where an idol of the ancient superstition remained. When

---

[1] Pippin died 14 December 714. At this juncture Radbod revolted, and during the disturbances that followed Willibrord retired to his monastery at Echternach.

[2] Charles Martel, the natural son of Pippin. He obliged Radbod to raise the siege of Cologne and then attacked the Neustrians at Compiègne, 26 Sept. 715, where he put them to rout. It was during this time that St. Boniface arrived with his companions in Utrecht, but, finding the conditions unpropitious for preaching, he returned home.

[3] Walcheren, where during the Roman occupation the goddess Nehelamia, protectress of navigation, had been worshipped. A later tradition at Echternach placed the scene of this story at Westcapelle and said that traces of Willibrord's blood could still be discovered. At this place a votive stone of Hercules Magusanus has been found.

the man of God, moved by zeal, smashed it to pieces before the eyes of the custodian, the latter, seething with anger, in a sudden fit of passion struck the priest of Christ on the head with a sword, as if to avenge the insult paid to his god. But, as God was protecting His servant, the murderous blow did him no harm. On seeing this, Willibrord's companions rushed forward to kill the wicked man for his audacity. The man of God goodnaturedly delivered the culprit from their hands and allowed him to go free. The same day, however, he was seized and possessed by the devil and three days later he ended his wretched life in misery. And thus, because the man of God followed the Lord's command and was unwilling to avenge the wrongs done to him, he was vindicated all the more by the Lord Himself, just as He had said regarding the wrongs which the wicked inflicted upon His saints: "Vengeance is mine; I will repay, saith the Lord."

On another occasion, when the blessed man was on his way to a cell belonging to him called Susteren, from the name of the stream that flows past it, he took a narrow path running through the cornfields of a certain wealthy landowner. When the keeper of the fields saw this he was furious and began to revile the man of God. Those who accompanied him [Willibrord] wanted to punish the man for insulting him, but the servant of God mildly restrained them, not wishing that anyone should perish on his account, since his whole happiness lay in bringing salvation to all. When he found it impossible to calm the fury of the foolish man, Willibrord did not persist but returned by the way he had come. Next day, however, the wretch who had not feared to heap insults upon the servant of God was struck down on that very spot with sudden death before a crowd of onlookers.

Whilst the divinely inspired man in his urgent desire to preach the Gospel was travelling through the coastal regions where the people were suffering from the lack of fresh water he noticed that his companions could hardly bear the pangs of thirst. So he called one of them and bade him dig a small trench inside his tent. There, upon his knees, he secretly prayed to God that He, who had brought forth water from the rock for his people whilst they were in the desert, would with like compassion bring forth water for his servants from the sandy soil. At once his prayer was heard and a spring of sweet water straightway filled the trench. His followers on seeing this gave thanks to God, who in this manner had glorified His saint and condescended to hear his prayer. And when they had drunk their fill they took with them as much water as they thought would satisfy their needs on the journey that lay before them.

Again, when the holy priest of God was pursuing his way in a certain place, he saw twelve poor beggars asking alms from the passers-by. Being extremely kind-hearted, he gazed on them with compassion and bade one of his companions take his own flask and give a drink to Christ's poor. All the twelve drank from it as much as they would, and the remarkable fact was that as the company went on their way they found that the flask from which so many had drunk was just as full as it was before of the most excellent wine. When they discovered this they all blessed the Lord, saying: " Indeed, the saying of Christ in the Gospels ' Give and it shall be given unto you ' has been fulfilled."

Once, the saintly man came to his monastery [at Echternach][1] to make a visitation, and after praying to God, greeting the brethren and speaking peaceably with them, the holy father went round the cells of each one of the brothers to see if anything in them might be improved. On going into the store-house, he found there only a small supply of wine in one cask, into which, as a sign of his blessing, he thrust his staff, praying the while, and then went out. The same night, the wine in the cask began to rise to the brim and then to overflow. When the steward noticed it he was astounded at the unexpected increase, and, knowing it to have been wrought by God's mercy through the blessing of His servant, he did not dare to keep it secret. Next morning, he ran after the holy father and, falling at his feet, reported what he had seen. Willibrord, as usual, gave thanks to God, but, bearing in mind our Lord's command to His disciples not to make public the glory of the Transfiguration before the day of the Resurrection,

---

[1] The property for this foundation had been given to Willibrord in 714 by Plectrude, wife of Pippin II.

he forbade the steward to speak to anyone of the miracle he had witnessed until the day of his [Willibrord's] death.

A further miracle of the same kind was wrought by Christ our God through Willibrord's blessing. On one occasion the servant of God came with his companions to the house of a friend of his and wished to break the tedium of the long journey by taking a meal at his friend's house. But it came to his ears that the head of the house had no wine. He gave orders that four small flasks, which were all that his companions carried with them for their needs on the journey, should be brought to him. Then he blessed them in the name of Him who at the marriage feast of Cana changed water into wine—and, remarkable to relate, after this gracious blessing about forty people drank their fill from these small bottles, and with great thanksgiving and joyful hearts said one to another: " The Lord Jesus has in truth fulfilled His promise in the Gospel: ' He that believeth in me will do the deeds I do, and greater than these shall he do.' "

Once, when this holy preacher was going in haste towards Frisia in order, as usual, to preach the Gospel, he wanted to pasture his horses, worn out by the fatigue of the journey, in the meadows of a certain wealthy landowner. The man, seeing horses feeding in his meadows, began to beat them and drive them out of his pastures with great arrogance. The man of God accosted him with peaceable words and said: " Brother, do us no harm. Our purpose in wishing to rest in these meadows is not to do you harm but to meet our own needs. We are under obligation to pursue the work of God, and you also might share in its rewards if, as far as lies in your power, you help us in a friendly spirit, mindful of the sweet promise of Christ: ' He that receiveth you, receiveth me, and he that receiveth me, receiveth him that sent me.' Be at peace, and rather as a friend take a drink with us by way of refreshment. Then when we have gone on our way, return to your house with the blessing of God." The man, however, persisted in his ill-will and would not listen to the reasonable words of the man of God, but, on the contrary, repeated his abuse and continued to insult him. " You ask me to drink with you," he said, " and make peace: be assured that I set no store

whatever upon drinking with you." The man of God took the
words out of his mouth and said: "If you will not drink with
me, then do not drink at all." Thereupon, as soon as his companions were ready, he went on his way. The obstinate man also
hurriedly went home, but was seized almost at once with a burning
thirst which he tried in vain to assuage with wine, for the mouth
that had cast reproaches upon the man of God was unable to
swallow a single draught. Thus the man who would not of his own
accord make peace with the servant of God was now compelled
to bear within himself the penalty of his fault. Doctors were called
to relieve his thirst and to restore to the sufferer his power of
drinking. His whole being cried out for relief, but no one could
get a drop of wine to reach his parched throat. At last, struck with
remorse, he came to his senses, and, discovering that the saintly
man he had reviled was Willibrord, he began to yearn intensely
for his return. In the following year, Willibrord came back by
the same way, and on hearing of his approach the sick man
hurried out to meet him. Confessing his sin and telling him of
the suffering he had endured, he besought him for the love
of Christ to release him from it. The man of God was moved with
pity, released him from his punishment and allowed him to drink
from his own cup. Thereupon the man who was released drank
and returned to his own house cured.

In the town of Trèves there is a convent of nuns,[1] which in the
days of Willibrord was visited with a terrible plague. Many of
the nuns died of the infection, others were confined to bed by
severe sickness, whilst the rest were in a state of extreme terror,
expecting death at any moment. At a short distance from this town
stands the monastery of the holy man, called Echternach, in which
his body reposes to this day and which his successors are known
to have held by lawful bequest of the said father and through the
goodwill of pious kings. Learning that the holy man was coming
thither, the women of the above-mentioned convent sent a deputa-
tion beseeching him to come to them without delay. When he
heard their request, the man of God, instructed by the gracious

---

[1] Probably St. Marien-ad-Martyres, where the portable altar of St. Willibrord is still preserved.

example of St. Peter, Prince of the Apostles, who went from Joppa to Lydda at the request of the widows of Christ in order to raise holy Tabitha to life, went to their assistance without delay. On arriving at the convent, he immediately celebrated Mass for the sick and then blessed water and ordered it to be sprinkled about the buildings and given to the nuns to drink. Through the mercy of God they speedily recovered and there were no more deaths in that convent from the plague.

It happened that a head of a family and his household were afflicted by a terrible visitation of devilish sorcery, and it became quite obvious from the horrors and evil tricks that occurred there that the house was haunted by a wicked spirit. For it would suddenly siezc food and clothing and other household goods and throw them into the fire. Once, indeed, whilst the parents were asleep, it snatched their little boy as he rested in their arms and hurled him into the fire, and it was only with great difficulty that the parents, roused by the child's screams, rescued him from the flames. Many were the ill turns that the family had to endure at the hands of this execrable spirit and no priest was able to exorcize it. Eventually the holy man Willibrord, at the father's urgent request, sent them some holy water and directed them to sprinkle it over all the furniture after it had been taken out of doors, for the man of God foresaw that the whole house would be consumed by fire. When they had done this, a conflagration broke out in the very place where the bed had stood, and, quickly enveloping the house, reduced it to ashes. After another house had been built on the site of the old one and blessed with holy water the family suffered no more from their former trial and thenceforth lived in peace, giving thanks to the Lord who had deigned to deliver them through the hands of His servant.

The same holy man, who was pleasing to God, also prophesied certain things that were subsequently verified by the course of events. He baptized Pippin the Short, son of the valiant Charles Martel, King of the Franks and father of the present illustrious Charles, who governs the Franks at the present day in triumph, dignity and glory. Of Pippin, father of the last named, Willibrord uttered the following prediction in the presence of his disciples: " Know that this child will be highly exalted and renowned. He will be greater than all the kings of the Franks who have gone before him." The truth of this prophecy has been fulfilled in our times and there is no need to prove what is universally acknowledged throughout the whole kingdom. For all the people know what wonderful victories this illustrious conqueror has gained, how widely he has extended the bounds of his empire, how devotedly he has promoted the Christian religion and how he has defended the Holy Church of God abroad. All these things can be more clearly seen with the eye than set forth in words.

Now this holy man was distinguished by every kind of natural quality: he was of middle height, dignified mien, comely of face, cheerful in spirit, wise in counsel, pleasing in speech, grave in character and energetic in everything he undertook for God. His forbearance is shown by the actions we have recorded above. How great was his zeal in preaching the Gospel of Christ and how he was sustained in the labour of preaching by the grace of God we need not set forth in writing, since it is vouched for by the testimony of all. His personal life can be inferred from his vigils and prayers, his fasting and singing of psalms, the holiness of his conduct and his many miracles. His charity is made manifest in the unremitting labours which he bore daily for the name of Christ.

This holy man, who progressed every day of his life in the work of God, who was pleasing to God and friendly to all the people, was laid to his fathers in the time of the elder Charles, the valiant ruler of the Franks. He was then an old man coming to the end of his days and was about to receive from God a generous reward for his labours. He forsook this world to take possession of heaven and to behold Christ for ever in eternal glory, in whose love he had never ceased to labour as long as he lived in our midst. On the sixth of November, that is, the eighth day before the Ides, he passed from this place of pilgrimage to the eternal country and was buried in the monastery of Echternach, which, as we have said before, he had built to the glory of God. There to this day, through the mercy of God, miracles of healing are constantly performed beside the relics of the holy priest of God. That some of these should be appended to our account of his life we regard as redounding to the glory of our Lord Jesus Christ, who so often deigned to perform them at the request of His servant.

His venerable body was laid to rest in a marble sarcophagus, which at first was found to be six inches too short to hold the entire body of God's servant. The brethren were greatly concerned at this, and, being at a loss to know what to do, they discussed the matter again and again, wondering where they could find a suitable resting-place for his sacred remains. Wonderful to relate, however, through the loving-kindness of God the sarcophagus was suddenly discovered to be as much longer than the holy man's body as previously it had been shorter. Therein they laid the remains of the man of God, and to the accompaniment of hymns and psalms and every token of respect it was interred in the church of the monastery which he had built and dedicated in honour of the Blessed Trinity. A sweet and marvellous fragrance filled the air, so that all were conscious that the ministry of angels had been present at the last rites of the holy man.

The death of the holy man was revealed to one of his religious disciples who was stationed at some distance from the monastery as he was keeping watch in prayer. He testifies that he saw the soul of his saintly father surrounded by a bright radiance as it was being carried by a host of angels towards the realms above, all singing his praises. Likewise many of the brothers have testified that they have frequently seen a wonderful light over the bed on which he gave back his blessed soul to his Creator, and perceived there a ravishing fragrance and most sweet odour. From these signs one can only surmise that the denizens of heaven used to visit the spot from which his saintly soul had passed to the Lord.

Many sick persons, through the grace of God and assisted by their own faith, have been cured after being anointed with the oil from the lamp which burns over the relics of the holy man. Penitents also frequently came to the church wearing rings on their arms,[1] as the custom then was, and the links were broken and they were loosed from their bonds. Evidence of this are the rings which hang in the church to this day.

---

[1] It was the custom to fasten iron rings on the limbs of penitents as a sign of their sinful state.

There was a certain woman suffering from paralysis and who had been tormented for seven years with severe pain, whose infirmity had increased so much from day to day that she had completely lost the use of her limbs and had to rely upon the help of others. So frail was she that she could scarcely breathe. This woman was carried by her relatives to the church in which the saint of God lay at rest and placed near the casket of his relics. There, with many tears, she prayed that God in His mercy might have pity on her through the intercession of His holy servant. Her prayer was heard by the Lord our God, and suddenly she was delivered from all her infirmities and restored to health. And she, who had previously been carried into the church by others, ran home upon her own feet, joyfully giving thanks to God.

In like manner a young man afflicted with sickness was brought by his friends to the body of the blessed prelate. He trembled in every limb and was totally unable to raise his head, which lolled and twisted this way and that as if it had not been fixed on his neck. Sometimes, too, he became so inert as to appear completely lifeless. This young man, as we have said, was placed near the body of the saint by his friends, and through the mercy of God was so quickly cured, in the presence of all the onlookers, that no trace remained of his former infirmity and long-standing affliction.

A certain man who held the office of deacon in the church of the saint (though he was quite unworthy of it) did not scruple to steal, among other things that had been offered to the church, a golden cross which the holy man used to carry with him on his travels. The brethren were distressed at this, and, though ignorant of the perpetrator of this sacrilege, they felt confident that through the prayers of the saint of God so heinous a crime could not long be concealed. They tried, nevertheless, in their brotherly kindness to bring the culprit to repentance, not wishing to encompass his downfall. But the man who had committed the crime hardened his heart and despised his own salvation, even as, according to Solomon, " the wicked man continues when he comes to the depths of his evil deeds ". The unhappy wretch thought that the deed, which had been committed in secret and unseen by others, would remain undetected, but it could not be hidden from the eye of God, to whom all things lie open and who is often not slow to avenge the wrongs done to His servants. For the miserable wretch who had not scrupled to commit the offence was suddenly seized with sickness and died a miserable death, and in his dying moments confessed his guilt to some of the brethren and divulged the place where he had hidden the stolen objects. You see, brethren, what a fearful judgment was visited upon the man who presumed to desecrate the church of God's saint by stealing. I beseech you, therefore, to keep your manner of life pure in this house, so that in His mercy and through the intercession of the apostolic man St. Clement He may deign to hear your prayers when you make your petitions, just as we have already told you how he heard the prayers of the sick in this same church, enabling them to return home with the good health they had long yearned for. Nor need we doubt that just as he deigned visibly to heal their bodily diseases, so also through the intercession of the saint on our behalf, whose body rests here and whom we believe to be present in the spirit, listening to our prayers, he will continue daily to cure the hidden disorders of our souls, if with firm faith and sincere confession we pour out our hearts with tears in that place before the merciful face of Him who in His mercy is quick to pardon if we are not slow to ask. Praise and glory be His for ever and ever.

It only remains now to speak of blessed Wilgils, who, as we have said, was the father of this holy man, for as the first chapter of this story began with him, so the last must close with a reference to him. It was on the anniversary of the sacred death of Wilgils that the good abbot Aldberct, successor to the venerable archbishop, proposed to eat and rejoice with the brethren after the solemnities of the Mass and the thanksgiving due to God. In the monastery, unfortunately, there were left only two flagons of wine; and since one of them had been drunk at the midday meal, the other was put by for supper. Accordingly, after Vespers had been sung in honour of that day the brethren returned to the refectory; and when they came to the end of the reading the abbot addressed the brethren with these words: " It is fitting, reverend Fathers, that we should celebrate the feast days of our venerable predecessors with spiritual rejoicing and should allow our bodies somewhat more indulgence than our usual strictness permits, not from motives of gluttony but of love. Now if there were anything in the monastery that I could offer you beyond this single flagon of wine which is left over from the midday meal I should certainly not withhold it from you. But God is able through the prayer of His saints to make even this prove more than sufficient for our needs, alike to honour them as to gladden us, and to demonstrate to us, unworthy as we are, the kindly power of Him who once through the blessing of our former father, the holy Willibrord, condescended to satisfy forty men from four flagons. Let us drink what we have with rejoicing and with hope."

After all the brethren had drunk from the bottle a first and a second time the server found it as full as before. When the abbot was acquainted with this he joined the brethren in giving thanks to God; and, doing honour to the divine mercy, they drank soberly but gladly that night as much as they desired.

O happy father to beget such a son and to be deemed worthy by God of having such an heir! In thee is fulfilled the blessing which is read in Deuteronomy: " Blessed shalt thou be, and blessed shall be the fruit of thy body."

THE LIFE OF ST. BONIFACE
BY WILLIBALD

The following Life was written in answer to the many requests from Boniface's friends in Britain, France and Germany, who wished, like Bishop Milret of Worcester, to have " an account of the life and glorious end " of their hero. These requests were sent to Boniface's successor in the bishopric of Mainz, Lull, and Willibald was a chosen by him and Bishop Megingoz of Wurzburg to satisfy their demand.

Willibald is not to be confused with the Bishop of Eichstatt, whose biography appears elsewhere in this volume. The writer of the Life was a simple priest who had never come into direct contact with Boniface and what he says is based upon the facts that he was able to collect from those who had been Boniface's disciples. That he was an English missionary is proved by the many indications given in his treatment of names. Whilst he always employs the correct spelling and endings for Anglo-Saxon words, he anglicizes the spelling of names and places of Frisian or Germanic origin. He wrote not long after the death of Boniface—to be precise, within thirteen years, for Megingoz, to whom the book is dedicated, died 26 September 768.

The work has been composed on a systematic plan. Each chapter opens with a prologue in which the events to be narrated are briefly outlined, and ends with a verse from the New Testament. Only in the eighth and ninth chapters does this plan fail, and for this reason it has been thought that the whole Life has not been preserved. A number of explanations have been put forward to account for this—for example, the censorship of Bishop Lull on those parts which might have reflected on his conduct—but it is more likely that the author himself did not fully carry out his intentions.

The chief defects of the work are twofold: first, the style is inflated and obscure, due no doubt to his attempt to model himself on St. Aldhelm's writings; second, the comparative meagreness of the facts. In spite of this, the book was much read and even imitated. The proof of this lies in the biographies of Boniface's companions and disciples, where passages can be readily recognized—for instance in Rudolf's Life of Leoba, Leoba's Life of Willibald and Eigil's Life of Sturm.

THE LIFE OF ST. BONIFACE
BY WILLIBALD

PROLOGUE[1]

To MY venerable and dear fathers in Christ, Bishops Lull[2] and Megingoz,[3] Willibald, an unworthy priest in the Lord.

With all the deference and obedience that is due to your Lordships, but with little confidence in my own literary craft, I have cheerfully accepted the injunction laid upon me. In spite of my incapacity, I have undertaken the heavy task you enjoined upon me and carried it through to the end. If the result should fall short of your expectations I beg you in fairness to myself to compare the difficulty of the charge with my lack of skill and to consider as a convincing proof of my regard the willing acquiescence I have shown in bearing this heavy burden. If, on the other hand, I succeed in producing a book that is worthy of these times and useful to my contemporaries, ascribe its success to the help of God and to your personal intervention and desire, for the stimulus given to me by your earnest entreaties may be likened to the hand that controls the winepress, which by exerting pressure, squeezes out the precious juice of knowledge and hands it round for the refreshment of the thirsty.

Your Holiness has seen fit to place me on a level with, and indeed to exalt me, ignorant as I am, above, the wise: to choose me, in spite of my incompetence, instead of a more experienced writer and to commit to me, though an unlettered man, a task you might so easily have deputed to a scholar. Since, therefore, you have brought pressure to bear on me, I beg of you to support me with continual prayer. May my mind, now dulled by sloth,

---

[1] The words and ideas of the prologue have been borrowed from Victorinus of Aquitaine, from the prefatory letter sent to Archdeacon Hilary of Rome in A.D. 457.
[2] Lull, Bishop of Mainz, 754–85.
[3] Archbishop of Wurzburg, who died between 763 and 769.

be roused by your love and entreaties, so that I may compose in clear and vigorous language[1] the biography which you have called on me to write.

It is at the request of Catholic and religious-minded men from Tuscany, Gaul, Germany, Britain and all the other countries where the fame and miracles of St. Boniface the martyr are known that you have urged me to describe his life from its beginning to its close; and you have counselled me to model it on the classic biographies of saints written by the Fathers, basing my facts upon personal knowledge and on the accounts of those who for a long time were his close disciples. As Hegesippus, who, after the abrogation of the Old Covenant and the dawning of the New, is related to have gone to Rome during the reign of Pope Anacletus[2] and to have published for the edification of his readers a history of the Church in five volumes; and as Eusebius of Caesarea, the celebrated historian, and his assistant, Pamphilius the martyr, recorded the events of their own and previous ages in several well-written volumes; and as the learned and great Pope Gregory[3] of blessed memory described the lives of the holy confessors in four books, remarkable for their form and style, books which, being placed to this day in the libraries of our churches, furnish posterity with facts ascertained only by immense labour—so you bid me unfold to my contemporaries and future ages the life, virtues, practical piety and ascetic habits of St. Boniface. For the telling of so wonderful a story I am quite unfitted, but in spite of my lack of literary skill I will make an attempt to discharge this duty. Without presuming on my own powers, but rather putting my trust in the kindly help of my fellow-Catholics, I shall try in writing this book not to increase my personal reputation but to furnish my readers with a story that will serve them as an example, and so by drawing encouragement from the model I put forward they may be led towards the pursuit of better things.

---

[1] " eleganti verborum ambage ", an excellent description of Willibald's inflated and obscure style.

[2] Anicetus, Bishop of Rome, 157 ?–68: known as Anacletus I.

[3] Gregory the Great, Pope 590–604.

HERE BEGINS THE LIFE OF ST. BONIFACE

How, in childhood, he began to serve God

What I am attempting to do here is to describe the blessed life and character of St. Boniface, the archbishop, in so far as I have learned the facts from holy men who lived in daily contact with him and who, therefore, knew his manner of life and were in a position to recall those details which they have heard or witnessed. Though I labour under the disadvantage of having had only an indirect acquaintance with him, my design is to weave into the texture of my narrative and to present in as brief a form as possible all the facts ascertainable by a thorough investigation into his holiness and divine contemplation.

In his very early childhood, after he had been weaned and reared with a mother's usual anxious care, his father lavished upon him more affection than upon the rest of his brothers. When he reached the age of about four or five he conceived a desire to enter the service of God and began to think deeply on the advantages of the monastic life. Even at this early age he had subdued the flesh to the spirit and meditated on the things that are eternal rather than on those that are temporal.

When priests or clerics, travelling abroad, as is the custom in those parts, to preach to the people, came to the town and the house where his father dwelt the child would converse with them on spiritual matters and, as far as the capacity of his tender years permitted, would ask them to advise him on the best means of overcoming the frailties of his nature. After some time, when he had given long consideration to the things of God and his whole nature craved for a future life, he revealed his desires to his father and begged him to take his confidences in good part. His father, taken aback at the views he expressed, rebuked him with violence and, whilst forbidding him to leave his side, enticed him with promises of worldly success, hoping by this means to retain the boy as guardian, or rather heir of his worldly possessions. Employing all the subtle craft of human wisdom, he endeavoured by long discussions to dissuade the boy from carrying out his purpose, and mingled promises with flattery in the hope of persuading him that life in the world would be more congenial for one of his age than the austere regime of the monastic and contemplative life. In order to turn the boy aside from pursuing his purpose he paraded before him all the inducements of pleasure and luxury. But the saint, even at that early age, was filled with the spirit of God. The more his father attempted to hold him back, the more stoutly and doggedly he determined to pursue the heavenly ideal and to devote himself to the study of sacred letters. And in accordance with the workings of divine mercy it fell out in a remarkable way that divine providence not only confirmed him in his undertaking but also changed the obstinate mood of his father, for at one and the same instant his father was struck down by a sudden and fatal sickness, whilst the boy's intentions, long frustrated, grew in strength and were, by the help of God, brought to their fulfilment.

When, by the inscrutable judgment and dispensation of God, the saint's father fell sick, he suddenly changed his previous obstinate attitude and, after calling together all the members of his family, sent the boy under the care of trustworthy messengers to the Monastery of Examchester,[1] which was ruled at that time by Abbot Wulfhard. There, surrounded by his friends, he made known to the abbot his desire to enter the monastic life and, in a manner mature for his years, presented his petition according to the instructions previously given to him by his parents. The father of the monastery thereupon took counsel with the rest of the brethren and, after receiving their blessing as is prescribed by the monastic rule,[2] gave his consent. In this way the man of God was bereaved of his earthly father and embraced the adoptive Father of our redemption. He thus renounced all worldly and transitory possessions for the sake of acquiring the eternal inheritance in order that, to quote the words of the Gospel, by forsaking father and mother and lands and the other things of this world he might receive a hundredfold hereafter and possess everlasting life.

---

[1] Boniface's childhood was spent not far from Exeter. The tradition that he was born at Crediton is traced to John de Grandisson, Bishop of Exeter, 1327–69.
[2] Rule of St. Benedict, cap. 3.

CHAPTER II

How in the beginning he overcame the passions of youth and clave to all that was good.

The first part of our narrative, though briefly expressed, is now completed. We shall now describe the virtuous habits in which the saint trained himself at the beginning of his monastic life. Then, after we have established our work on a firm basis, we can raise the structure little by little to its crowning point.

After he had increased in age and strength and knowledge and, completing the years of childhood, had reached the bloom of youth[1], the grace of God, as later events in this book will show, endowed him with wonderful intellectual qualities. He modelled his behaviour on the lives of the early saints, submitted with due humility to the regulations of the fathers of the monastery and became conspicuous for his genuine and many-sided virtues. Moreover, he was endowed with a spark of divine genius and so assiduously fostered it by study that every hour and moment of his long and active life only served to increase the divine gifts which had been showered upon him. The longer he continued in the service of the priesthood, the more, as we are told by his trusted and intimate friends, did his continual studies and his protracted endeavours in the literary field stimulate him in his search for eternal bliss. This was a marvellous protection against the enticements and diabolical suggestions which beset young men in the flower of their youth and which cloud their minds with a kind of darkness. As a result, the fiery passions of youth and the fleshly lusts which at first made violent assaults upon him lost their power through his ceaseless vigilance and his assiduous enquiries into the meaning of Sacred Scripture. His studies, pursued with increasing ardour, led him inevitably to undertake the task of teaching others, a labour which after a short time and in accordance with episcopal and ecclesiastical ordinances he duly carried out. He spurned the fleeting successes of this world and

---

[1] According to Isidore of Seville, youth began at the age of fourteen.

continued under the able guidance of Abbot Wulfhard to follow
faithfully and conscientiously the true pattern of monastic observance. When he had outgrown his boyhood and youth his
enthusiasm for study and the lack of suitable teachers moved him
to seek permission from the abbot and community to pass over
to a neighbouring monastery. He prayed constantly and per-
severingly for the approval of God on his undertaking, and finally,
under the inspiration of divine grace, he went to the monastery
which to this day is called Nursling.[1] There, attracted by the
desire for learning, he became a disciple of the venerable abbot
Winbert,[2] of blessed memory, and joined the community of the
brethren who dwelt there with him in the Lord. Thus united to
the servants of God, he showed great zeal for meditation, devotion
to the service of God, perseverance in watching and assiduity
in the study of the Scriptures. In this way he became proficient
not only in grammar and rhetoric and the writing of verses[3] but
also in the literal and spiritual exposition of the Bible.[4] In the
end he became so renowned for his profound understanding of the
Scriptures and for his skill in imparting his knowledge to others
that he was accepted as a trustworthy guide in traditional doctrine.
As a teacher he was a model, because he did not refuse to learn
from his pupils, for it is a principle in monastic houses that no
one should presume to rule others unless he has previously learned
to submit. No man who has failed to render obedience to the
superiors set over him by God can rightly exact obedience from his
inferiors. Such obedience as befits a monk was given by the saint
to all the members of the community, and particularly to the abbot,
and he applied himself assiduously, as the Rule of St. Benedict
prescribes, to the daily manual labour and the regular performance

---

[1] Nursling, between Southampton and Winchester.
[2] Abbot Winbert, a notary at court, seems to have become abbot about 701.
Boniface wrote to Bishop Daniel later in life (Letter 30) asking for Winbert's
copy of the prophets.
[3] To this period may be assigned the grammatical and metrical writings of
Boniface, of which a specimen can be seen in M.G., Poetae Aevi Carolini, i,
pp. 16–17.
[4] Cassian in his Collations (xiv, 8, 1) says: " The three kinds of spiritual
knowledge are tropology, allegory and anagogy." Miss Beryl Smalley in her
Study of the Bible in the Middle Ages (ch. I) gives an excellent account of the
methods of interpreting Scripture.

of his duties. In this way he was an example to all both in word, deed, faith and purity. All could profit by his good deeds, whilst he on his side shared in their common eternal reward. But God alone, from whom nothing is concealed, knew the hidden depths of his heart and the extent of his humility and charity which had won for him an ascendancy over all his brethren. They looked upon him with love mingled with fear; and though he was their companion in the pursuit of divine love, they considered him, as St. Paul says, as their father. His kindliness towards the brethren and the extent of his learning increased to such a degree that his fame as a teacher spread far and wide among monasteries both of men and women. Of their inmates great numbers of men, attracted by a desire for learning, flocked to hear him and under his guidance studied the whole extent of the Scriptures; but the nuns, who were unable continually to come to his lectures, stimulated by his vast wisdom and his spirit of divine love, applied themselves with diligence to the study of the sacred texts, scanning page after page as they meditated on the sacred and hidden mysteries.

Guided and sustained as he was by supernatural grace, he followed both the example and the teaching of the Apostle of the Gentiles, holding fast the form of sound doctrine in the faith and love of Jesus Christ, studying to show himself approved unto God, a workman that need not be ashamed, rightly handling the word of truth.

CHAPTER III

How he gave instruction to all and assumed the office of teacher, not at his own whim but on the attainment of the proper age.

We will now turn our attention for a moment to the general tenor of the saint's daily contemplation and to his perseverance in fasting and abstinence. In this way, making gradual progress, we shall relate with conciseness and brevity his wonderful deeds, follow his life to its close and examine it in greater detail. By balancing one aspect of his life against another we shall show

Boniface to be an example of the Christian life and a perfect model of apostolic learning. He trod in the footsteps of the saints, climbed the steep path that leads to knowledge of heavenly things and went before his people as a leader who opens the gate of paradise through which only the upright shall enter.

From the early days of his childhood even to infirm old age he imitated in particular the practice of the ancient Fathers in daily committing to memory the writings of the prophets and Apostles, the narratives of the passion of the martyrs and the Gospel teaching of our Lord. To quote the words of the Apostle: whether he ate or drank or whatsoever else he did, he always praised and thanked God both in heart and word; as says the Psalmist: " I will praise the Lord at all times: His praise shall be continually in my mouth." To such a degree was he inflamed with a love of the Scriptures that he applied all his energies to learning and practising their counsels, and those matters which were written for the instruction of the people he paraphrased and explained to them with striking eloquence, shrewdly spicing it with parables. His discretion was such that his rebukes, though sharp, were never lacking in gentleness, whilst his teaching, though mild, was never lacking in force. Zeal and vigour made him forceful, but gentleness and love made him mild. Accordingly he exhorted and reproved with equal impartiality the rich and powerful, the freedmen and the slaves, neither flattering and fawning upon the rich nor oppressing and browbeating the freedmen and slaves, but, in the words of the Apostle, he became all things to all men that he might gain all.

He did not take upon himself the office of preacher either as an expression of his caprice or before the appointed time, nor did he seek the position through contumacy and greed. But he waited, as was in keeping with his humble character, until he had reached the age of thirty[1] or more, when, by the recommendation and choice of his superior and brethren, he was ordained in accordance with the rules laid down by the ecclesiastical decrees. As a priest he received divers gifts and presents, and as far as he was

---

[1] The Council of Neocesarea (cap. 11) forbade elevation to the priesthood before the age of thirty.

allowed by the severity of the Rule and the monastic life he gave himself up to almsgiving and works of mercy. He always rose before the hours of vigils and occupied himself in the laborious exercise of prayer. Anger could not undermine his patience, rage did not shake his forbearance. Lust was impotent in presence of his chastity, and gluttony was unable to break down his abstemious-ness. He subdued himself by fasting and abstinence to such a degree that he drank neither wine nor beer and in this imitated the great figures of the Old and New Testament. With the Apostle of the Gentiles he could say: " I subdue my body and bring it into subjection, lest by any means, when I have preached to others, I myself should become a castaway."

Chapter IV

How he was sent to Kent by all the nobles, and how afterwards he went to Frisia.

In the previous chapter we collected together some isolated examples of St. Boniface's admirable virtues. We consider that the others which follow, which have been elicited from trustworthy witnesses and which we shall attempt to recount, should not be passed over in silence. These are concerned with his constancy in the projects he had undertaken and his zeal in bringing others to their desired end. When he had trained himself over a long period in the virtues already mentioned and had given proof during his priesthood of many outstanding qualities, there arose a sudden crisis during the reign of Ina, King of the West Saxons [688-725], occasioned by the outbreak of a rebellion. On the advice of the king the heads of the churches immediately sum-moned a council of the servants of God, and as soon as they were all assembled a discussion, satisfactory from every point of view, took place among the priests. They adopted the prudent measure of sending trustworthy legates to Bertwald, the Archbishop of Canterbury, fearing that if they made any decision without the advice of the archbishop they would be accused of presumption and temerity. At the conclusion of the discussion, when the entire gathering had reached an agreement, the king addressed all the servants of Christ, asking them whom they would choose to deliver their message. Without hesitation Winbert, the senior abbot present, who ruled over the Monastery of Nursling, Wintra, the Abbot of Tisbury,[1] Beorwald, the Abbot of Glastonbury and many others who professed the monastic life summoned the saint and led him into the presence of the king. The king entrusted the message and the principal responsibilities of the embassy to him and, after giving him companions, sent him on his way in peace. In accordance with the commands of his superiors he set out with the message and, after a prosperous journey, came to Kent, where he skilfully made known to the archbishop all the matters, from first to last, which the king had told him. On receiving an immediate reply, he returned home after a few days and delivered the archbishop's answer to the king as he sat with the servants of God, bringing great joy to them all. Thus by the wonderful dispensation of God his good name was made known on all sides, and his reputation was high both among the lay nobility and the clergy. From that moment his influence increased by leaps and bounds, so that he became a regular member of their synodal assemblies.

But because a mind intent on God is not elated nor dependent upon the praise and approbation of man, he began carefully and cautiously to turn his mind to other things, to shun the company of his relatives and acquaintances and to set his heart not on remaining in his native land but on travelling abroad. After long deliberation on the question of forsaking his country and his relatives, he took counsel of Abbot Winbert, of blessed memory, and frankly disclosed to him the plans which up to that moment he had carefully concealed. He importuned the holy man with loud and urgent requests to give his consent to the project, but Winbert, astounded, at first refused to grant his permission, thinking that delay might turn him away from carrying out his proposals. At last, however, the providence of God prevailed and Boniface's petition was granted.

[1] Tisbury near Salisbury, Wilts.

So great was the affection of the abbot and brethren, with whom he had lived under the monastic rule, that they willingly provided the money for his needs and continued long afterwards to pray to God on his behalf: and so he set out upon his journey and, with God's help, safely completed it.

Much strengthened by their spiritual support and liberally supplied with earthly goods, the saint lacked nothing necessary for soul and body. Accompanied by two or three of the brethren on whose bodily and spiritual comfort he depended, he set out on his journey; and after travelling wide stretches of countryside, happy in the companionship of his brethren, he came to a place where there was a market for the buying and selling of merchandise. This place is called Lundenwich[1] by the Anglo-Saxons even to this day. After a few days, when the sailors were about to embark on their return home, Boniface asked permission of the shipmaster to go on board, and after paying his fare he set sail and came with a favourable winds to Dorsteb,[2] where he tarried for a while and gave thanks to God night and day.

But a fierce quarrel which broke out between Prince Charles, the noble Duke of the Franks, and Radbod, the King of the Frisians, as a result of a hostile incursion by the pagans, caused great disturbances among the population of both sides, and through the dispersion of the priests and the persecution of Radbod the greater part of the Christian churches, which previously had been subject to the Frankish empire, were laid waste and brought to ruin. Moreover, the pagan shrines were rebuilt and, what is worse, the worship of idols was restored. When the man of God perceived the wicked perversity of Radbod he came to Utrecht and, after waiting for a few days, spoke with the king, who had also gone there. And having travelled about the country and examined many parts of it to discover what possibility there might be of preaching the Gospel in future, he decided that if at any time he could see his way to approach the people he would minister

[1] London.
[2] Now Wijk bij Duurstede on the river Lek, about twelve miles south of Utrecht; it was the chief emporium of the region until it fell into the hands of the Danes in the ninth century.

to them the Word of God. On this purpose of his, his glorious martyrdom many years later set its seal.

A strange thing in the sanctity of the saints is that when they perceive that their labours are frustrated for a time and bear no spiritual fruit they betake themselves to other places where the results are more palpable, for there is nothing to be gained if one stays in a place without reaping a harvest of souls. With this in mind, when the saint had spent the whole of the summer in the country of the Frisians to no purpose and the autumn was nearing its end, he forsook the pastures that lay parched through lack of heavenly and fruitful dew, and, taking several companions with him for the journey, he departed to his native land. There in the seclusion of his monastery he spent two winters and one summer[1] with the brethren, who received him with open arms. In this manner he fulfilled that passage in the writings of the Apostle of the Gentiles, where it says: " For there I have determined to pass the winter."

CHAPTER V

How after the death of his abbot he tarried a short time with the brethren and then went to Rome.

Having now touched briefly on the virtues of the saint, we shall make known the subsequent events of his life as we have ascertained them from reliable witnesses, that his life and character may be made more clearly manifest to those who wish to model themselves on the example of his holy manner of life.

After accomplishing his dangerous journey and escaping unharmed from the perils of the sea, he returned to his native soil and rejoined once more the fellowship of his brethren. But when he had enjoyed their company for many days a deep sorrow began to gnaw at his heart and grief weighed heavily on his soul, for as the days went by he noticed that the ageing limbs of his master were growing weaker and weaker, and as a violent sickness shook

[1] That is, two winters and one summer: autumn 716 to spring of 718.

and troubled his body he saw the day of his master's death approaching. At length Wimbert laid aside the prison of his body and breathed his last sigh whilst the monks looked sadly on. Often in the hearts of the saints the feeling of compassion for those who are overtaken by trouble wells up with particular force. For a time they themselves may be sad at heart, but through putting their trust in the words of the Apostle they receive everlasting consolation in the Lord.

On this occasion the saint addressed the brethren with words of comfort and, ever mindful of the tradition of the Fathers, exhorted them in a spiritual discourse always to preserve down to their smallest detail both the formal prescriptions of the Rule and the decrees laid down by the Church. He counselled them also to choose someone as their spiritual father. Then all of one accord and with one voice earnestly implored the holy man, who at that time was called Winfrith, to take upon himself the abbatial office. But since he had already forsaken the comfort of his native land and put aside all idea of ruling others, particularly as he was now eagerly preparing to put his own plans into execution, he tactfully declined.

Now when the winter season was over and the summer was well advanced he called to mind his intention of the previous year and carefully set about preparing the journey which had been deferred. Provided with letters of introduction from Bishop Daniel, of blessed memory, he tried to set out on his way to the tombs of the Apostles. But for a long time he was detained by the needs of the brethren, who, now bereft of a superior, opposed his departure. Faced with their tears and wailings, he was restrained from leaving them through his feelings of affection and compassion; but so great a mental anguish oppressed him that he knew not which way to turn, for he was afraid that if he forsook the flock which had been committed to his master's care and which was now without a watchful guardian it might be exposed to ravening wolves, but on the other hand he was anxious not to miss the opportunity of going abroad in the autumn season. And when Almighty God, not unmindful of his paternal love, desired to deliver His servant from his perplexity, anxiety and grief, and to provide a suitable superior for the community, Bishop Daniel[1] busied himself with the brethren's needs and set over the monastery a man of sterling character named Stephen. Thereupon he sped the holy man safely on his pilgrim way.

Bidding farewell to the brethren, he departed, and after travelling a considerable distance he came at length, in fulfilment of his desire, to the town which, as we have said, is called Lundenwich. He embarked immediately on a small swift ship and began to cross the pathless expanse of the sea. The sailors were in good spirits, the huge sails bellied in the north-west wind, and, helped along by a stiff following breeze, they soon came after an uneventful crossing in sight of the mouth of the river called Cuent.[2] Here, safe from shipwreck, they set foot on dry land. At Cuentwick[3] they pitched their camp and waited until the remainder of the party came together.

When they had all met they set out straightway on their journey, for with the passing of the days the threat of winter hung over them. Many a church they visited on their way to pray that by the help of Almighty God they might cross in safety the snowy peaks of the Alps, find greater kindness at the hands of the Lombards and escape with impunity from the savage ferocity of the undisciplined soldiery.[4] And when at last, through the prayers of the saints and the providence of God, the saint and his whole retinue had reached the tomb of St. Peter the Apostle unharmed, they immediately gave thanks to Christ for their safe journey. Afterwards they went with deep joy to the Church of St. Peter, chief of the Apostles, and many of them offered up gifts, begging absolution of their sins. Now after several days had passed, the saint had audience with His Holiness Pope Gregory the Second, of blessed memory[5] (the one who preceded the present Pope of that name), who in the common parlance of the Romans is called the Younger. To him he explained in all its details the reason of his journey and his visit. He described the

[1] Daniel, Bishop of Winchester, 704–45.
[2] Cuent or Canche, a small stream a few miles south of Boulogne.
[3] Not far from Étaples, but no longer existing.
[4] The Byzantine troops that garrisoned the Exarchate of Ravenna.
[5] Pope Gregory II, 715–31.

work which was closest to his heart and for which he had laboured so anxiously and so long. The saintly Pope, suddenly turning his gaze upon him, enquired with cheerful countenance and smiling eyes whether he had brought with him any letter of introduction from his bishop. Boniface, coming to himself, drew back his cloak and produced a note, which, conformably to usage, was sealed and folded,[1] and with it the letter of recommendation from his bishop. These he handed over to the Pope. As soon as His Holiness had taken the letter he made a sign to the saint to withdraw. When the Pope had read the letter and examined the note of introduction he discussed the saint's project with him every day until the summer season, in which he had to set out on the return journey, was near. When the end of April had passed and it was already the beginning of May the saint begged and received the apostolic blessing and was sent by the Pope[2] to make a report on the savage peoples of Germany. The purpose of this was to discover whether their untutored hearts and minds were ready to receive the seed of the divine Word.

And so, collecting a number of relics of the saints, he retraced his steps in the company of his fellows and reached the frontiers of Italy, where he met Liudprand,[3] King of the Lombards, to whom he gave gifts and tokens of peace. He was honourably received by the king and rested awhile after the weary labours of the journey. After receiving many presents in return, he crossed the hills and the plains and scaled the steep mountain passes of the Alps.

He then traversed the territories of the Bavarians and their German neighbours, unknown to him till then, and, in accordance with the injunction of the Apostolic See, proceeded on his journey of inspection into Thuringia.[4] Thus like the busy bee which, borne along by its softly buzzing wings, flits over fields and

---

[1] " Carta ex more involuta ": an ecclesiatical letter authenticated by a numerical key known only to the initiates. Good examples of the *epistola formata* are given in M.G.H., *Leges*, sect V, pp. 557–68. In addition to this, Boniface carried an open letter of introduction, probably the one preserved and printed here, No. 2.

[2] Letter 3, dated 15 May 719.

[3] Liudprand, 712–44.

[4] Territory east of the Rhine and north of the Danube.

meadows and picks its way among a thousand different sweet-smelling flowers, testing with its discriminating tongue the secret hoards of honey-bearing nectar and completely ignoring all bitter and poisonous juices, and then comes back with nectar to its hive and, to use an illustration from the words of the Apostle, " proves all things but holds fast to that which is good "—so in Thuringia the saint followed out the instructions given to him by the Holy See. He spoke to the elders of the Churches and the princes of the people with words of spiritual exhortation, recalling them to the true way of knowledge and the light of understanding which for the greater part they had lost through the perversity of their teachers. By preaching the Gospel and turning their minds away from evil towards a life of virtue and the observance of canonical decrees he reproved, admonished and instructed to the best of his ability the priests and the elders, some of whom devoted themselves to the true worship of Almighty God, whilst others, contaminated and polluted by unchastity, had forsaken the life of continence to which, as ministers of the altar, they were vowed.

Afterwards, accompanied by his brethren, he went into France, and, on learning of the death of Radbod,[1] King of the Frisians, being desirous that Frisia also should hear the Word of God, he joyfully took ship and sailed up the river. In this way he reached districts that had hitherto been left untouched by the preaching of the Gospel. The ending of the persecution raised by the savage King Radbod permitted him to scatter abroad the seed of Christian teaching and to feed with wholesome doctrine those who had been famished by pagan superstition. The results of this work, so close to his heart, were swift and spontaneous. The divine light illumined their hearts, the sovereignty of Duke Charles over the Frisians was established, the word of truth was blazened abroad, the voice of preachers filled the land, and the venerable Willibrord[2] with his fellow-missioners propagated the Gospel.

When he saw that the harvest was abundant and the labourers were few the holy servant of God offered his services for three

---

[1] Radbod, 679–719: see Letter 4, where Abbess Bugga congratulates Boniface on the removal of Radbod.
[2] Willibrord, born c. 657–8.

years to Archbishop Willibrord[1] and laboured indefatigably. He destroyed pagan temples and shrines, built churches and chapels, and with the help of Willibrord gained numerous converts to the Church. When Willibrord grew old and was becoming infirm he decided on the suggestion of his disciples to appoint an assistant to relieve him of the burden of the ministry in his declining years and to choose from his small flock some man of faith who would be able to govern so numerous a people. He summoned to him the servant of God and urged him with salutary words of advice to accept the responsibility and dignity of the episcopal office and to assist him in governing the people of God. The saint in his humility hastily declined, answering that he was unworthy of the episcopal office, that so great a responsibility ought not to be imposed upon him at so young an age and that he had not yet reached the age of fifty required by canon law. All these excuses he put forward to avoid being raised to this exalted position. Archbishop Willibrord therefore sternly reproved him and urged him to accept the work offered him, adducing, as a final argument, the extreme need of the people over whom he ruled. When not even Willibrord's reproof could bring the saint to acquiesce and every kind of argument had been employed, they amicably agreed to differ. The saint on the one hand, held back by the feeling of humility, declined so high a position of honour; Willibrord on the other, intent on spiritual gain, thought only of the salvation of souls. Accordingly, after they had expressed their personal views, the servant of God, as if taking part in a kind of spiritual contest, at last brought forward an unanswerable argument. He said: " Most holy Bishop, you, as spiritual leader here, know full well that I came to Germany at the express command of Pope Gregory, of holy memory. As the envoy of the Apostolic See sent to the barbarian countries of the West, I freely gave my services to you and to your diocese without the knowledge of my master, to whose service I am bound by vow even to this day. Therefore without the counsel and permission of the Apostolic See and without its express command I dare not accept so exalted and sublime an office." To this rejoinder he

[1] Fellow-worker, 719–22.

added a reasonable request in these words: " I beseech you, therefore, to send me, bound as I am by the ties of my own promise, to those lands to which originally I was despatched by the Holy See."

As soon as Willibrord had learned the reason of the saint's solemn promise, he gave him his blessing and granted him permission to depart. Thereupon the saint set out and reached the place called Amanburch,[1] " nourished ", as the Apostle says, " in the word of faith and good doctrine whereunto he attained ".

Chapter VI

We have given, step by step, proofs of this holy man's virtue and of his perseverance in the work of the Lord in order that we may recall to memory, both in general and in detail, the subsequent examples of his good deeds.

When he had converted to the Lord a vast number of people among the Frisians and many had come through his instruction to the knowledge of the truth, he then travelled, under the protection of God, to other parts of Germany to preach there and in this way came, with the help of God, to the place already mentioned, called Amanburch. Here the rulers were two twin brothers named Dettic and Devrulf, whom he converted from the sacrilegious worship of idols which was practised under the cloak of Christianity. He turned away also from the superstitions of paganism a great multitude of people by revealing to them the path of right understanding, and induced them to forsake their horrible and erroneous beliefs. When he had gathered together a sufficient number of believers he built a small chapel. In this way he delivered from the captivity of the devil the people of Saxe-Hesse, who up to that time had practised pagan ritual.

Having converted many thousands of people from their long-standing heathen practices and baptized them, he sent to Rome

---

[1] Amoeneburg in Hesse-Nassau on the river Ohm; it lies about seven miles east of Marburg.

an experienced and trustworthy messenger, Bynnan by name, with a letter in which he made known to the Supreme Pontiff, Bishop of the Apostolic See, all the matters which by God's grace had been accomplished, and the number of people who, through the operation of the Holy Spirit, had received the sacrament of Baptism. In addition he asked for guidance on certain questions concerning the day-to-day needs of the Church and the progress of the people, for he wished to have the advice of the Apostolic See. When the aforesaid messenger had tarried in Rome for some days and the time for his return journey drew near, the Bishop of the Apostolic See gave him a letter in reply to the message he had brought on his embassy. Returning immediately, he quickly brought to his master the letter dictated by the Pope.

On reading the missive brought to him by the messenger, he learned that he was summoned to Rome, and with all haste he prepared to carry out this injunction in a spirit of complete obedience. Without delay he set out on his journey accompanied by a large retinue and a number of his brethren. Passing through France and Burgundy, he crossed the Alps and descended through the marches of Italy and the territory held by the soldiers. Eventually he came in sight of the walls of Rome and, giving praise and thanks to God on high, went quickly to the Church of St. Peter, where he fortified himself in long and earnest prayer. After he had rested his weary limbs for a brief space of time a message was sent to Blessed Gregory, Bishop of the Apostolic See, saying that the servant of God had arrived; he was then welcomed with great kindness and conducted to the pilgrim's lodge.

A convenient day was fixed for a meeting, and at the appointed time the Pontiff came down to the basilica of St. Peter the Apostle, and the servant of God was summoned to his presence. After they had exchanged a few words of greeting, the Pontiff interrogated him on his teaching, on the creed and on the tradition and beliefs of his Church. To this the man of God gave an immediate and humble reply, saying: " My Lord Pope, as a stranger I am conscious that I lack the skill in the use of the tongue with which you are familiar, but grant me leisure and time, I beseech you, to write down my confession of faith, so that my words and not my tongue may make a reasonable presentation of the truths I believe." To this the Pontiff agreed at once and commanded him to bring his written statement as quickly as possible. Within a short time he presented his written confession of faith, expressed in polished, eloquent and learned phrases, and delivered it to the aforesaid Pontiff. He then waited patiently for some days.

At length he was once more invited to meet the Pope, and, being conducted within the Lateran Palace, he cast himself prostrate upon his face at the feet of the Apostolic Pontiff and begged for his blessing. The Pope quickly raised him from the ground, and, after giving into the hands of the servant of God the document in which the pure and uncontaminated truth of the faith was clearly expressed, he invited him to sit at his side. With wise counsel and wholesome doctrine he admonished him to preserve at all times the deposit of the faith and to the best of his ability to preach it vigorously to others. They discussed and debated many other matters relating to holy religion and the true faith, and in this exchange of views they spent almost the whole day. At last the Pope enquired how the people who previously had been steeped in error and wickedness received his preaching of the true faith. On learning that a vast number had been converted from the sacrilegious worship of idols and admitted to the communion of the Church, the Pope told him that he intended to raise him to the episcopal dignity and set him over peoples who up to that time had been without a leader to guide them and who, in the words of our Lord, " languished as sheep without a shepherd ". The saint, not daring to contradict this great Pontiff who ruled the Apostolic See, thereupon gave his consent and obeyed. And so the Supreme Pontiff, who holds the highest authority in the Church, appointed the thirtieth day of November as the day of his consecration.

When the holy day for the sacred solemnity dawned, which was both the feast day of St. Andrew and the day set aside for his consecration, the Holy Pontiff of the Apostolic See conferred upon him the dignity of the episcopate and gave him the name of

Boniface.[1] He put into his hands the book in which the most sacred laws and canons of the Church and the decrees of episcopal synods have been inscribed or compiled,[2] commanding him that henceforth this norm of church conduct and belief should be kept inviolate and that the people under his jurisdiction should be taught on these lines. He also offered to him and to all his subjects the friendship of the Holy Apostolic See thenceforth and for ever.[3] He also wrote letters[4] in which he placed the servant of God under the protection and loving care of the sovereign power of Duke Charles.[5]

After Boniface had passed by devious ways through the densely populated territories of the Franks he came at last into the presence of the aforesaid prince and was received by him with marks of reverence. He delivered to him the letters of the Bishop of Rome and of the Apostolic See, and after acknowledging the prince as his lord and patron, returned with the duke's permission to the land of the Hessians in which he had previously settled.

Now many of the Hessians who at that time had acknowledged the Catholic faith were confirmed by the grace of the Holy Spirit and received the laying-on of hands. But others, not yet strong in the spirit, refused to accept the pure teachings of the Church in their entirety. Moreover, some continued secretly, others openly, to offer sacrifices to trees and springs, to inspect the entrails of victims; some practised divination, legerdemain and incantations; some turned their attention to auguries, auspices and other sacrificial rites; whilst others, of a more reasonable character, forsook all the profane practices of heathenism and committed none of these crimes. With the counsel and advice of the latter persons, Boniface in their presence attempted to cut down, at a place called Gaesmere,[6] a certain oak of extraordinary size called

---

[1] Boniface's ordination oath is preserved: see Letter 5. The date of consecration is uncertain, either 722 or 723.

[2] Probably the manual of canon law of Dionysius Exiguus.

[3] This special relationship was renewed by Pope Gregory III in 731: see Letters 27 and 46, to Pope Zacharias and Stephen III.

[4] Letter 9: several letters given by Gregory under this date, December 722, to Thuringians and Old Saxons; preserved by Otloh, *Vita Bonifatii*, i, 16.

[5] Charles' letter is No. 22 (ed. Tangl).

[6] The Teutonic rendering of *Thor*. There are several places with the name Geismar.

by the pagans of olden times the Oak of Jupiter. Taking his courage in his hands (for a great crowd of pagans stood by watching and bitterly cursing in their hearts the enemy of the gods), he cut the first notch. But when he had made a superficial cut, suddenly the oak's vast bulk, shaken by a mighty blast of wind from above, crashed to the ground shivering its topmost branches into fragments in its fall. As if by the express will of God (for the brethren present had done nothing to cause it) the oak burst asunder into four parts, each part having a trunk of equal length. At the sight of this extraordinary spectacle the heathens who had been cursing ceased to revile and began, on the contrary, to believe and bless the Lord. Thereupon the holy bishop took counsel with the brethren, built an oratory from the timber of the oak and dedicated it to St. Peter the Apostle. He then set out on a journey to Thuringia, having accomplished by the help of God all the things we have already mentioned. Arrived there, he addressed the elders and the chiefs of the people, calling on them to put aside their blind ignorance and to return to the Christian religion which they had formerly embraced. For, after the sovereignty of their kings came to an end, Theobald and Heden[1] had seized the reins of government. Under their disastrous sway, which was founded more upon tyranny and slaughter than upon the loyalty of the people, many of the counts had been put to death or seized and carried off into captivity, whilst the remainder of the population, overwhelmed by all kinds of misfortunes, had submitted to the domination of the Saxons. Thus when the power of the dukes, who had protected religion, was destroyed, the devotion of the people to Christianity and religion died out also, and false brethren were brought in to pervert the minds of the people and to introduce among them under the guise of religion dangerous heretical sects. Of these men the chief were Torchtwine, Zeretheve, Eaubercht and Hunraed, men living in fornication and adultery, whom, in the words of the Apostle, God has already judged. These individuals stirred up a violent conflict against the man of God; but when they had been unmasked and shown to be in opposition to the truth, they received a just penalty for their crimes.

[1] Heden gave donations to Willibrord in 704 and 717.

When the light of faith had illumined the minds of the people and the population had been loosed from its bonds of error, when also the devil's disciples and the insidious seducers of the people, whom we have already mentioned, had been banished, Boniface, assisted by a few helpers, gathered in an abundant harvest. At first he suffered from extreme want and lacked even the necessaries of life, but, though in straitened circumstances and in deep distress, he continued to preach the Word of God. Little by little the number of believers increased, the preachers grew more numerous, church buildings were restored and the Word of God was published far and wide. At the same time the servants of God, monks of genuinely ascetic habits, were grouped together in one body and they established a monastery[1] with their own hands like the Apostles, procuring food and raiment for their needs.

By this means the report of his preaching reached far-off lands so that within a short space of time his fame resounded throughout the greater part of Europe. From Britain an exceedingly large number of holy men came to his aid, among them readers, writers and learned men trained in the other arts. Of these a considerable number put themselves under his rule and guidance, and by their help the population in many places was recalled from the errors and profane rites of their heathen gods. Working in widely scattered groups among the people of Hesse and Thuringia, they preached the Word of God in the country districts and villages. The number of Hessians and Thuringians who received the sacraments of the faith was enormous and many thousands of them were baptised. On the death of Gregory the Second,[2] of blessed memory, ruler of the Apostolic See, the renowned Gregory the Younger[3] ascended the papal throne. Once more the saint's messengers journeyed to Rome and spoke with the Bishop of the Apostolic See, presenting to him the pledge of friendship which his predecessor had previously bestowed upon St. Boniface and his people. They assured the Pope of the saint's devoted and humble submission to the Holy See both in the past and for the

[1] Ohrdruf, near Gotha. This monastery was governed for some years by Wigbert, Abbot of Fritzlar, on the orders of Boniface.
[2] 11 February 731.
[3] Pope Gregory III, 731–41.

future, and begged the Pontiff, in accordance with the instructions they had received, to allow his loyal subject to remain in the brotherhood and communion of the Pope and the Apostolic See. To this the Pontiff gave an immediate reply and granted to St. Boniface and to all those under his care fraternal and friendly communion both with himself and the Apostolic See.[1] Furthermore, he gave the archiepiscopal pallium to the envoys, loaded them with gifts and the relics of divers saints and despatched them homewards.

On their arrival home, the envoys related to St. Boniface the benevolent answer of the Pope, which filled him with joy. Deeply comforted by the liberal support of the Holy See and supported by the assistance of divine grace, he built two churches. One was in Frideslare,[2] which he dedicated to St. Peter, Prince of the Apostles. The other was in Amanburch, which he dedicated to St. Michael the Archangel. He attached two small monasteries to these two churches and invited a large number of monks to serve God there, with the result that even to this day praise and blessing and thanksgiving are offered to the Lord our God.

When all these arrangements had received their final completion he set out on a journey to Bavaria where Duke Hugobert was then.[3] Here he continued to preach and to make visitations of all the churches. So great was his zeal and spiritual courage that he condemned and expelled in accordance with canonical decrees a certain schismatic named Eremwulf, who was imbued with heretical opinions. Boniface then converted the people of this misguided sect from their worship of idols. After this he departed from them and returned to the people of his own diocese, being moved by a desire, as the Apostle puts it, to come to his own brethren.

---

[1] Letter 28 (ed. Tangl).
[2] Fritzlar. The Saxons attempted to burn it down in 774, but in vain. To this monastery, after the death of Wigbert, Boniface sent a letter of instruction: see Letter 40 (ed. Tangl).
[3] Hugobert, died 736.

CHAPTER VII

How he expelled the heretics from the provinces of Bavaria and divided it into four dioceses.

We have spent no little time in recounting some of the merits of St. Boniface in order that we may describe, though not in detail, the powerful religious sense which guided him throughout the whole of his life. For, as history shows, it is a characteristic of the saints that, setting the example of others before their own eyes, they arouse in themselves the desire for better things, and as their life draws to its close they increase the love of God in their hearts.

When a considerable number of churches had been built in Hesse and Thuringia and a superior had been appointed over each church he set out on a journey to Rome for the third time, accompanied as usual by a group of disciples. His intention was to have further discussions with the Holy Father and to commend himself in his declining years to the prayers of the saints. When at the end of his long and painful journey he was brought into the presence of His Holiness Pope Gregory III, the second Pope to be called " The Younger ", he was received with great kindness and was held in such veneration by everyone, as well Romans as strangers, that many flocked together to listen to his preaching.[1] Many Franks, Bavarians and Saxons who had arrived from Britain and other countries followed his teaching with the closest attention.

When he had spent the better part of a year in these parts, visiting and praying at the shrines of the saints, he took his leave of the venerable Bishop of the Apostolic See and returned home, carrying with him many gifts and sacred relics of the saints. After traversing Italy, he came to the walls of the city of Picena, and, as his limbs were weary with old age, he rested awhile with Liudprand, King of the Lombards.

On his departure from Italy he made a visit to the Bavarians, not only because Duke Odilo had sent him an invitation but also

---

[1] Among his hearers was Wynnebald, brother of St. Willibald. Both these brothers eventually worked with Boniface.

because he himself was desirous of seeing them. He remained among them for some time preaching the Word of God, restored the sacraments of the faith to their primitive purity, and banned those men who destroyed the churches and perverted the people. Some of these had arrogated to themselves the dignity of bishops, others the office of priests, whilst others, by these and a thousand other lying pretexts, had led the greater part of the populace into error. The saint, who had dedicated himself to God's service from his earliest childhood and was therefore ill able to brook the insult offered to his Lord, compelled Duke Odilo and his subjects to forsake their evil, false and heretical doctrines and put them on their guard against the deceitfulness of immoral priests. With the consent of Duke Odilo he divided the province of Bavaria into four dioceses and appointed over them four bishops, whom he consecrated for this purpose. Of these, the first, John by name,[1] was appointed to the see in the town which is called Salzburg. The second was Erembert, who took upon himself the obligation of governing the church in the city of Regensburg.[2] When everything was set in order in Bavaria, a Christian form of life established and the prescriptions of canon law enforced, Boniface returned home to his own diocese. He governed the people committed to his care, diligently provided for the needs of his flock, appointed priests to defend the faithful and deliver them from the attacks of ravening wolves.

The temporal rule of Duke Charles eventually came to an end[3] and the reins of power passed into the strong hands of his two sons Carloman and Pippin. Then by the help of God and at the suggestion of the archbishop St. Boniface the establishment of the Christian religion was confirmed, the convening of synods by orthodox bishops was instituted among the Franks and all abuses were redressed and corrected in accordance with canonical authority. On the saint's advice the unlawful practice of concubinage among the layfolk was suppressed whilst the sacrilegious marriages of the clergy were annulled and the sinful parties

[1] John, Bishop of Salzburg, 745–84.
[2] The fourth bishop, Vivilo, had been ordained by Gregory III: see Letter 45 (ed. Tangl).
[3] Charles Martel died October 741.

separated. So great was the religious fervour kindled by the teaching of St. Boniface that Carloman and Pippin freed the faithful to a large extent from the evil practices in which through long neglect they had become deeply rooted and through which, partly by giving rein to their own passions, partly by being misled by the insidious doctrines of heretics, they had forfeited their right to eternal bliss. For so thoroughly had the heretics quenched the light of religious teaching among the people that a dark impenetrable gloom of error had settled down over a large section of the Church. Two of the heretics, for example, named Adalbert and Clement, led astray by this greed for filthy lucre, strove with all their might to turn away the people from the truth. But when the archbishop St. Boniface with the co-operation of Dukes Carloman and Pippin forcibly ejected them from the communion of the Church they were, in accordance with the apostolic words, " delivered unto Satan for the destruction of the flesh that their spirit might be saved in the day of the Lord ".

CHAPTER VIII

How throughout his whole life he preached with zeal and how he departed from this world.

During the reign of Carloman all the bishops, priests, deacons and clerics and everyone of ecclesiastical rank gathered together at the duke's instance and held four synodal councils. At these Archbishop Boniface presided, with the consent and support of Carloman and of the metropolitan of the see and city of Mainz. And being a legate of the Roman Church and the Apostolic See, sent as he was by the saintly and venerable Gregory II and later by Gregory III, he urged that the numerous canons and ordinances decreed by these four important and early councils should be preserved in order to ensure the healthy development of Christian doctrine.[1] For as at the Council of Nicaea, held

[1] Willibald condenses the history of the four main Councils from Isidore of Seville, *Etymologiae*, vi, 16, 5.

under Constantine Augustus, the errors and blasphemies of Arius were rejected; as under Theodosius[1] the Elder an assembly of one hundred and fifty bishops condemned Macedonius, who denied the divinity of the Holy Spirit; as in the city of Ephesus[2] under Theodosius two hundred bishops excommunicated Nestorius for declaring that there are two Persons in Christ; and as at the Council of Chalcedon[3] an assembly of six hundred and thirty bishops, basing their decision on an earlier one of the Fathers, pronounced an anathema against Eutyches, an abbot of Constantinople, and Dioscorus, who defended him, for attacking the foundations of the Catholic faith—so in the Frankish territories, after the eradication of heresy and the destruction of wicked conspirators, he urged that later developments of Christian doctrine and the decrees of the General Councils should be received. With this in view there should be a meeting of the bishops in synod each year in accordance with the aforesaid decree of the General Council. This holding of synods had fallen into desuetude through the constant fear of war and the hostility and attacks of the surrounding barbarian tribes and through the attempts of hostile enemies to destroy the Frankish realm by violence. They had been forgotten so completely that no one could recall such an assembly's having taken place within living memory. For it is in the nature of the world to fall into ruin even though it is daily restored, whilst if no attempt is made to reform it it quickly disintegrates and rushes headlong to its predestined doom. Therefore if in the course of this mortal life means have been discovered to remedy such evils they should be preserved and strongly defended by Catholics and fixed indelibly in the mind. Otherwise human forgetfulness and the enticement of pleasure, both of them instigated by the devil, will prove a stumbling-block. For this reason the holy bishop, in his anxiety to deliver his people from the baleful influence of the devil, repeatedly urged Carloman to summon the episcopal synods already mentioned in order that both present and later generations should learn spiritual wisdom and should make the knowledge of Christianity available

[1] In 381.   [2] In 431.
                     [3] In 451.

to all. Only in this way could unsuspecting souls escape being ensnared.

After he had set before all ranks of society the accepted norm of the Christian life and made known to them the way of truth, Boniface, now weak and decrepit, showed great foresight both as regards himself and his people by appointing a successor to his see, as ecclesiastical law demands. So, whether he lived or whether he died, the people would not be left without pastors and their ministration. He promoted two men of good repute to the episcopate, Willibald and Burchard, dividing between them the churches which were under his jurisdiction in east France and on the frontiers of Bavaria.[1] To Willibald he entrusted the diocese of Eichstatt,[2] to Burchard that of Wurzburgh, putting under his care all the churches within the borders of the Franks, Saxons and Slavs. Nevertheless, even to the day of his death he did not fail to instruct the people in the way of life.

On the death of Carloman,[3] Pippin,[4] his brother, succeeded to the Frankish kingdom, and after the disorders among the people had abated he was proclaimed king. From the outset he conscientiously carried out the vows he had sworn to the Lord, to put into effect without delay the synodal decrees, and he renewed the canonical institutions which his brother, following the advice of the archbishop St. Boniface, had so dutifully set on foot. He showed the saint every mark of veneration and friendship and obeyed his spiritual precepts. But because the saint, owing to his physical infirmities, was not able to attend the synodal assemblies, he decided, with the king's approval and advice, to appoint a suitable person to minister to his flock. To this purpose he appointed Lull,[5] a disciple of outstanding ability, whose duty it would be to continue his instruction to the people. He consecrated him bishop, and committed to his care the inheritance which he had won for Christ by his zealous efforts. Lull was the

---

[1] Letter 50 (ed. Tangl).
[2] Letters 50, 51, 53 (ed. Tangl).
[3] Carloman abdicated in 747 and became a monk, 749–51.
[4] Pippin, November 751.
[5] Letter 93 (ed. Tangl). It is not known when Lull was consecrated bishop; when he returned from Rome in 751 he was still a priest; by 753 he was a bishop.

man who had been his trusted companion on his journeys and who had been closely connected with him both in his sufferings and his consolations.

When the Lord willed to deliver his servant from the trials of this world and to set him free from the vicissitudes of this mortal life, it was decided, under God's providence, that he should travel in the company of his disciples to Frisia, from which he had departed in body though not in spirit. And this was done so that in dying there he might receive the divine recompense in the place where he had begun his preaching.

To Bishop Lull he foretold in an astonishing prophecy the approaching day of his death and made known to him the manner in which he would meet his end. Then he drew up plans for the construction of further churches and for the evangelization of the people. " My wish," he said, " is to complete the journey on which I have set my heart, and nothing can prevent me from doing so. The day of my departure from this life draws near and the time of my death is approaching. In a short time I shall lay aside the burden of my body and receive the prize of eternal bliss. But do thou, my dear son, bring to completion the building of the churches which I began in Thuringia. Earnestly recall the people from the paths of error, finish the construction of the basilica at Fulda, which is now in process of building, and bring thither this body of mine now wasted by the toil of years." When he had ended his instructions he added the following words, or words to this effect: " Carefully provide everything which we shall need on our journey, not forgetting to place in the chest, where my books are kept, a linen sheet in which my aged body may be wrapped."

At these sad words Bishop Lull could not restrain his tears and gave vent to his profound sorrow; but Boniface, having expressed his last wishes, went about his business unconcerned. After the lapse of a few days, he still persevered in his decision to set out on the journey, and so, taking with him a few companions, he went on board a ship and sailed down the Rhine.[1] Eventually he reached the marshy country of Frisia, crossed

---

[1] The journey took place in the early summer (after 23 May) of 753-4.

safely over the stretch of water, which in their tongue is called
Aelmere,[1] and made a survey of the lands round about, which up
till then had borne no fruit. After bravely hazarding the perils
of the river, the sea and the wide expanse of the ocean, he passed
through dangerous places without fear of danger, and visited the
heathen Frisians, whose land is divided into many territories
and districts by intersecting canals. These territories, though
bearing different names, are, nevertheless, the property of one
nation. But since it would prove tedious to give a list of
these districts one after the other, we will merely mention one or
two of them by name to prove the veracity and add to the
continuity of our narrative. In this way the place and its name
will bear witness to the activities of the saint as we relate
them and show the kind of death which took him from this
world.

This, then, is how he traversed the whole of Frisia,[2] destroy-
ing pagan worship and turning away the people from their
heathen errors by his preaching of the Gospel. The heathen
temples and gods were overthrown and churches were built in
their stead. Many thousands of men, women and children were
baptized by him, assisted by his fellow missionary and suffragan
bishop Eoban, who, after being consecrated and appointed to the
diocese of Utrecht, was summoned to Frisia to help Boniface in
his old age. He was also assisted in his labours by a number of
priests and deacons whose names are subjoined: Wintrung,
Walthere, Ethelhere, priests; Hamrind, Scirbald and Bosa,
deacons; Wachar, Gundaecer, Illehere and Hathowulf, monks.
These in company with St. Boniface preached the Word of
God far and wide with great success and were so united in spirit
that, like the Apostles, they had but one heart and one soul,
and thus deserved to share in the same crown of martyrdom and
the same final and eternal reward.

When, as we have already said, the faith had been planted
strongly in Frisia and the glorious end of the saint's life drew near,
he took with him a picked number of his personal followers and

[1] Now Zuyder Zee.
[2] According to Eigil, *Vita Sturmi*, this was in the second summer of the
Frisian ministry after an intervening winter spent in Germany.

pitched a camp on the banks of the river Bordne[1] which flows through the territories called Ostor and Westeraeche and divides them. Here he fixed a day on which he would confirm by the laying-on of hands all the neophytes and those who had recently been baptized; and because the people were scattered far and wide over the countryside, they all returned to their homes, so that, in accordance with the instructions laid down by the holy bishop, they could meet together again on the day appointed for their confirmation.

But events turned out otherwise than expected. When the appointed day arrived and the morning light was breaking through the clouds after sunrise, enemies came instead of friends, new executioners in place of new worshippers of the faith. A vast number of foes armed with spears and shields rushed into the camp brandishing their weapons. In the twinkling of an eye the attendants sprang from the camp to meet them and snatched up arms here and there to defend the holy band of martyrs (for that is what they were to be) against the insensate fury of the mob. But the man of God, hearing the shouts and the onrush of the rabble, straightway called the clergy to his side, and, collecting together the relics of the saints, which he always carried with him, came out of his tent. At once he reproved the attendants and forbade them to continue the conflict, saying: " Sons, cease fighting. Lay down your arms, for we are told in Scripture not to render evil for good but to overcome evil by good. The hour to which we have long looked forward is near and the day of our release is at hand. Take comfort in the Lord and endure with gladness the suffering He has mercifully ordained. Put your trust in Him and He will grant deliverance to your souls." And addressing himself like a loving father to the priests, deacons and other clerics, all trained to the service of God, who stood about him, he gave them courage, saying: " Brethren, be of stout heart, fear not them who kill the body, for they cannot slay the soul, which continues to live for ever. Rejoice in the Lord; anchor your hope in God, for without delay He will render to you the reward of eternal bliss and grant you an abode with the

[1] Boorne, Dutch province of Friesland.

angels in His heaven above. Be not slaves to the transitory pleasures of this world. Be not seduced by the vain flattery of the heathen, but endure with steadfast mind the sudden onslaught of death, that you may be able to reign evermore with Christ."

Whilst with these words he was encouraging his disciples to accept the crown of martyrdom, the frenzied mob of heathens rushed suddenly upon them with swords and every kind of warlike weapon, staining their bodies with their precious blood.[1]

When they had sated their lust for blood on the mortal remains of the just, the heathenish mob seized with exultation upon the spoils of their victory (in reality the cause of their damnation) and, after laying waste the camp, carried off and shared the booty; they stole the chests in which the books and relics were preserved and, thinking that they had acquired a hoard of gold and silver, carried them off, still locked, to the ships. Now the ships were stocked with provisions for the feeding of the clerics and attendants and a great deal of wine still remained. Finding this goodly liquor, the heathens immediately began to slake their sottish appetites and to get drunk. After some time, by the wonderful dispensation of God, they began to argue among themselves about the booty they had taken and discussed how they were to share out the gold and silver which they had not even seen. During the long and wordy discussion about the treasure, which they imagined to be considerable, frequent quarrels broke out amongst them until, in the end, there arose such enmity and discord that they were divided into two angry and frenzied factions. It was not long before the weapons which had earlier murdered the holy martyrs were turned against each other in bitter strife. After the greater part of the mad freebooters had been slain, the survivors, surrounded by the corpses of their rivals for the booty, swooped down upon the treasure which had been obtained by so much loss of life. They broke open the chests containing the books and found, to their dismay, that they held manuscripts instead of gold vessels, pages of sacred texts instead of silver plate. Disappointed in their hope of gold and silver, they littered the fields with the books they found, throwing some of them into reedy marshes, hiding

[1] Thirty suffered with him, of whom the best known is Eoban.

away others in widely different places. But by the grace of God and through the prayers of the archbishop and martyr St. Boniface the manuscripts were discovered, a long time afterwards, unharmed and intact,[1] and they were returned by those who found them to the monastery,[2] in which they are used with great advantage to the salvation of souls even at the present day.

Disillusioned by the loss of the treasure on which they had reckoned, the murderers returned to their dwellings. But after a lapse of three days they were visited with a just retribution for their crimes, losing not only all their worldly possessions but their lives also. For it was the will of the omnipotent Creator and Saviour of the world that He should be avenged of His enemies; and in His mercy and compassion he demanded a penalty for the sacred blood shed on His behalf. Deeply moved by the recent act of wicked savagery, He deigned to show the wrath He had concealed so long against the worshippers of idols. As the unhappy tidings of the martyr's death spread rapidly from village to village throughout the whole province and the Christians learned of their fate, a large avenging force, composed of warriors ready to take speedy retribution, was gathered together and rushed swiftly to their neighbours' frontiers. The heathens, unable to withstand the onslaught of the Christians, immediately took to flight and were slaughtered in great numbers. In their flight they lost their lives, their household goods and their children. So the Christians, after taking as their spoil the wives and children, men and maid-servants of the pagan worshippers, returned to their homes. As a result, the pagans round about, dismayed at their recent misfortune and seeking to avoid everlasting punishment, opened their minds and hearts to the glory of the faith. Struck with terror at the visitation of God's vengeance, they embraced after Boniface's death the teaching which they had rejected whilst he still lived.

The bodies of the holy bishop and of the other martyrs were

---

[1] Three books, the so-called *Codices Bonifatiani*, are preserved in the Landesbibliothek at Fulda. One of these, almost cut through, is traditionally identified with the book mentioned in the *Vita Bonifatii* by Radbod of Utrecht.

[2] Cathedral of Fulda, probably.

brought by boat across the water called Aelmere, an uneventful voyage of some days, to the city of Utrecht, which we mentioned earlier. There the bodies were deposited and interred until some religious and trustworthy men of God arrived from Mainz. From there they had been sent in a ship by Bishop Lull, the successor of our holy bishop and martyr, to bring the body of the saint to the monastery built by him during his lifetime on the banks of the river Fulda. Of these men there was one named Hadda, remarkable for his continence and chastity, who planned the journey and organized the party. On him particularly and on all the brethren who accompanied him Lull imposed the obligation of setting out on the journey and of bringing back the sacred body in order that greater honour and reverence might be paid to the holy man and greater credence might be given to all the facts they saw and heard.

This venerable and holy company came to the city of Utrecht and was met by a small throng of people. But the count of the city declared in the hearing of all that an edict had been issued by King Pippin forbidding anyone to remove the body of Bishop Boniface from that place. As, however, the power of Almighty God is greater than the strength of men, suddenly in their presence a marvellous miracle took place, wrought through angelic rather than human intervention. The bell of the church, untouched by human hands, began to ring, as if the body of the saint was issuing a warning; and every person present, smitten by a sudden feeling of awe, was struck with terror and cried out that the body of this holy man should be given up. The body, consequently, was handed over at once and was taken away in great honour by the brethren already mentioned. And so, to the accompaniment of psalms and hymns, without having to row against the current of the stream, the body was brought, thirty days after the saint's decease, to the city of Mainz. It fell out by the wonderful providence of God that on one and the same day, although no fixed arrangement had been made, there assembled together for the interment of this great man not only the envoys who had brought the sacred body but also many men and women of the faith from distant and widely scattered districts, just as if they had been forewarned of the event. Moreover, Lull, the saint's successor, who at that time was engaged at the royal palace and was not informed of the arrival of the sacred body and was quite ignorant of what was afoot, came to Mainz almost at the same hour and moment.[1] And though all strangers and citizens alike were weighed down with sorrow and grief, yet they experienced a great joy. For whilst they were struck with grief when they considered the circumstances of his death, they felt, on the other hand, that he would protect them and their heirs for all time to come. Therefore the people with the priests, deacons and all ranks of the clergy carried the sacred body, with hearts torn by conflicting emotions, to the spot which he had decided upon during his lifetime. A new sarcophagus was made in the church and the body was laid in it with all the customary rites of burial. When the ceremony was over they all returned to their homes, strengthened and comforted in the faith.

From that moment the spot in which the sacred body was interred became the scene of many divine blessings through the intercession of the saint; many of those who came there, troubled by various sicknesses and diseases, were healed in soul and body. Some who were at death's door and practically lifeless, deprived of everything except their last breath, were restored to vigorous health. Others, whose eyes were dim with blindness, received their sight; others, bound fast by the snares of the devil, unbalanced in mind and out of their senses, regained their peace of mind and after their cure gave praise and thanks to God. God deigned to honour and enrich His servant, who possessed this great gift, and glorified him in the eyes of present and future ages, forty years after his pilgrimage was over, i.e., 716, which year is reckoned as the year of the Incarnation of our Lord seven hundred and fifty-five, the eighth indiction.[2] He occupied the episcopal chair thirty-six years, six months and six days. Thus, in the manner described above, on the fifth day of June, crowned with the palm of martyrdom, he departed to the Lord, to whom be honour and glory for ever and ever. Amen.

---

[1] According to Eigil, Lull wished to keep the body at Mainz.
[2] Tradition at Fulda says 754, a date supported by Tangl.

Chapter IX

How in the place where the blood of the martyrs was shed a living fountain appeared to those who were surveying the site for a church.

Now that we have narrated the outstanding events in the saint's childhood, boyhood, youth, middle life, old age, let us return to the marvellous happenings which were wrought by the help of God after his life's work was over, and make known to men the sanctity of his life.

Let us recall to memory a miracle which people still remember and recount. This story was told to us by the venerable Bishop Lull, who learned it from King Pippin, who in turn heard it from eyewitnesses. The story as related by Lull goes as follows: A plan was drawn up with the advice of the ecclesiastical authorities and the majority of the Frisian people to raise an enormous mound of earth on the spot where some years before the precious blood of the holy martyr had been spilt. This was because the violent neap and spring tides at different times of the year affect the ocean swell and cause disturbances in the incoming and outgoing floods of water. On the mound they proposed to build a church[1] (as was done later) and to construct on the same spot a monastery for the servants of God. But when the mound had been raised and the work of building it up had been completed, the residents and inhabitants of the district began to discuss on their return home the difficulty of obtaining fresh water, for throughout almost all Frisia this is a great problem both for man and beast. At last a certain man named Abba, who was an administrator under King Pippin and director of the work in question, taking some attendants with him, mounted his horse, rode over the hill and inspected the mound. Suddenly and unexpectedly the horse of one of the attendants, which had barely trod upon the ground, felt it sinking and giving way altogether. With its forelegs held firmly in the soil, the horse rolled helplessly about until those who were more active and experienced

[1] The church was dedicated to SS. Paul and Boniface.

hurriedly dismounted from their horses and extricated it as it lay fast in the earth. At once an astonishing miracle happened, worthy to be remembered by all those who were present and saw it. A fountain of water much clearer than any found in that country, extraordinarily sweet and pleasant to the taste, came bubbling up and flowed out through innumerable channels until it formed a considerable stream. Astounded at this miracle, they returned to their homes in joy and gladness, spreading the news in the churches of what they had seen.

THE CORRESPONDENCE OF
ST. BONIFACE

The correspondence of St. Boniface as edited by Tangl contains many letters which belong to several other people in his circle, such as Lull, and to various correspondents in England and in Rome. Since some of these are of no particular interest, it has been thought better to concentrate on those letters which are intimately concerned with the progress of his missionary work in Germany and with those facets of his character which emerge most clearly in the execution of his plans. The more homely and affectionate side of his nature appears in his letters to nuns, his preoccupation with the education of his disciples and subjects in his letters to abbots and bishops in England; whilst the difficulties of conversion, of organization, of church reform and many other matters are the subject of his letters to the Popes. Nowhere else in this period do we find so vivid a picture of the discouraging conditions amongst which the missionaries laboured and died. But in spite of the moral degradation of the Frankish clergy whom he strove to reform, in spite also of the poverty, dangers, ostracism and opposition which he met, there is no echo in these letters of discouragement, self-pity or weariness. We see him forging patiently and with complete confidence the instruments by which Europe was to be converted—the establishment of convents and monasteries, the foundation of bishoprics, centres of education and schools, submitting all to the ever-watchful guidance of the Popes, to whose devoted and constant service he had pledged himself at the outset of his missionary career.

THE CORRESPONDENCE OF ST. BONIFACE

BONIFACE ADVISES NITHARD TO CONTINUE HIS STUDIES
(A.D. 716–19)

To MY dear friend and companion, who was drawn to me not by gifts of perishable gold nor by the smooth tongue of flattery but by the similarity of our ideals and the bonds of unfailing love, Wynfrith, a suppliant, sends greetings for eternal welfare in Jesus Christ.

Lowly as I am, noble youth, I beg you not to disregard the words of Solomon the wise: " In all thy works remember thy last end and thou shalt never sin."[1] Walk whilst you have the light lest the darkness of death come upon you.[2] Temporal things pass swiftly away, but the eternal that never fade will soon be upon us. All the treasures of this world, such as gold, silver, precious stones of every hue, succulent and dainty food and costly garments, melt away like shadows, vanish like smoke, dissolve like foam on the sea. The psalmist uttered the truth when he said: " Man's days are like grass: like the flower of the field he flourishes."[3] And again: " My days are like a shadow that declineth and I am withered like grass."[4]

Men who wallow in luxury are said in Holy Scripture to pass sleepless nights through anxiety, spinning their fragile webs that catch only dust or a breath of wind, for as the psalmist says: " They gather together treasure and know not for whom they gather it."[5] And at the moment when death, the minion of baneful Pluto, barks at the door, foaming at the mouth and gnashing his teeth, they faint with fear; then, deprived of heavenly consolation, they lose in an instant both their precious souls and the deceitful gains for which they have slaved like misers night and day. Finally,

[1] Ecclus. vii. 40.
[2] John xii. 35.
[3] Ps. cii. 15.
[4] Ps. ci. 12.
[5] Ps. xxxviii. 7.

they are snatched by the claws of fiends and borne off to the gloomy caverns of Erebus, there to suffer everlasting torments.

There is no doubting the truth of this. In all earnestness and affection I beg you to consider this matter very carefully. Give rein to your natural gifts and abilities; do not stifle your literary talents and your keen spiritual understanding with gross pleasures of the flesh. Keep in mind the words of the psalmist: "His delight is in the words of the law of the Lord; in his law he meditates day and night ":[1] and elsewhere: " O how I love thy law, it is my meditation all the day."[2] Call to mind also the words of Moses: " This book of the law shall not depart out of thy mouth, but thou shalt meditate therein day and night."[3] Put aside all harmful obstacles; strive with unflagging zest to pursue your study of the scriptures and thereby acquire that nobility of mind which is divine wisdom. It is more precious than gold, more beautiful than silver, more lustrous than onyx, clearer than crystal, more costly than topaz,[4] and, according to the opinion of the Preacher, all things that may be desired are not to be compared with it.[5]

Can there be a more fitting pursuit in youth or a more valuable possession in old age than a knowledge of Holy Writ? In the midst of storms it will preserve you from the dangers of shipwreck and guide you to the shore of an enchanting paradise and the everlasting bliss of the angels. Of it the same wise man has remarked: "Wisdom overcometh evil: it stretches from end to end mightily and disposes all things sweetly. Her have I loved from my youth and have become enamoured of her form."[6]

If God allows me to return home, for such is my intention, I promise to remain steadfast at your side, helping you in your study of Sacred Scripture to the best of my ability.

(Tangl, 9)

[1] Ps. i. 2.
[2] Ps. cxviii. 97.
[3] Josue. i. 8.
[4] Job xxviii. 17, 19.
[5] Prov. viii. 11.
[6] Wisd. viii. 1.

2

BISHOP DANIEL OF WINCHESTER[1] GIVES WYNFRITH A LETTER OF INTRODUCTION

(718)

To godly and merciful kings, all dukes, reverend and beloved bishops, priests and holy abbots and to all the spiritual sons of Christ, Daniel, a servant of the servants of God.

Though the commandments of God should be observed by all the faithful with sincerity and devotion, Holy Scripture lays special stress on the obligation of offering hospitality to travellers and shows how pleasing to God is the fulfilment of this duty. As a reward for his kindly hospitality, Abraham was judged worthy of receiving the blessed angels in person and of enjoying their holy converse. Lot also on account of this same service was snatched from the flames of Sodom.

So it will redound to your eternal welfare if you extend to the bearer of this letter, Wynfrith, a holy priest and servant of almighty God, a warm welcome such as God loves and enjoins. In receiving the servants of God you receive Him whom they serve, for he promised: " He who receiveth you, receiveth me."

Do this with heartfelt devotion and you will fulfil the divine command, and by placing your trust in God's promises you will receive an everlasting reward.

May the grace of God protect you from harm.

(Tangl, 11)

---

[1] Daniel, Bishop of Winchester, was a pupil, like Aldhelm of Malmesbury, of Maelduff and is ranked as one of the most learned, energetic and influential bishops of the period. He assisted Bede in the compilation of his *Ecclesiastical History* by providing him with material relating to the Church in Wessex, Sussex and the Isle of Wight. In 721 he visited Rome. He resigned his see in 744 through failing sight and retired to Malmesbury, where he died in the following year.

3

POPE GREGORY II[1] ENTRUSTS BONIFACE WITH A MISSION TO THE HEATHENS

(15 May 719)

Gregory, the servant of the servants of God, to Boniface, a holy priest.

Your holy purpose, as it has been explained to us, and your well-tried faith lead us to make use of your services in spreading the Gospel, which by the grace of God has been committed to our care. Knowing that from your childhood you have been a student of Sacred Scripture and that you now wish to use the talent entrusted to you by God in dedicating yourself to missionary work, we rejoice in your faith and desire to have you as our colleague in this enterprise. Wherefore, since you have humbly submitted to us your plans regarding this mission, like a member of the body deferring to the head, and have shown yourself to be a true member of the body by following the directions given by the head, therefore, in the name of the indivisible Trinity and by the authority of St. Peter, Prince of the Apostles, whose government we administer in this See by the dispensation of God, we now place your humble and devout work upon a secure basis and decree that you go forth to preach the Word of God to those people who are still bound by the shackles of paganism. You are to teach them the service of the kingdom of God by persuading them to accept the truth in the name of Christ, the Lord our God. You will instil into their minds the teaching of the Old and New Testaments, doing this in a spirit of love and moderation, and with arguments suited to their understanding. Finally, we command you that in admitting within the Church those who have some kind of belief in God you will insist upon using the sacramental discipline prescribed in the official ritual formulary of the Holy Apostolic See. Whatever means you find lacking in the

[1] Gregory was known as " The Younger ", 715-31. It was to him that Abbot Ceolfrid brought the famous *Codex Amiatinus*, so precious for establishing the text of the Vulgate, and on his encouragement that King Ina, on his visit to Rome, founded the Schola Anglorum, later the nursery of many martyrs during the Reformation period.

furtherance of your work, you are to report to us as opportunity occurs.

Fare you well.

Given on the Ides of May in the third year of our most august Lord, Leo, by God crowned emperor, in the third year of his consulship, in the second indiction.

(Tangl, 12)

4

THE ABBESS BUGGA[1] CONGRATULATES BONIFACE ON HIS SUCCESS IN FRISIA

(720)

Be it known to you, my gracious father, that I give thanks without ceasing to Almighty God because, as I learned from your letter, He has shown His mercy to you in many ways and jealously guarded you on your way through strange and distant lands. First, He inspired the Pontiff who sits in the chair of Peter to grant the desire of your heart. Afterwards He humbled at your feet King Radbod, the enemy of the Catholic Church; finally He revealed to you in a dream that you would reap God's harvest and gather many souls into the barn of the heavenly kingdom. I am led to believe that, no matter what our circumstances on earth may be, nothing can separate me from the affectionate care you have always shown. The strength of my love increases the more I perceive for certain that through the support of your prayers I have come into a haven of security and peace. And so again I humbly beg you: deign to offer your earnest intercession to God for my unworthy self, so that through your protection His grace may keep me safe from harm.

Know also that I have been unable to obtain a copy of *The Sufferings of the Martyrs* which you asked me to send you, but I shall send it to you as soon as I can. And you, my best beloved,

[1] Bugga, or St. Eadburga, was Abbess of Minster in the Isle of Thanet. She was the daughter of King Centwin of the West Saxons. Her predecessor at Minster was St. Mildred, whose incorruptible body she laid to rest in a new church built by her and consecrated by Cuthbert, Archbishop of Canterbury. She was of great assistance to Boniface, especially by her gifts of books. Leoba also learned much from her. She died about 751 and her feast was kept on 27 December.

comfort me in my weakness by sending me some select passages of Holy Scripture in fulfilment of the promise made in your last letter. I beg you also to offer some holy Masses for the soul of a relative of mine, who was dear to me beyond all others and whose name was N ——.

By this same messenger I am sending you fifty shillings and an altar cloth, because I was unable to get for you a more precious gift. Small as they are, they are sent with great love.

Farewell in this world, " in love unfeigned ".

(Tangl, 15)

5

THE OATH[1] TAKEN BY BONIFACE
(30 November 722)

In the name of God and of our Saviour Jesus Christ.

In the sixth year of Leo, by the grace of God crowned emperor, the sixth year of his consulship, the fourth of his son the Emperor Constantine, the sixth indiction.

I, Boniface, by the grace of God bishop, promise to you, blessed Peter, chief of the Apostles, and to your vicar, the blessed Pope Gregory, and to his successors, in the name of the indivisible Trinity, Father, Son and Holy Ghost, and on thy most sacred body, that I will uphold the faith and purity of holy Catholic teaching and will persevere in the unity of the same faith in which beyond a doubt the whole salvation of a Christian lies. I will not agree to anything which is opposed to the unity of the Universal Church, no matter who may try to persuade me, but in all things I will show, as I have said, complete loyalty to you and to the welfare of your Church on which, in the person of your vicar and his successors, the power to bind and loose has been conferred.

Should it come to my notice that some bishops deviate from the teaching of the Fathers I will have no part or lot with them, but as far as in me lies I will correct them, or, if that is impossible, I will report the matter to the Holy See. And if (which God forbid)

---

[1] This oath is based upon one usually taken by the bishops of the sub-urbicarian sees, but here there is no expression of loyalty to the emperor—it has been changed into submission to the Holy See.

I should be led astray into any course of action contrary to this my oath, under whatsoever pretext, may I be found guilty at the last judgment and suffer the punishment meted out to Ananias and Sapphira, who dared to defraud you by making a false declaration of their goods.

This text of my oath, I, Boniface, a lowly bishop, have written with my own hand and placed over thy sacred body. I have taken this oath, as prescribed, in the presence of God, my Witness and my Judge: I pledge myself to keep it.

(Tangl, 16)

6

POPE GREGORY II COMMENDS BISHOP BONIFACE TO THE CHRISTIANS OF GERMANY

(1 December 722)

Bishop Gregory, servant of the servants of God, to all the very reverend and holy brethren, fellow-bishops, religious priests and deacons, dukes, provosts, counts and all Christian men who fear God.

Knowing that some of the peoples in the parts of Germany that lie on the eastern bank of the Rhine have been led astray by the wiles of the devil and now serve idols under the guise of the Christian religion, and that others have not yet been cleansed by the waters of holy Baptism, but like brute beasts are blind to their Creator, we have taken great care to send the bearer of these letters, our revered brother and fellow-bishop Boniface, into these parts to enlighten them and to preach the word of faith, so that by his preaching he may teach them the way of eternal life, and when he finds those who have been led astray from the path of true faith or been misled by the cunning of the devil he may reprove them, bring them back to the haven of salvation, instruct them in the teachings of this Apostolic See and confirm them in the Catholic faith.

We exhort you, then, for the love of our Lord Jesus Christ and the reverence you bear to His apostles, to support him by all the means at your disposal and to receive him in the name of Jesus Christ, according to what is written of His disciples: " He who receiveth you, receiveth me." See to it that he has all he requires; give him companions to escort him on his journey, provide him with food and drink and anything else he may need, so that with the blessing of God the work of piety and salvation committed to him may proceed without hindrance, and that you yourselves may receive the reward of your labours and through the conversion of sinners may find treasure laid up for you in heaven.

If, therefore, any man assists and gives succour to this servant of God sent by the Apostolic See for the enlightenment of the heathen, may he enjoy through the prayers of the princes of the Apostles the fellowship of the saints and martyrs of Jesus Christ.

But if (which God forbid) any man should attempt to hinder his efforts and oppose the work of the ministry entrusted to him and his successors, may he be cursed by the judgment of God and condemned to eternal damnation.

Fare ye well.

(Tangl, 17)

7

GREGORY INVESTS BONIFACE WITH EPISCOPAL AUTHORITY

(1 December 722)

Gregory, the servant of the servants of God, to the clergy and people [of Thuringia], greeting in the Lord.

Acceding without delay to your praiseworthy desire, we have raised our colleague Boniface to the episcopal dignity. We have commanded him not to ordain a man who has been married twice or one who has married a woman not a virgin, or one who is not fully instructed, or a man suffering from a physical defect, or who is notorious for a crime whether civil or ecclesiastical, or who is known to be subject to some liability. If he finds such persons in office he shall not advance them. Under no circumstances whatsoever should he accept Africans who dare to apply for admission to ecclesiastical orders, because some of them are Manichaeans and others are known to have received Baptism several times. He shall endeavour not to diminish but rather to increase the services and adornments of the churches and whatsoever endowments they possess. He is to divide the revenue and the offerings of the faithful into four parts: one for himself, another to the clergy for their ministrations, a third to the poor and pilgrims, and a fourth for the fabric of the churches, for all of which he must render an account at the judgment seat of God. The ordination of priests and deacons is to take place only at the quarter tenses of April, July and October and at the beginning of Lent. Baptism must be conferred only at Easter and Whitsuntide, except in the case of those who are in danger of death, for otherwise they might perish eternally.

As long as he continues to carry out the injunctions of this our see you are to show him unquestioning obedience, that the body of the Church may be without blame and in perfect peace, through Jesus Christ our Lord, who liveth and reigneth with Almighty God and the Holy Spirit for ever and ever.

May God preserve you from all harm, beloved sons.

Given on the kalends of December in the seventh year of the reign of our august Lord, Leo, by the grace of God crowned emperor, in the fourth year of his son Constantine the Great, the sixth indiction.

(Tangl, 18)

8

POPE GREGORY II COMMENDS BONIFACE TO THE LEADERS OF THURINGIA

(December 722)

Pope Gregory to his distinguished sons Asulf, Godolaus, Wilareus, Gundhar, Alvold and all the faithful of Thuringia who are beloved of God.

The report of your loyalty to Christ and of your steadfast answers to the heathen when they urged you to return to the worship of idols that you would rather die than break faith with Christ once you had accepted Him filled us with great joy. We give thanks to our God and Redeemer, the Giver of all good.

We pray that in the strength of His grace you may advance to higher and greater things, whilst you cling with all your might to the beliefs and teaching of the Holy Apostolic See.

We pray also that as far as the work of our holy religion requires, you will seek consolation from this Holy Apostolic See, who is the spiritual mother of all believers, for as you are her sons and joint heirs of a kingdom that has a royal Father it is fitting that you do so.

We bid you to show obedience in all things to our dearest brother Boniface, now consecrated bishop, who is well grounded in all the traditions of this Apostolic See. We send him to you to preach and instruct you in the faith and we urge you to co-operate with him in working out your salvation in the Lord.

(Tangl, 19)

9

POPE GREGORY II COMMENDS BONIFACE TO CHARLES MARTEL
(December 722)

To the glorious Lord, our son, Duke Charles.

Having learned, beloved son in Christ, that you are a man of deeply religious feeling, we make known to you that our brother Boniface, who now stands before you, a man of sterling faith and character, has been consecrated bishop by us, and after being instructed in the teachings of the Holy Apostolic See, over which by God's grace we preside, is being sent to preach the faith to the peoples of Germany who dwell on the eastern bank of the Rhine, some of whom are still steeped in the errors of paganism, while many more are plunged in the darkness of ignorance.

For this reason we commend him without more ado to your kindness and goodwill, begging you to help him in all his needs and to grant him your constant protection against any who may stand in his way. Know for certain that any favour bestowed on him is done for God, who on sending His holy Apostles to convert the Gentiles said that any man who received them received Him.

Instructed by us in the teachings of these Apostles, the bishop aforesaid is now on his way to take up the work assigned to him.

(Tangl, 20)

10

CHARLES MARTEL[1] TAKES BONIFACE UNDER HIS PROTECTION
(723)

To the holy lords and apostolic fathers, bishops, dukes, counts, regents, servants, lesser officials and friends, Charles, Mayor of the Palace, hearty greetings.

Let it be known that the apostolic father Bishop Boniface has come into our presence and begged us to take him under our protection. Know then that it has been our pleasure to do this.

Furthermore, we have seen fit to issue and seal with our own hand an order that wheresoever he goes, no matter where it shall be, he shall with our love and protection remain unmolested and undisturbed, on the understanding that he shall maintain justice and receive justice in like manner.

And if any question or eventuality arise which is not covered by our law, he shall remain unmolested and undisturbed until he reach our presence, both he and those who put their trust in him, so that as long as he remains under our protection no man shall oppose or do him harm.

And in order to give greater authority to this our command, we have signed it with our own hand and sealed it below with our ring.

(Tangl, 22)

11

BISHOP DANIEL OF WINCHESTER ADVISES BONIFACE ON THE METHOD OF CONVERTING THE HEATHEN
(723-4)

To Boniface, honoured and beloved leader, Daniel, servant of the people of God.

Great is my joy, brother and colleague in the episcopate, that your good work has received its reward. Supported by your deep

---

[1] Charles Martel (688–741) was the natural son of Pippin of Heristal. He received the appellation Martel (the Hammer) from his victory over the Saracens at Tours, upon the issue of which depended the fate of Christendom.

faith and great courage, you have embarked upon the conversion of heathens whose hearts have hitherto been stony and barren; and with the Gospel as your ploughshare you have laboured tirelessly day after day to transform them into harvest-bearing fields. Well may the words of the prophet be applied to you: " A voice of one crying in the wilderness, etc."

Yet not less deserving of reward are they who give what help they can to such a good and deserving work by relieving the poverty of the labourers, so that they may pursue unhampered the task of preaching and begetting children to Christ. And so, moved by affection and good will, I am taking the liberty of making a few suggestions, in order to show you how, in my opinion, you may overcome with the least possible trouble the resistance of this barbarous people.

Do not begin by arguing with them about the genealogies of their false gods. Accept their statement that they were begotten by other gods through the intercourse of male and female and then you will be able to prove that, as these gods and goddesses did not exist before, and were born like men, they must be men and not gods. When they have been forced to admit that their gods had a beginning, since they were begotten by others, they should be asked whether the world had a beginning or was always in existence. There is no doubt that before the universe was created there was no place in which these created gods could have subsisted or dwelt. And by " universe " I mean not merely heaven and earth which we see with our eyes but the whole extent of space which even the heathens can grasp in their imagination. If they maintain that the universe had no beginning, try to refute their arguments and bring forward convincing proofs; and if they persist in arguing, ask them, Who ruled it? How did the gods bring under their sway a universe that existed before them? Whence or by whom or when was the first god or goddess begotten? Do they believe that gods and goddesses still beget other gods and goddesses? If they do not, when did they cease and why? If they do, the number of gods must be infinite. In such a case, who is the most powerful among these different gods? Surely no mortal man can know. Yet man must take care not to offend this god who is more powerful than the rest. Do they think the gods should be worshipped for the sake of temporal and transitory benefits or for eternal and future reward? If for temporal benefit let them say in what respect the heathens are better off than the Christians. What do the heathen gods gain from the sacrifices if they already possess everything? Or why do the gods leave it to the whim of their subjects to decide what kind of tribute shall be paid? If they need such sacrifices, why do they not choose more suitable ones? If they do not need them, then the people are wrong in thinking that they can placate the gods with such offerings and victims.

These and similar questions, and many others that it would be tedious to mention, should be put to them, not in an offensive and irritating way but calmly and with great moderation. From time to time their superstitions should be compared with our Christian dogmas and touched upon indirectly, so that the heathens, more out of confusion than exasperation, may be ashamed of their absurd opinions and may recognise that their disgusting rites and legends have not escaped our notice.

This conclusion also must be drawn: If the gods are omnipotent, beneficent and just, they must reward their devotees and punish those who despise them. Why then, if they act thus in temporal affairs, do they spare the Christians who cast down their idols and turn away from their worship the inhabitants of practically the entire globe? And whilst the Christians are allowed to possess the countries that are rich in oil and wine and other commodities, why have they left to the heathens the frozen lands of the north, where the gods, banished from the rest of the world, are falsely supposed to dwell?

The heathens are frequently to be reminded of the supremacy of the Christian world and of the fact that they who still cling to outworn beliefs are in a very small minority.

If they boast that the gods have held undisputed sway over these people from the beginning, point out to them that formerly the whole world was given over to the worship of idols until, by the grace of Christ and through the knowledge of one God, its Almighty Creator and Ruler, it was enlightened, vivified and reconciled to God. For what does the baptizing of the children of Christian parents signify if not the purification of each one from the uncleanness of the guilt of heathenism in which the entire human race was involved?

It has given me great pleasure, brother, for the love I bear you, to bring these matters to your notice. Afflicted though I am with bodily infirmities, I may well say with the psalmist: " I know, O Lord, that thy judgment is just and that in truth thou hast afflicted me."[1] For this reason, I earnestly entreat Your Reverence and those with you who serve Christ in the spirit to pray for me that the Lord who made me taste of the wine of compunction may quickly aid me unto mercy, that as He has punished me justly, so He may graciously pardon and mercifully enable me to sing in gratitude the words of the prophet: " According to the number of my sorrows, thy consolations have comforted my soul."[2]

I pray for your welfare in Christ, my very dear colleague, and beg you to remember me.

(Tangl, 23)

12

POPE GREGORY REPLIES TO A REPORT FROM BONIFACE
(4 December 723)

To his most reverend brother and fellow-bishop Boniface, Gregory, the servant of the servants of God.

Moved by our anxiety for the charge committed to us and by the words of the Gospel, which says, " You must ask the lord to whom the harvest belongs to send labourers out to the harvesting ", we sent you just as the Lord sent the Apostles with the command: " Go out all over the world and preach the Gospel: freely you have received, freely give."

We sent you to shed some light on the people of Germany who sit in the shadow of death, so that, like the servant with the single talent, you might make some profit for God. And as we see that through your obedience the ministry of the Word has succeeded

---

[1] Ps. cxviii. 75.   [2] Ps. xciii. 19.

and, as we hear, by your preaching great numbers have been converted to the faith, we give thanks to God that He from whom all good proceeds and whose will it is that all men should be led to recognize the truth, should second your efforts and bring this people by His powerful inspiration from darkness to light.

For this reason we believe that a bountiful reward is laid up by Almighty God for us in heaven. If you are steadfast, you will be able to say with the Apostle: " I have fought the good fight, I have finished the race, I have redeemed my pledge." To gain the prize, you must persevere, for God promises it only to those who are steadfast to the end.

Do not be frightened by threats or discouraged by fears. Keep your trust fixed on God and proclaim the word of truth. Provided your will is constant in good works, God will crown it by His help. Therefore, the more people you convert from the errors of their ways (and that this is so we know from your letter), the more we shall rejoice and thank God for the gaining of souls.

As for the bishop who was too lazy to preach the Word of God and now claims a part of your diocese, we have written to our son, Duke Charles, asking him to restrain him, and we believe that he will put a stop to it. For your part, however, continue to preach in season and out of season.

We have written to the people of Thuringia and Germany regarding matters which concern their spiritual welfare, ordering them among other things to erect bishoprics and build churches. For He who desires not the death of the sinner but his conversion will grant an increase in everything.

May God preserve you.

(Tangl, 24)

13

POPE GREGORY II COMMENDS BONIFACE TO THE PEOPLE OF THURINGIA

(December 724)

Our Lord, Jesus Christ, came down from heaven and, true God as He was, became Man, suffered and was crucified for our sakes, was buried and the third day rose again from the dead and ascended into heaven. But to His holy Apostles he said: " Go, teach all nations, baptizing them in the name of the Father and of the Son and of the Holy Ghost ", promising eternal life to all those who believed.

Wherefore, desiring that you should rejoice with us for all eternity where there is no end, no suffering nor any bitterness, but only glory for evermore, we have sent you our most holy brother Boniface as your bishop, so that he may baptize you, teach you the faith of Christ and lead you from error to the path of salvation, whereby you may be saved and enjoy everlasting life. Obey him in all things, respect him as your father and submit your hearts to his teaching, because we have sent him to seek, not earthly gain, but the profit of your souls.

Wherefore, love God and receive Baptism in His name, because the Lord our God had prepared what the eye of man hath not seen nor the heart conceived for those who love Him. Put aside your evil ways and do good. Adore not idols nor make bloody sacrifices, because God does not accept them; but in all things carry out and observe the injunctions of our brother Boniface, and then both you and your children will be saved for evermore.

Build him a house, therefore, where he can dwell as your father and bishop; build churches where you can pray: and may God have mercy on your sins and grant you everlasting life.

(Tangl, 25)

14

POPE GREGORY II REPLIES TO QUESTIONS PUT BY BONIFACE
(22 November 726)

Gregory, the servant of the servants of God, to Boniface, our most holy brother and colleague in the episcopate.

Your devout messenger Denual has brought us the welcome news that you are well and that, by the help of God, you are making progress in the work for which you were sent. He also delivered to us letters from you reporting that the field of the Lord which had long lain fallow and was overgrown with the weeds of pagan customs has now been ploughed up and sown with the truth of the Gospel, producing an abundant harvest of souls.

In the same report you included a number of questions concerning the faith and teaching of the Holy Roman and Apostolic Church. This is a commendable practice, for here St. Peter the Apostle held his see and the episcopate had its beginning. And since you seek our advice on matters dealing with ecclesiastical discipline, we will state with all the authority of apostolic tradition what you must hold, though we speak not from our own insufficiency but relying on the grace of Him who opens the mouths of the dumb and makes eloquent the tongues of babes.

Your first question is: Within what degrees can marriage be solemnized? Our answer is that if the parties know themselves to be related by blood they should not marry; but since moderation weighs more with these savage people than strict legal duties, they should be allowed to marry after the fourth degree of consanguinity.

As to what a man shall do if his wife is unable through illness to allow him his marital rights, it would be better if he remained apart and practised continence. But since this is practicable only in the case of men of high ideals, the best course if he is unable to be continent would be for him to marry.[1] Nevertheless, he should continue to support the woman who is sick, unless she has contracted the disease through her own fault.

As regards a priest or bishop who has been accused by the people, if the evidence for the charge against him is not substantiated by reliable witnesses he should protest his innocence on oath before God, from whom nothing is concealed, and retain the rank which is his due. For once a man has been ordained or consecrated he cannot be ordained or consecrated anew.

In the sacred ceremony of the Mass that rite must be observed which our Lord transmitted to His Disciples, for he took the chalice and gave it to them, saying: " This is the chalice of the New Testament in my blood: do this as often as you shall drink

---

[1] This legislation is recorded by Gratian, *Decreta*, pt. ii, ch. 32, q. 7, can. 18, but attributed to Gregory III.

it." Therefore it is not fitting that two or three chalices should be placed on the altar during the celebration of Mass.

As to foods offered in sacrifice to idols, you ask whether a believer is permitted to eat them or not after he has first made a sign of the cross over them. A sufficient answer to this question is provided in the words of St. Paul when he said: " If any man says to you, This has been offered in sacrifice, eat not for the sake of the man who mentioned it and for conscience sake."

You ask further: If a father or mother gives a child during its early years to a monastery to be brought up in monastic discipline, is it lawful for that child, after reaching the age of puberty, to leave the cloister and enter into matrimony? This we strictly forbid, for it is an impious thing to allow children who have been offered to God by their parents to follow their baser instincts for pleasure.

You mention also that some have been baptized by adulterous and unworthy priests without being questioned on their belief in the articles of the Creed. In such cases you must hold fast to the ancient custom of the Church, because whoever is baptized in the name of Father, Son and Holy Ghost cannot be baptized again. For he has received this grace not in the name of the minister but in the name of the Trinity. Hold fast the teaching of the Apostles, " One Lord, one faith, one baptism ". We require you to impart spiritual instruction to such people with particular earnestness.

As regards small children who have been separated from their parents and do not know whether they have been baptized or not, reason demands that you should baptize them, unless there is evidence to the contrary.

Lepers who belong to the Christian faith should be allowed to partake of the body and blood of the Lord, but they may not attend sacred functions with people in good health. In the case of a contagious disease or plague attacking a church or monastery you ask whether those who have not been infected may escape danger by flight. We declare this to be utterly foolish; no man can escape the hand of God.

At the end of your letter you state that some priests and bishops are so vicious that their lives are a continual reproach to the priesthood and you enquire whether it would be lawful to eat and speak with them provided they are not heretics. We answer that you are to admonish and correct them with our apostolic authority and so bring them back to the purity of ecclesiastical discipline. If they obey, they will save their souls, and you, on your side, will attain your reward. Do not refuse to eat and speak with them at the same table. It often happens that where correction fails to bring men to an acknowledgment of the truth, the constant and gentle persuasion of their table companions leads them back to the paths of goodness. You should follow this same rule in dealing with the nobles who are of assistance to you.

This, my dear brother, is all that need be said with the authority of the Apostolic See. For the rest, we call upon the mercy of God, which has sent you, under our apostolic authority, to shed the light of truth on those regions of darkness, to crown your work with success so that you may receive the reward of your labours and the forgiveness of our sins.

May God keep you from all harm, most reverend brother.

Given on the tenth of the kalends of December in the tenth year of the reign of our august emperor Leo, in the seventh of his son Constantine the Great, the tenth indiction.

(Tangl, 26)

15

BONIFACE GIVES ADVICE TO ABBESS BUGGA ABOUT HER PILGRIMAGE TO ROME
(Before 738 (725?))

Be it known to you, dear sister, that in regard to the matter on which you have sought my advice I cannot presume, on my own responsibility, either to forbid your pilgrimage or to encourage it. I can only say how the matter appears to me. If for the sake of solitude and divine contemplation you have forsaken the monastic life and the care of your subjects, the servants and handmaidens of God, how can you bring yourself to submit to the orders and whims of men of this world and the labour and anxiety they entail? It appears to me that if, through the interference of seculars, you cannot find freedom and peace of mind in your native land, you should try (provided you have the will and the power to do so) to find freedom for contemplation by making a pilgrimage abroad. This is what our sister Wilthburga did. She has told me by letter that she has found at the shrine of St. Peter the kind of quiet life which she had long sought for in vain. Since I had written to her about your intentions, she sent me word that you would do better to wait until the attacks and the threats of the Saracens against Rome had died down and until she herself could send you an invitation. To me also this seems the better plan. Make all necessary preparations for the journey, wait for word from her and afterwards do what God's grace shall inspire you to do.

In regard to copying out the passages of Scripture for which you asked me, please excuse my remissness, for I have been so much occupied in preaching and travelling about that I could not find the time to complete it. But when I have finished it I will send it to you.

I thank you for the presents and the vestments which you have sent and pray God that He will reward you with eternal life among his angels and archangels on high. I beg of you, therefore, my dear sister, nay more, my very dear mother and mistress, to pray for me, because for my sins I am wearied with many trials and vexed both in mind and body. Rest assured that our long-standing friendship shall never fail. Farewell in Christ.

(Tangl, 27)

16

POPE GREGORY II INVESTS BONIFACE WITH THE PALLIUM
(732)

Gregory, the servant of the servants of God, to our most reverend and holy brother Bishop Boniface, sent by this apostolic Church of God for the enlightenment of the German people who live in the shadow of death, steeped in error.

It was a source of great satisfaction to us to learn from a repeated reading of your letter that by the grace of God many heathens have turned away from error and embraced the truth. And because we are taught in the parable that he to whom five talents was given gained also another five, we, and the whole Church with us, congratulate you on your success. Hence we have sent the sacred pallium to you as a gift, desiring with the authority of the Apostolic See that you accept it and wear it; and it is our wish that you be recognized as one of the archbishops divinely appointed. How you are to use it you will learn from the instructions of the Apostolic See, namely: you must wear it only during the celebration of Mass and when in the course of your episcopal duty you consecrate a bishop.

But since, as you say, you are unable to deal with all the matters involved in imparting the means of salvation to the multitudes of those who, by the grace of God, have been converted in those parts, we command you in virtue of our apostolic authority to consecrate bishops wherever the faithful have increased. This you must do in accordance with the sacred canons, choosing men of tried worth so that the dignity of the episcopate may not fall into disrepute.

As regards the priest whom you say came to us and was absolved from his nefarious crimes, we would like you to know that he made no confession to us, nor did he receive absolution so that he could pursue his lustful desires. If you find that he has fallen into error again we command you by the authority of the Holy See to correct and discipline him in accordance with the sacred canons, as also any other person you should meet like him. For when he came here he said, " I am a priest ", and he asked for letters of recommendation to our son Charles. We gave him no other favour. If his conduct is blameworthy we desire you to shun him, together with the rest.

Those whom you say were baptized by pagans and the case is proved should be baptized again in the name of the Trinity.

You say, among other things, that some eat wild horses and many eat tame horses. By no means allow this to happen in future, but suppress it in every possible way with the help of

Christ and impose a suitable penance upon offenders. It is a filthy and abominable custom.

You ask for advice on the lawfulness of making offerings for the dead. The teaching of the Church is this—that every man should make offerings for those who died as true Christians and that the priest should make a commemoration of them [at Mass]. And although all are liable to fall into sin, it is fitting that the priest should make a commemoration and intercede for them. But he is not allowed to do so for those who die in a state of sin even if they were Christians.

It is our command that those who doubt whether they were baptized or not should be baptized again, as also those who were baptized by a priest who sacrifices to Jupiter and partakes of sacrificial offerings. We decree that each one must keep a record of his consanguinity to the seventh degree.

If you are able, forbid those whose wives have died to enter into second marriages.

We declare that no one who has slain his father, mother, brother or sister can receive the Holy Eucharist except at the point of death. He must abstain from eating meat and drinking wine as long as he lives. He must fast on every Monday, Wednesday and Friday and thus with tears wash away the crime he has committed.

Among other difficulties which you face in those parts, you say that some of the faithful sell their slaves to be sacrificed by the heathen. This, above all, we urge you to forbid, for it is a crime against nature. Therefore, on those who have perpetrated such a crime you must impose a penance similar to that for culpable homicide.

As often as you consecrate a bishop, let two or three other bishops join with you so that what you do may be pleasing to God, may be done with their assistance and sanctioned by their presence.

These matters, dearest brother, we wish you carefully to observe. Pursue the work of salvation on which you have so piously embarked so that you may receive from our Lord God the eternal reward of your labours.

The privilege for which you asked is sent together with this letter. We pray God that under His protection you may achieve complete success in turning the heathens from the errors of their ways. May God protect you from harm, most reverend brother.

(Tangl, 28)

17

THE ENGLISH NUN LEOBA[1] BEGS BONIFACE'S PRAYERS FOR HER PARENTS

(Soon after 732)

To the most reverend Boniface, dearly beloved in Christ and related to me by kinship, the lowest servant of those who bear the sweet yoke of Christ, wishes for eternal welfare.

I beseech you in your kindliness to be mindful of the past friendship which you formed with my father Dynne long ago in the west country. It is now eight years since he passed from this world, so I beg you not to fail to pray for his soul. I ask you also to remember my mother Aebbe, who, as you are well aware, is related to you by ties of kinship. She is still alive but suffers from ill health and for many years now has been afflicted with infirmity. I am my parent's only child, and, though I am not worthy of so great a privilege, I would like to regard you as my brother, for there is no other man in my family in whom I can put my trust as I can in you. I venture to send you this little gift not because it is worthy of your attention but because I wish to remind you of my lowly self, so that, in spite of the distance that separates us, you may not forget me but rather be knit more closely to me in the bond of true affection. This boon particularly I beg of you, beloved brother, that by the help of your prayers I may be shielded from all temptation. Would you also, if you please, correct the homely style of this my letter and send me as a model a few words of your own, for I deeply long to hear them.

The little verses written below have been composed according

---

[1] The nun mentioned here appears later in this volume: see her biography by Rudolf of Fulda. Her mistress Eadburga was the Abbess of Minster in Thanet, as mentioned earlier.

to the rules of prosody. I made them, not because I imagine myself
to have great ability, but because I wished to exercise my budding
talents. I hope you will help me with them. I learned how to do
it from my mistress Eadburga, who continues with increasing
perseverance in her study of the Scriptures.

Farewell; pray for me; may you enjoy a long life here and a
happier life to come.

> " Arbiter omnipotens, solus qui cuncta creavit,
>   In regno patris semper qui lumine fulget,
>   Qua iugiter flagrans sic regnet gloria Christi
>   Inlesum servet semper te iure perenni."

(Tangl, 29)

18

Boniface Thanks Abbess Eadburga for Sending Him Books
(735–6)

To his dear sister, Abbess Eadburga, long united to him by
spiritual ties, Boniface, a servant of the servants of God, greetings
in Christ without end.

May the Eternal Rewarder of good works give joy on high among
the choirs of angels to my dearest sister, who has brought light
and consolation to an exile in Germany by sending him gifts of
spiritual books. For no man can shed light on these gloomy
lurking-places of the German people and take heed of the snares
that beset his path unless he have the Word of God as a lamp to
guide his feet and a light to shine on his way.

Of your charity I earnestly beg you to pray for me, because
as a penalty for my sins I am tossed about by the storms of this
dangerous sea, begging God, who is high above us but stoops to
regard the lowly, to give me words to speak my mind boldly that
the Word of the Lord may run its triumphant course and the
Gospel of Christ may be glorified among the heathen.

(Tangl, 30)

19

BONIFACE ASKS ARCHBISHOP NOTHELM OF CANTERBURY[1] TO
FORWARD A COPY OF THE QUESTIONS SENT TO POPE GREGORY I
BY AUGUSTINE, APOSTLE OF ENGLAND

(735)

To his beloved master, Archbishop Nothelm, invested with the
insignia of the high priesthood, Boniface, a humble servant of
the servants of God, sincere greetings of eternal love in Christ.

I earnestly beg you to remember me in your holy prayers and
so bring peace to my mind, tossed as it is by the anxieties of this
mission in Germany. Unite me to you in a bond of brotherhood
such as was granted to me by your predecessor, Archbishop
Bertwald, of revered memory, at the time I left my native country.
May my brethren and the companions of my wanderings be
counted worthy also to be united to you in the bond of the spirit,
in the ties of love, in the faith of Christ and the sweetness of
charity.

I pray you in the same way to obtain for me a copy of the
letter containing, it is said, the questions of Augustine, first
archbishop and apostle of the English, and the replies made to
them by Pope Gregory I. In this letter it is stated among other
things that marriages between Christians related in the third
degree are lawful. Will you have a careful search made to discover
whether or not this document has been proved to be an authentic
work of St. Gregory? For the registrars say that it is not to be
found in the archives of the Church at Rome among the other
papers of the said Pope.

Further, I would like your advice as regards a sin which I
have unwittingly committed by allowing a certain man to marry.
It happened in this way. The man, like many others, had stood
as godfather to the child of another man and then on the father's

---

[1] Nothelm was first archpriest of St. Paul's, London, and consecrated Archbishop of Canterbury in 735, receiving the pallium from Gregory III in the
following year. He was a friend of Albinus, Abbot of St. Augustine's, Canterbury, and conveyed information from him to Bede about the ecclesiastical
history of Kent. He died in October 739. Some writings have been attributed
to him, but they are spurious.

death married the mother. The people in Rome say that this is a sin, even a mortal sin, and state that in such cases a divorce is necessary. They maintain that under the Christian emperors such a marriage was punishable by death or exile for life. If you find that this is considered so great a sin in the decrees of the Fathers and in the canons or even in Holy Scripture, tell me so, because I would like to understand and learn the authorities for such an opinion. I cannot understand how spiritual relationship in marriage can be so great a sin, when we know that through Baptism we all become sons and daughters, brothers and sisters in the Church.

Would you also let me know in what year the first missionaries sent by St. Gregory came to England?

(Tangl, 33)

20

BONIFACE ASKS HIS FORMER PUPIL, ABBOT DUDDO,[1] TO SEND HIM CERTAIN MANUSCRIPTS

(735)

To his beloved son Abbot Duddo, Boniface also called Wynfrith, servant of the servants of God, heartfelt and loving greetings in Christ.

I hope, my dear son, that you recall the saying of a certain wise man, " keep thy old friend ", and forget not in old age the early friendship we formed in youth and have kept up till now. Remember your father, now failing in strength and going the way of all flesh.

Though I was but poorly equipped as a teacher, yet I tried to be the most devoted of them all, as you yourself well know. Be mindful of my devotion and take pity on an old man worn out by troubles in this German land. Support me by your prayers to God, and help me by supplying me with the Sacred Writings and the inspired works of the Fathers. It is well known that books are most helpful to those who read the Holy Scriptures, so I beg you

---

[1] Duddo is known only through a rather suspect charter. He was probably abbot of a monastery in the west of England.

to procure for me as an aid to sacred learning part of the commentary on the Apostle Paul which I need. I have commentaries on two Epistles—that to the Romans and the First to the Corinthians. If you have anything in your monastic library which you think would be useful to me and of which I may not be aware, or of which I have no copy, pray let me know about it; help me as a loving son might an ignorant father, and send me also any notes of your own.

Let us also agree mutually to render such service to each other. In accordance with what my son, the priest Eoban,[1] the bearer of my letters, may tell you about the marriage of a woman to the godfather of her children, kindly search the records to find out by what authority this is held to be a capital crime at Rome. If you find in ecclesiastical writings any discussion of this sin, please let me know at once.

Health and prosperity in Christ.

(Tangl, 34)

21

BONIFACE ASKS ABBESS EADBURGA TO MAKE HIM A COPY OF the EPISTLE OF ST. PETER IN LETTERS OF GOLD

(735)

To the most reverend and beloved sister, Abbess Eadburga, Boniface, least of the servants of God, loving greetings.

I pray Almighty God, the Rewarder of all good works, that when you reach the heavenly mansions and the everlasting tents He will repay you for all the generosity you have shown to me. For, many times, by your useful gifts of books and vestments, you have consoled and relieved me in my distress. And so I beg you to continue the good work you have begun by copying out for me in letters of gold the epistles of my lord, St. Peter, that a reverence and love of the Holy Scriptures may be impressed on the minds of the heathens to whom I preach, and that I may ever have before my gaze the words of him who guided me along this path.

[1] Eoban is probably to be identified with the Bishop Eoban of Utrecht, who later suffered martyrdom with Boniface at Dokkum.

The materials [gold] needed for the copy I am sending by the priest Eoban.

Deal, then, my dear sister, with this my request as you have so generously dealt with them in the past, so that here on earth your deeds may shine in letters of gold to the glory of our Father who is in heaven.

For your well-being in Christ and for your continual progress in virtue I offer my prayers.

(Tangl, 35)

22

BONIFACE ARRANGES THE AFFAIRS OF THE ABBEY OF FRITZLAR AFTER THE DEATH OF ABBOT WIGBERT[1]

(737-8)

To my beloved sons, Tatwin, Wigbert, priests, and to Bernard, Hiedde, Hunfrid and Sturm, Boniface, a servant of the servants of God, greetings in the Lord for evermore.

With fatherly love I entreat you, my friends, now that our father, Wigbert is dead, to preserve the rule of your monastic life with even greater strictness. Let the priest Wigbert and the deacon Megingoz expound the Rule to you; let them observe the canonical Hours and the Offices of the Church, administer correction, instruct the children and preach the Word of God to the brethren. Let Hiedde be prior and keep the servants in order, and let him have the assistance of Hunfrid if necessary. Sturm should take charge of the kitchen. Let Bernard do the manual labour and build us small houses to dwell in as they are needed. And on all matters seek the advice of Abbot Tatwin as occasion arises, and follow out his suggestions.

Let each one of you, according to his strength and character, try to preserve his chastity and to assist the others in the common life. So may you abide in brotherly love until, God willing, I

---

[1] The Life of St. Wigbert was written by Servatus Lupus, Abbot of Ferrières. He came from Dorset and was made Abbot of Fritzlar by Boniface, who also gave him the Abbey of Orhdruf because of his reputation for discipline. He died at Fulda. Megingoz afterwards became Bishop of Wurtzburg; Sturm was the founder and first Abbot of Fulda. Nothing certain is known of the remaining monks mentioned in this letter.

return to you once more. Then, together, we shall all praise God and give thanks to Him for all His benefits. Farewell in Christ.

(Tangl, 40)

23

BONIFACE TELLS HIS DISCIPLES ABOUT HIS RECEPTION BY GREGORY III[1]

(738)

To our beloved sons Geppan, Eoban, Tatwin, Wigbert and to all our brethren and sisters, Boniface, a servant of the servants of God, loving greetings in Christ.

We should like you to know and give thanks to God that when we safely reached the threshold of St. Peter, Prince of the Apostles, the Apostolic Pontiff welcomed us with joy and gave a satisfactory reply to the matters for which we came. He counselled and commanded us to return once more to you and to persevere in the work we have undertaken.

At the moment we are waiting for the opening of a council of bishops, but we do not know when the Apostolic Pontiff will order it to sit. As soon as it is over, we shall hasten back to you, if God so wills and our health is spared. In this knowledge wait our coming with fraternal love and in the unity of faith, bearing one another's burdens. So doing, you will fulfil the law of Christ and renew your joy.

Fare ye well and pray for us.

(Tangl, 41)

24

POPE GREGORY III WRITES TO BONIFACE ABOUT THE ORGANIZATION OF THE CHURCH IN BAVARIA

(29 October 739)

To our most reverend and holy brother Boniface, Gregory, servant of the servants of God.

---

[1] This letter was written to inform his disciples that Boniface's request to the Pope to allow him to resign and go elsewhere had not been accepted.

A sentence of the teacher of all nations, the celebrated Apostle St. Paul, tells us that everything helps to secure the good of those who love God. Therefore when we learned from your report that God in His mercy had loosed a great number of the German people from the toils of paganism and had brought as many as a hundred thousand souls into the Church through your efforts and those of Prince Charles, we raised our hands in prayer and thanked God, the Giver of all good, for having opened the gates of mercy and love to make known to the West the path of salvation. Glory be to Him for ever.

You tell us that you have made a journey into Bavaria and found the people there living in a manner contrary to the ordinances of the Church, and that, because they have no bishops except Vivilo, whom we consecrated some time ago, you have, with the approval of Odilo, Duke of Bavaria, and the nobles of the province, consecrated three other bishops. You say also that you have divided the province into four districts, so that each bishop may have his own diocese. In carrying out our commands and in performing the task that was enjoined upon you you have acted wisely and well.

Continue, reverend brother, to teach them the holy, Catholic and apostolic traditions of the See of Rome, so that the ignorant may be enlightened and may follow the path that leads to eternal bliss.

As to the priests whom you have found there, if the bishops who ordained them are not known to you and a doubt remains whether they were true bishops or not, let them be ordained by a bishop and fulfil their sacred charge, provided they are Catholics of blameless life, trained to the service of God, well versed in the teachings of the Church and fitted to hold office.

Those who were baptized with a formula expressed in a heathen tongue, provided their Baptism was performed in the name of the Trinity should be confirmed with sacred chrism and the laying-on-of-hands.

Bishop Vivilo was consecrated by us. If, however, he has deviated from orthodox teaching in any point, correct and instruct him according to the traditions of the Church of Rome, as you have learned them from us.

We command you to attend the council which is to be held on the banks of the Danube and, vested with Apostolic authority, to act as our representative. As far as God shall grant you strength, continue to preach the word of salvation, so that the Christian faith may increase and multiply in the name of the Lord.

You have no permission, brother, to remain in one district once your work there has been completed. Strengthen the minds of your brethren and the faithful who are scattered throughout the West and continue to preach wherever God grants you opportunity to save souls. When the need arises consecrate bishops according to canon law in your capacity as our representative, and instruct them to observe apostolic and Catholic doctrine. In this way you will assure yourself of a great reward and win over to Almighty God a perfect people. Do not shrink, beloved brother, from difficult and protracted journeys in the service of the Christian faith, for it is written that small is the gate and narrow the road that leads on to life.

Continue, then, brother, the exemplary work you have begun, so that in the day of Christ you may be entitled to say in the presence of the saints at the day of judgment: " Here stand I and these children the Lord has given me. I have not lost any of them whom thou has entrusted to me." And again: " It was five talents thou gavest me, see how I have made profit of five talents besides." Then you will deservedly hear the voice of God saying: " Well done, my good and faithful servant: since thou hast been faithful over little things, I have great things to commit to thy charge: come and share the joy of thy Lord."

May God preserve you, most reverend brother.

Given on the fourth day of the kalends of November, in the twenty-third year of our loving and august lord Leo, by the grace of God emperor, in the twenty-third year of his consulship and the twentieth year of the Emperor Constantine, in the eighth indiction.

(Tangl, 45)

25

BONIFACE WRITES TO THE ENGLISH, ASKING PRAYERS FOR THE CONVERSION OF THE SAXONS

(738)

To all his most reverend colleagues in the episcopate, to the venerable priests, deacons, canons, clerics, abbots and abbesses of communities, to the lowly monks who obey for Christ's sake, to the consecrated and devout virgins and all professed nuns of Christ, indeed to all those Catholics of the English race who fear God, Boniface, a native of the same race, legate of the Universal Church in Germany and servant of the Apostolic See, formerly called Wynfrith, but now, through no deserts of his own, archbishop: greetings in the humble communion and sincere love of Christ.

With humble prayer, we beseech you, brethren, of your charity to remember our lowly selves in your prayers, that we may escape the cunning snares of the devil and the buffetings of evil men, that the word of the Lord may prosper and be glorified. We beg you to be instant in prayer that God and our Lord Jesus Christ, who desires all men to be saved and to come to the knowledge of the truth, may convert the hearts of the pagan Saxons to the faith, may make them repent of the devilish errors in which they are entangled and unite them to the children of Mother Church. Have pity on them, because their repeated cry is: " We are of one and the same blood and bone." Remember that we go the way of all flesh and in hell no man praises the Lord nor can death honour Him.

Be it known that in this undertaking I have the agreement and support and blessing of two Pontiffs of the Roman See. Act, then, on this prayer of mine, that your reward among the angels of heaven may be manifest and enlarged.

May the Almighty Creator keep your unity and common bond of love in force for evermore.

(Tangl, 46)

26

BONIFACE ASKS PROTECTION FOR HIS MISSION IN THURINGIA FROM GRIFO,[1] MAYOR OF THE PALACE

(741)

Boniface, servant of the servants of God, greetings in Christ to Grifo, son of Charles.

I beg and entreat Your Highness in the name of God the Father Almighty, of Jesus Christ, His Son, and of the Holy Ghost, by the Trinity and Unity of God, that in the event of your coming to power you will help the clerics, priests, monks, nuns and all the servants of God in Thuringia, and that you will protect the Christians from the hostility of the heathens so that they may not be destroyed by them. Thus you will reap an everlasting reward at the judgment seat of Christ. Be assured that you are constantly in our prayers to God: this, your father desired during his life-time as did also your mother. We pray God, the Saviour of the world, to guide your steps through life, so that your soul may be saved and you may abide in the grace of God for evermore.

Meanwhile, my son, recall the words of the psalmist: " Man's life is like the grass, he blooms and dies like a flower in the fields." And the Apostle : " The whole world about us lies in the power of evil." And Truth Himself says in the Gospel: " How is a man the better for gaining the whole world if he loses himself? " And again in the Gospel, speaking of the glory of the just: " Then, at last, the just will shine out, clear as the sun, in their Father's kingdom." And Paul, the Apostle, said about the bliss of eternal life: " Things no eye has seen, nor ear heard, no human heart conceived, is the welcome God has prepared for those who love Him."

So conduct yourself, my son, that your reward may shine ever more brightly in the high vault of heaven.

---

[1] Grifo was step-brother to Pippin the Short and Carloman, being the son of Charles Martel and the Bavarian Sonnichilde. When this letter was written Charles Martel had just died and the struggles between the brothers for power had not yet begun. Grifo was eventually eliminated and Pippin and Carloman gained complete control.

Our wish is that it may be well with you till the end of your days in Christ.

(Tangl, 48)

27

BONIFACE TO POPE ZACHARIAS[1] ON HIS ACCESSION TO THE PAPACY

(742)

To our beloved lord Zacharias, who bears the insignia of the supreme pontificate, Boniface, a servant of the servants of God.

We confess, Father and Lord, that after we had learned through messengers that your predecessor Gregory, of holy memory, had departed this life, nothing gave us greater comfort and happiness than the knowledge that God had appointed Your Holiness to enforce the canonical decrees and govern the Apostolic See. Kneeling at your feet, we earnestly beg that, as we have been devoted servants and humble disciples to your predecessors in the See of Peter, we may likewise be counted obedient servants, under canon law, of Your Holiness.

It is our firm resolution to preserve the Catholic faith and the unity of the Church of Rome, and I shall continue to urge as many hearers and disciples as God shall grant me on this mission to render obedience to the Apostolic See.

We must also inform you, Holy Father, that owing to the conversion of the German people we have consecrated three bishops and divided the province into three dioceses. We humbly desire you to confirm and establish as bishoprics, both by your authority and in writing, the three towns or cities in which they were consecrated. We have established one episcopal see in Wurzburg, another in Buraburg and a third in Erfurt, formerly a city of barbarous heathens. These three places we urgently beg you to uphold and confirm by a charter embodying the authority of the Holy See, so that, God willing, there may be in Germany three

[1] Pope Zacharias (741–52) was of Greek extraction. He seems to have been less understanding of Boniface's difficulties than the previous Popes, though to him must be ascribed the confirmation of the synods and much else that Boniface undertook. It was through his efforts that the Synod of Cloveshoe in England, 747, was held.

episcopal sees founded and established by St. Peter's word and the Apostolic See's command, which neither present nor future generations will presume to change in defiance of the authority of the Apostolic See.

Be it known to you also, Holy Father, that Carloman, Emperor of the Franks, summoned me to his presence and desired me to convoke a synod in that part of the Frankish kingdom which is under his jurisdiction. He promised me that he would reform and re-establish ecclesiastical discipline, which for the past sixty or seventy years has been completely disregarded and despised. If he is truly willing, under divine inspiration, to put his plan into execution, I should like to have the advice and the instructions of the Apostolic See. According to their elders, the Franks have not held a council for more than eighty years; they have had no archbishop nor have they established or restored in any place the canon law of the Church. The episcopal sees, which are in the cities, have been given, for the most part, into the possession of avaricious laymen or exploited by adulterous and unworthy clerics for worldly uses. If I am to undertake this task at your bidding and on the invitation of the Emperor I must have at once, with the appropriate ecclesiastical sanctions, both the command and the decision of the Apostolic See.

Should I discover among these men certain deacons, as they are called, who have spent their lives since childhood in debauchery, adultery and every kind of uncleanness, who have received the diaconate with this reputation, and who even now, when they have four or five or even more concubines in their beds at night, are brazen enough to call themselves deacons and read out the Gospel: who enter the priesthood, continue in the same career of vice and declare that they have the right to exercise the priestly functions of making intercession for the people and offering Mass, and who, to make matters worse, are promoted, despite their reputations, to higher offices and are eventually nominated and consecrated bishops, may I in such cases have a written and authoritative statement regarding the procedure to be followed, so that they may be convicted as criminals and condemned by apostolic authority? Among them are bishops who deny the charges of fornication and adultery but who, nevertheless, are shiftless drunkards, addicted to the chase, who march armed into battle and shed with their own hands the blood of Christians and heathens alike. Since I am recognised as the servant and legate of the Apostolic See, my decisions here and your decisions in Rome ought to be in complete agreement when I send messengers to receive your judgment.

In another matter, also, I must crave your advice and permission. Your predecessor of holy memory bade me, in your presence and hearing, to appoint a certain priest as my successor to rule this diocese after my death. If this be the will of God, I concur. But now I have my doubts whether it is feasible, for in the meantime a brother of that priest has murdered the duke's uncle, and at the moment I see no possibility of settling the quarrel.

I beg you, therefore, to give me your authority to act on the advice of my colleagues regarding the choice of a successor, so that in common we may do what is most advantageous for God, the Church and the safeguard of the faith. May I have your permission to act in this matter as God shall inspire me, for without defying the wishes of the duke the former choice seems impossible.

I have further to seek your advice, Holy Father, in connection with a perplexing and scandalous report that has lately reached our ears. It has greatly disturbed us and filled the bishops of the Church with shame. A certain layman of high rank came to us and asserted that Gregory, of blessed memory, Pontiff of the Apostolic See, had granted him permission to marry his uncle's widow. This woman had previously married her own cousin and deserted him during his lifetime. She is known to be related in the third degree to the man who wishes to marry her and who now declares that the necessary permission has been granted. Furthermore, before her first marriage she had made a solemn vow of chastity and, after taking the veil, threw it aside.

For this marriage the man states that he has permission from the Holy See. This we cannot accept as true. For, at a Synod of the Church beyond the sea, where I was born and bred, namely, the Synod of London, convoked by the disciples of St. Gregory, the archbishops, Augustine, Laurence, Justus and Mellitus, such a marriage was declared on the authority of Holy Scripture to be a heinous crime, an incestuous and execrable union and a damnable sin. For this reason, I beg you, Holy Father, to state the truth of the matter, so that it may not give rise to scandals, dissensions and new errors among the clergy and the faithful.

Because the sensual and ignorant Allemanians, Bavarians and Franks see that some of these abuses which we condemn are rife in Rome, they think that the priests there allow them, and on that account they reproach us and take bad example. They say that in Rome, near the church of St. Peter, they have seen throngs of people parading the streets at the beginning of January of each year, shouting and singing songs in pagan fashion, loading tables with food and drink from morning till night, and that during that time no man is willing to lend his neighbour fire or tools or anything useful from his own house. They recount also that they have seen women wearing pagan amulets and bracelets on their arms and legs and offering them for sale. All such abuses witnessed by sensual and ignorant people bring reproach upon us here and frustrate our work of preaching and teaching. Of such matters the Apostle says reprovingly: " You have begun to observe special days and months, special seasons and years. I am anxious over you: has all the labour I have spent on you been useless? "

And St. Augustine says: " The man who puts his faith in such nonsense as incantations, fortune-tellers, soothsayers, amulets or prophecies of any sort, even though he fasts and prays and runs continually to church, giving alms and doing all kinds of penances, gains nothing as long as he clings to such sacrilegious practices."

If Your Holiness would put an end to these heathen customs in Rome it would redound to your credit besides promoting the success of our teaching of the faith.

Frankish bishops and priests, whose reputation as adulterers and fornicators was notorious, whose children, born during their episcopate or priesthood, are living witnesses to their guilt, now declare on their return from Rome that the Roman Pontiff has granted them full permission to exercise their offices in the Church.

Our answer to them is that we have never heard of the Apostolic See giving judgment contrary to the canonical decrees.

All these matters, beloved master, we bring to your notice, in order that we may give these men an authoritative reply. May we, under your guidance and instruction, overcome and destroy these ravening wolves and prevent the sheep from being led astray.

Finally, we are sending you some small gifts, a warm rug and a little silver and gold. Though they are too trifling to be offered to Your Holiness, they come as a token of our affection and our devoted obedience.

May God protect Your Holiness and may you enjoy health and long life in Christ.

(Tangl, 50)

28

ANSWERS OF POPE ZACHARIAS TO BONIFACE
(April 743)

Zacharias, servant of the servants of God, to his very reverend and holy brother and fellow bishop Boniface.

When we received your letter, most holy brother, which was brought to us by your priest Denehard, and heard that you were in good health (as we hope you may always be), we gave thanks to Almighty God who has deigned to crown your labours with success. Our heart is always filled with great joy on the receipt of your letters, because we find in them reports about the salvation of souls and the conversion of new peoples through your preaching to our Holy Mother, the Church.

Your latest letter tells us that you have established three bishops in three separate places to govern the people whom God, through your intervention, has brought into his fold. You ask that these episcopal sees may be confirmed by our authority. You should, however, first consider and carefully examine whether this is advisable and whether the places and the number of inhabitants warrant the establishment of bishoprics. You will recall, beloved, that the sacred canons decree that bishops should not be attached to villages and small cities lest the dignity of the episcopate be lessened.

However, in response to your earnest appeal we hasten to grant your request. By our apostolic authority we ordain that bishoprics be fixed there and that a worthy succession of bishops shall govern the people and instruct them in the faith: there shall be one in the fortress called Wurzburg, a second in the town of Buraburg and a third in the place called Erfurt. Let no one dare to violate in the future what we have laid down and confirmed by the authority of the blessed Apostle Peter.

You tell us that our son Carloman[1] summoned you to meet him and to arrange for a synod to be held in that part of the Frankish kingdom which is under his rule because of the complete collapse of church discipline in that province, a matter which we deeply regret. For a long time no council has been held there, and as a result many who call themselves priests hardly know what the priesthood is. When Carloman has put his promises into effect and you take your place by his side at the council, if you see bishops, priests or deacons living in adultery or having more than one wife in flagrant contradiction to the decrees and laws of the Fathers, or shedding the blood of Christians and pagans or acting in any other way contrary to ecclesiastical law, you must suspend them, on apostolic authority, from their priestly duties: for such individuals stand condemned by their own conduct as false priests and are worse than those layfolk who give rein to their lusts, foster infamous unions and commit murder. On what grounds do they consider themselves to be priests? And how do they interpret God's word: " Let my priests marry once "? Or the words of the Apostle: " Faithful to one wife "? And this is valid only before receiving the priesthood, for afterwards they are forbidden to marry. How do they think they can perform priestly duties when they are obviously steeped in such crimes as are unthinkable even in laymen? Are they not afraid to handle the sacred mysteries? How can they have the effrontery to offer prayers for the sins of the people, when the sacred canons pre-

---

[1] Carloman was one of the sons of Charles Martel. Brought up at Saint Denys, he was more religious than his brother Pippin the Short and was of great assistance to Boniface. He eventually abdicated and entered the monastic life.

scribe that not even a simple cleric who has not been ordained may contract a second marriage? These men, on the contrary, are guilty of sins worse than those of laymen not only because, being priests, they refuse to give up one wife, but because they take several wives when they know quite well that their state precludes even the taking of one.

But they attach no importance to this and proceed to call down on themselves the wrath of God by committing the still greater crime of murder: and so it comes about those whom they should baptize and cleanse from their sins and whom they should save from hell by the administration of the sacraments are slain by their sacrilegious hands. How can any reasonable man regard them as priests if they neither restrain their lust nor keep their hands free from blood? Who can believe that their sacrifices are pleasing to God when the prophet says: " Bloodthirsty and treacherous men the Lord holds in abhorrence "?

As I have said previously, we command you to suspend them from the performance of priestly duties and the handling of the sacred mysteries. If you find that they have acted contrary to the laws of the Church in any other matters, consult the canons and decrees of the Fathers and make your decisions accordingly.

You say that you are entitled to name your successor and to choose a bishop to take your place during your lifetime: this we cannot allow under any consideration. It is in open contradiction to the law of the Church and the opinions of the Fathers. But we will allow you to have an assistant to help you to preach the Gospel of Christ, according to the Apostle's words: " Those who have served well in the diaconate will secure for themselves a sure footing and great boldness in proclaiming the faith." It would obviously be quite wrong for us to appoint a substitute for you during your lifetime. We command you to offer up continual prayer as long as God grants you life to find you a successor pleasing to Him, able to govern the people whom you have brought to His grace and capable of leading them along the path of life. Even if we wanted to satisfy your desire, we could not do so, for we are all frail and mortal, not knowing what the coming day may bring and unable to foretell who may die first. However, if God allows him to outlive you and you find that he is suitable and you persevere in your intention, then as soon as you become aware that your death is not far off you may designate your successor in the presence of others and send him to me to be consecrated. But this is a privilege which we grant to you out of our affection: we cannot allow it to be conferred on any other person.

As regards the man who wishes to marry his uncle's widow, it appears that the woman was previously married to her own cousin after having taken the veil, and the story has been put about that our predecessor, of blessed memory, gave him permission to contract this scandalous marriage with her. God forbid that our predecessor should have allowed such a thing. The Holy See never countenances anything in open violation of the teaching of the Fathers and the laws of the Church. Continue to warn, exhort and urge them to break off so detestable a marriage, lest they perish eternally. Recall to their minds that they have been redeemed by the blood of Christ and that they must not wittingly hand themselves over to the power of the devil in this incestuous marriage. Let them dedicate themselves to Christ and the Holy Ghost in whose name they have been snatched from the claws of that ancient foe. Impress upon them, most holy brother, the words of Scripture: " To bring back erring feet into the right path means saving a soul from death, means throwing a veil over a multitude of sins."

As regards the New Year celebrations, auguries, amulets, incantations and other practices, which you say are observed in pagan fashion at the church of St. Peter, the Apostle, or in the city of Rome, we consider them to be sinful and pernicious not only for us but for all Christians, according to God's word in the Scriptures: " Jacob needs no soothsayer, Israel no divination: time will reveal the marvellous things God does to them." We consider also that auguries and divinations should be avoided, for we have been taught that such practices were repudiated by the Fathers. Because these evils were cropping up again, we strove to abolish them from the very outset of our pontificate, when by divine favour we were elected to fill the place of the Apostle. We desire you to instruct your people on the same lines and so lead them to eternal life. All such practices were conscientiously and thoroughly suppressed by our predecessor and teacher, Gregory of sacred memory, together with many others, which, on the instigation of the devil, were beginning to make their appearance in the fold of Christ.

In fulfilment of your request, we are sending separate letters of confirmation to each of your three bishops and we ask you to deliver them with your own hand.

We have sent letters also to our son Carloman urging him to carry out his promises at the earliest possible opportunity and to give you his support.

These, beloved brother, are our answers to the enquiries you made previously, given as God has inspired us for the suppression of all the scandals and deceits of the devil. If other disorders arise among your people, do your best to counteract them, framing your decisions on the laws of the Church. We have no right to teach anything except the traditions of the Fathers, but if some new situation arises through the wiles of the devil and no solution is suggested in the provisions of the Church canons do not hesitate to refer the matter to us, so that with God's help we may quickly give you an answer and attend to the wellbeing of your newly converted people.

Be assured that you have a special place in our affections and that it would give us great pleasure to have you always by our side as a minister of God in charge of the churches of Christ.

Finally, beloved brother, take strength in God. Persevere manfully in the work to which God, in His mercy, has called you; for the great reward which God has promised to all those who love Him awaits you. And sinners though we are, we will never cease to implore Him to bring to perfection the generosity He has inspired in you. May blessed Peter, Prince of the Apostles, assist you in everything which you do in obedience to Him to the best of your desire.

May God keep you safe, most reverend and holy father.

Given on the kalends of April in the 24th year of our pious and august lord Constantine, by God crowned Emperor, in the second year of his consulship, in the eleventh indiction.

(Tangl, 51)

29

Acts of the Synod of 25 October 745, Condemning Aldebert and Clemens

In the name of our Lord, Jesus Christ. In the twenty-sixth year of the reign of our august lord, the Emperor Constantine, in the fifth year of his consulship, the 25th of October, the fourteenth indiction, the holy and blessed Pope Zacharias presided over a council held in the Lateran Basilica, at which the following bishops and venerable priests were present: Epiphanius of Selva Candida, Benedict of Mentana, Venantius of Palestrina, Gregory of Porto, Nicetas of Gabii, Theodore of Ostia, Gratiosus of Velletri, the archpriest John, Gregory, Stephen, Dominic, Theodore, Anastasius, George, Sergius, Jordan, Leo, another Leo, Gregory, Stephen, Eustathius, Procopius and Theophanius.

After the holy Gospels had been placed in the middle of the assembly, Gregory, the regional notary and nomenclator, announced in the presence of the deacons and the whole body of the clergy: The devout priest Denehard, who has been sent to Your Apostolic Holiness by Boniface, the Bishop of the province of Germany, is waiting behind the veil and begs for admittance. What is your command? The order was given: Let him come in.

When he came in, Zacharias, the blessed Pope of the Holy, Catholic, Apostolic Church of the city of Rome, said: You brought us a document some days ago from our revered and holy brother, the Archbishop Boniface. In that document he gave his opinion regarding the best course to follow. Why, then, have you asked a second time to be present at our meeting?

Then Denehard, the priest, replied: My Lord, when Bishop Boniface, your devoted servant and my master, convoked the synod in the Frankish province in accordance with your injunction, he discovered there two false priests, heretics and schismatics, named Aldebert and Clement. After he had deprived them of their episcopal dignity he obtained the approval of the Frankish princes to put them into custody. They are not performing their penance in accordance with the sentence passed upon them but, on the contrary, they are still leading the people astray. For this reason, I have been despatched with this letter from my master and I offer it to Your Apostolic Holiness that it may be read out before this sacred council.

The reply was: Let the letter be taken up and read in our presence.

Then Theophanius, the regional notary and treasurer, took the letter and read it aloud as follows:

" To the Supreme Father and Apostolic Pontiff, who holds the power and authority of Peter, Prince of the Apostles, Boniface, the lowest servant of the servants of God, warm greetings in the love of Christ.

" Ever since I dedicated myself, nearly thirty years ago, to the service of the Apostolic See, which I did at the instance and with the approval of Pope Gregory II, it has been my custom to relate to the Supreme Pontiff all my joys and sorrows, so that in joy we might unite together to praise God and in sorrow I might be comforted by his counsel. Let it be so now. I come as a suppliant to Your Holiness, for the Scripture says: ' Ask thy Father and he will instruct thee, thy elders and they will tell thee.'

" I wish you to know, Holy Father, that after you had ordered me, unworthy as I am, to preside at the episcopal council and synod of the Franks, an arrangement in which they concurred, I had to suffer many insults and much persecution particularly from false bishops, adulterous priests and deacons and vicious clerics. My greatest difficulties arose from the opposition of two well-known heretics, blasphemers against God and the Catholic faith. One is called Aldebert, a Gaul by birth, the other an Irishman called Clement. In the form that their heresy takes they differ from each other, but they are alike in their degree of error.

" Since I am weak, I beg Your Apostolic Holiness to protect me against them by your authority and to lead back the Franks and Gauls to the right path by a written statement, so that they may no longer accept the fables, false miracles and prophecies

of the precursors of Antichrist but turn once more to sober
truth. If after reading my account of their doctrines you consider it justified, order them to be thrust into prison. Let no
one communicate with them for fear of becoming contaminated
with their errors and perish in so doing, but make them live
apart and hand them over to Satan for the overthrow of their
corrupt nature, so that their spirits may find salvation in the
day of our Lord Jesus Christ. If they will not listen to the
Church, let them be counted as publicans and heathens, until
they learn not to blaspheme and to rend the tunic of Christ.
On their account I suffer persecution, enmity and the reproaches
of many people, whilst the work of the Church is hindered in
its faith and teaching.

" Of Aldebert they say that I have deprived them of a saintly
apostle and robbed them of a patron and intercessor, a doer of
good deeds and a worker of miracles. But hear first the story
of his life and judge for yourself whether or not he is a wolf in
sheep's clothing.

" Quite early in life he deceived many people by saying that
an angel in the guise of a man had brought him from the other
end of the world relics of extraordinary but rather suspect
holiness, and that through their efficacy he could obtain from
God whatever he desired. By such pretence he was able by
degrees, as St. Paul says, to make his way into house after
house, captivating weak women whose consciences were
burdened by sin and swayed by shifting passions. He also
deceived great numbers of simple folk who thought that he was
a man of truly apostolic character because he had wrought
signs and wonders. He bribed ill-instructed bishops to consecrate him, in defiance of canon law and, finally, with unbridled
arrogance, put himself on the level of the Apostles. He in-
solently refused to consecrate churches to the honour of the
Apostles and martyrs and used to ask people what they expected
to gain by going on pilgrimage to the tombs of the Apostles.
Later, he dedicated small chapels to himself—or, to speak more
truthfully, desecrated them. In the fields or near springs or
wherever he had a mind he erected crosses and small chapels

and ordered prayers to be recited there. As a result, throngs of people absented themselves from the established churches, flouted the injunctions of the bishops and held their services in those places, saying: 'The merits of St. Aldebert will help us.'

" He distributed his hair and fingernails for veneration and had them carried round in procession with the relics of St. Peter the Apostle. Finally, he committed what I consider to be the greatest crime and blasphemy against God. Whenever anyone came to him and fell at his feet desiring confession he would say: 'I know all your sins: your secret deeds are open to my gaze. There is no need to confess, since your past sins are forgiven. Go home in peace: you are absolved.'

" In his dress, his bearing, his behaviour, in fact, in all the details described by Holy Scripture, he imitated the hypocrites.

" The other heretic, whose name is Clement, is opposed to the Church, denies and refuses to acknowledge the sacred canons and rejects the teaching of the holy Fathers St. Jerome, St. Augustine and St. Gregory. He despises all synodal decrees and declares on his own authority that, even though he has had two children born to him during his episcopate, he can still exercise the functions of a Christian bishop. He accepts the Old Testament ruling that a man can, if he wishes, marry his brother's widow and considers that the same doctrine is applicable to Christians. Contrary to the teaching of the Fathers, he affirms that Christ descended into hell to deliver all those, believers and unbelievers, servants of Christ as well as worshippers of idols, who were confined there. On the question of predestination he holds a number of damnable opinions which are contrary to Catholic belief.

" For these reasons I beg you to write to Duke Carloman about this heretic and have him put into prison so that he may be prevented from disseminating his doctrines more widely. Otherwise, one diseased sheep will infect the whole flock.

" I hope Your Holiness will enjoy good health, continued prosperity and long life."

When this was read out, Pope Zacharias said: " You have heard, my dear brethren, what has been stated in this letter concerning the heretics who proclaim to the people that they are apostles. This they do to their own condemnation." The holy bishops and the venerable priests replied: " We have heard, indeed. They are not apostles, they are the slaves of the devil and the precursors of Antichrist. For what Apostle ever distributed his hair or fingernails to the people as relics as did this sacrilegious and pestilent Aldebert? Your Holiness must punish these crimes, both in the case of Aldebert and in that of Clement, who shows contempt for the sacred canons and rejects the teachings of the Fathers, St. Ambrose, Augustine and the others. They should receive a sentence commensurate with their crimes."

Zacharias, the Pope, said: " It is rather too late today, but at the next session, when we have heard the account of his life, the prayer he composed for himself and the rest of his malpractices, we may, by the help of God, come to a unanimous decision on the best course to be followed in this matter."

The Second Session

In the name of our Lord Jesus Christ. In the twenty-sixth year of the reign of our august lord, the Emperor Constantine the Great, in the fifth year of his consulship, the 25th of October, the fourteenth indiction, the holy and blessed Pope Zacharias presided over a council held in the Lateran Basilica of Theodore at which the following bishops and venerable priests were present: Epiphanius of Selva Candida, Benedict of Mentana, Venantius of Palestrina, Gregory of Porto, Nicetas of Gabii, Theodore of Ostia, Gratiosus of Velletri, the archpriest John, Gregory, Stephen, Dominic, Theodore, Anastasius, George, Sergius, Jordan, Leo, another Leo, Gregory, Stephen, Eustathius, Procopius and Theophanius.

After the holy Gospels had been placed in the middle of the assembly, Gregory, the regional notary, announced: " In accordance with the instructions given by Your Holiness in the last session, Denehard, the priest, awaits behind the veil for admittance. What is your command?" The order was given: "Let him come in."

When he came in, Zacharias, the holy and blessed Pope, said: " Bring forward the life-story of the infamous man Aldebert, together with his writings which you had in your hands at the last session, and cause them to be read out before the present gathering." Then Theophanius, the regional notary and treasurer, took them and read aloud the following opening sentences:

" In the name of Jesus Christ. Here begins the life of the holy and blessed servant of God, Bishop Aldebert, born by the will of God. He was sprung from simple parents and was crowned by the grace of God. For whilst he was in his mother's womb the grace of God came upon him, and before his birth his mother saw, as in a vision, a calf issuing from her right side. This calf symbolized the grace which he had received from an angel before he came forth from the womb."

When the book had been read through to the end Zacharias, the Pope, asked: " What reply do you make to these blasphemies? "

Epiphanius, the holy Bishop of Selva Candida answered: " Apostolic Father, you were indeed acting under divine inspiration when you commanded our holy brother Archbishop Boniface and the Frankish princes to convoke an episcopal council in those provinces after so long an interval in order that these schisms and blasphemies should no longer be concealed from your Apostolic Holiness."

Zacharias, the holy and blessed Pope, said: " If Denehard, the priest, has anything further to bring to our notice which should be read out let him produce it."

Denehard, the priest, answered: " I have a letter here which he made use of in his teaching, saying that it was written by Jesus and came down from heaven."

Then Theophanius, the regional notary and treasurer, took it up and read out the following words:

" In the name of God. Here begins the letter of our Lord Jesus Christ, the Son of God, which fell from heaven in Jerusalem and was discovered by the archangel Michael near the gate of Ephraim. This very copy of the letter came into the hands of a priest named Icore, who read it and sent it to a priest named Talasius in the city of Jeremias. Talasius passed it on to another priest Leoban, who was living in a town of Arabia. Leoban sent the letter to the city of Westphalia, where it was received by a priest Macrius. He sent the letter to Mont St. Michel. In the end, through the intervention of an angel, the letter reached Rome, even the tombs of the Apostles, where the keys of the kingdom of heaven are. And the twelve dignitaries who are in the city of Rome fasted, watched and prayed for three days and three nights," etc.

Zacharias, the saintly and blessed Pope, said: " There is no doubt, beloved brethren, that this fellow Aldebert is out of his senses. Anyone who could pin his faith to such a letter must he childish, lacking in intelligence and like an hysterical woman. But to prevent him from deceiving simple-minded folks we must not delay to discuss the case against him and to pronounce sentence."

Then the holy bishops and venerable priests replied: We know that Your Holiness receives illumination from God and that all your utterances proceed from the Holy Ghost. Therefore, as you shall see fit, let judgment be pronounced against them both."

Zacharias, the Pope, said: " The matter must be considered in common with Your Reverences and not merely according to my own judgment. If it please God, sentence shall be promulgated at the next session on the basis of the documents laid before us, founded on the claims of justice and the inspiration of God."

Third Session

In the name of our Lord and Saviour Jesus Christ. In the twenty-sixth year of the reign of our august lord and emperor, Constantine the Great, in the fifth year of his consulship, the 25th of October, the fourteenth indiction, the holy and blessed Pope

Zacharias presided over a council assembled in the Lateran Patriarchate, in the basilica which is named after Theodore, at which the following bishops and priests were present: Epiphanius of Selva Candida, Benedict of Mentana, Venantius of Palestrina, Gregory of Porto, Nicetas of Gabii, Theodore of Ostia, Gratiosus of Velletri, the archpriest John, Gregory, Stephen, another Stephen, Dominic, Theodore, Anastasius, George, Sergius, Jordon, Leo, another Leo, Gregory, Stephen, Eustathius, Procopius and Theophanius.

When the Holy Gospels had been placed in the middle of the assembly, Gregory, the regional notary and nomenclator, announced in the presence of the deacons and the clergy: " In accordance with the command given by Your Holiness in the last session that Denehard, the priest, should appear before you today, he is waiting outside the door. What is your command? " The order was given: " Let him enter."

When he had come in, Zacharias, the Pope, said: " Have you any other writings belonging to those renegades which you ought to hand over to be read? " Denehard, the priest, replied: " Yes, my Lord. I have a prayer which Aldebert tried to compose for his own use. Here it is in my hand. Pray, take it."

And Theophanius, taking it, read it aloud, beginning with the following words:

" O Lord, Omnipotent God, Father of Christ, the Son of God, and our Lord Jesus Christ, *alpha et omega*, who sittest on the seventh throne above the cherubim and seraphim, immense love and wonderful sweetness is with Thee. O Father of the holy angels, who hast created heaven and earth, the sea and all the things that are in them, I invoke Thee, I cry out and summon thee to my aid, wretch that I am. Thou hast deigned to say: Whatsoever you shall ask the Father in my name, that will I give. To Thee I pray, to Thee aloud I cry, to the Lord Christ I commend my soul."

And as he was reading from beginning to end, he came to the passage where it said: " I pray and entreat and beseech you, angel

Uriel, Raguel, Tubuel, Michael, Adinus, Tubuas, Sabaoc, Simiel. . . ."

When he had read this sacrilegious prayer to the end, Zacharias, the Pope, said: " What is your comment upon this, dear brethren? " The holy bishops and venerable priests replied: " What else can we do except consign these writings, which have been read out to us, to the flames and to strike their authors with anathema? The names of the eight angels whom Aldebert invokes in his prayer are, with the exception of Michael, not angels but demons whom he has called to his aid. As we know from the teaching of the Apostolic See and divine authority, there are only three angels, Michael, Gabriel and Raphael. He has introduced demons under the guise of angels."

Zacharias, the Pope, replied: " Wisely have Your Reverences decided that his writings should be burned. But in order that they may serve for his condemnation and his everlasting confusion, it may be useful to preserve them in our archives. Now that the discussion is at an end, we will proceed to pass sentence upon the two delinquents mentioned earlier."

The whole assembly decreed: " As regards Aldebert, whose deeds and abominable writings have been read out to us, who thought fit to call himself an apostle and gave his hair and nails to the people as relics, leading them astray into various errors, who summoned demons to his aid under the guise of angels, let him be deprived of his episcopal office, do penance for his sins and cease to seduce the people any longer. If he persists in his errors and continues to deceive the faithful, let him be anathema and condemned by the eternal judgment of God, he and any other who agrees with him, or accepts his teaching or associates with him. In the same way let Clement, who in his foolhardiness rejected the decrees of the Fathers, accepted the Old Testament regulations in so far as he allowed a man to marry his brother's widow, and furthermore affirmed that our Lord Jesus Christ descended into hell to deliver all the godly and the ungodly, let him, we say, be stripped of his episcopal office, excommunicated and condemned by the everlasting judgment of God. This applies also to anyone who agrees with his sacrilegious teaching."

ZACHARIAS, *Bishop of the Holy Church of God and of the apostolic city of Rome.*

EPIPHANIUS, *Bishop of Selva Candida.*

BENEDICT, *Bishop of Mentana.*

VENANTIUS, *Bishop of Palestrina.*

GREGORY, *Bishop of Porto.*

NICETAS, *Bishop of Gabii.*

THEODORE, *Bishop of Ostia.*

GRATIOSUS, *Bishop of Velletri.*

JOHN, *Archpriest of Santa Susanna.*

etc.

(Tangl, 59)

30

BONIFACE TO BISHOP DANIEL DESCRIBING THE OBSTACLES TO HIS WORK

(742–6)

To Bishop Daniel, beloved in the Lord, Boniface, a servant of the servants of God, affectionate greetings in Christ.

It is the usual custom for men who are in trouble and anxiety to seek the consolation and advice of those on whose wisdom and affection they can rely. And so it is with me. Relying on your friendship and your experience, I come to lay before you all my difficulties and vexations of mind and beg you to support me with your comfort and advice. To quote the Apostle, all is conflict without and anxiety within; but in my case there are also conflicts within and anxiety without. This is caused in particular by false priests and hypocrites who set God at defiance, thereby rushing to their own damnation and leading the faithful astray by their scandals and errors. They say, in the words of the prophet, Peace, peace, but there is no peace. They strive to sow cockle among the wheat, to choke with weeds or pervert into a poisonous weed the Word of God, which we received from the Catholic and Apostolic Church and which, to the best of our ability, we endeavour to disseminate. But what we plant they make no attempt to water in order that it may grow; in order, rather, that it may wither away they use every effort to root it out by proposing to the faithful new sects and new falsehoods.

Some of them refrain from eating food which God created for our sustenance; others live on milk and honey whilst rejecting bread and other food; some, and these do most harm to the people, say that murderers and adulterers can be accepted for the priesthood even if they persist in their crimes. The people, as the Apostle says, grow tired of sound doctrine and provide themselves with a succession of new teachers as the whim takes them.

In our visits to the Frankish court to obtain assistance and protection, it is not possible, as required by canon law, wholly to avoid the company of such men. We are careful, however, not to communicate with them in the sacred body and blood of the Lord during the celebration of Mass. We also avoid taking their advice or asking their consent, for to such men, mixing with heathens and the common people, our toils and struggles are quite incomprehensible. When a priest, a deacon, a cleric or a monk, or any of the faithful, leaves the bosom of the Church, then he joins the heathens in abusing the members of the Church, and this raises terrible obstacles to the spread of the Gospel.

On all these matters we seek your help. We ask you particularly to intercede with God that we may fulfil our duties and our ministry without detriment to our soul. We beg you with most earnest prayer to intercede for us that God, the loving Consoler of those in distress, may deign to keep our souls amidst such trials unharmed and free from sin.

As regards my contacts with the priests already mentioned, I am anxious to have and to follow your considered advice. Without the patronage of the Frankish prince I can neither govern the faithful of the Church nor protect the priests, clerics, monks and nuns of God, nor can I forbid the practice of heathen rites and the worship of idols in Germany without his orders and the fear he inspires. When I come into his presence to secure his support for measures of this kind I cannot, as canon law requires, avoid personal contact with such men. All I can do is to avoid condoning their conduct. I am afraid of contracting sin by associating with them, for I remember that at the time of my consecration I took an oath over the body of St. Peter at Pope Gregory's command, promising that if I was unsuccessful in bringing them back to the right path I would avoid their company. On the other hand, if, in avoiding them, I fail to approach the Frankish prince, I fear that my missionary work amongst the people will greatly suffer.

Pray, resolve my doubts and hesitations by your advice, judgment and precept. For my own part, I feel that if I dissociate myself from them, especially in cases where their manner of life is not in conformity with the canons of the Church, and if I refrain from seeking their advice, from agreeing with their views and from taking part with them in the services of the Church, I shall have done enough.

There is one other comfort for my missionary labours that I should like to ask from you. May I be so bold as to beg of you to send me the *Book of the Prophets* which Winbert, of revered memory, my former abbot and teacher, left behind when he departed this life? It contains the text of the six prophets bound together in one volume, all written out in full with clear letters. Should God inspire you to do this for me, no greater comfort could be given me in my old age, nor could any greater reward be earned by yourself. A *Book of the Prophets*, such as I need, cannot be procured in this country, and with my failing sight it is impossible for me to read small, abbreviated script. I am asking for this particular book because all the letters in it are written out clearly and separately.

In the meantime I am sending you by the priest Forthere a letter and a small gift as a token of affection, a towel, not of pure silk but mixed with rough goat's hair, for drying your feet....

News was brought to me recently by a priest who came to Germany from your parts that you had lost your sight. You, my Lord, are more aware than I am who it is who said: " Where he loves, he bestows correction." And St. Paul says: " When I am weakest, then I am strongest of all "; and: " My strength is increased in infirmity." The author of the psalms adds: " Many are the trials of the innocent ", etc. You, my father, have eyes like those of Didimus, of whom Antony is related to have said that his eyes saw God and His angels and the blessed joys of the heavenly

Jerusalem. On this account, and because I know your wisdom and your patience, I believe that God has permitted you to be afflicted in this way so that your virtue and merit may increase and that you may gaze with the eyes of the spirit on those things which God loves and commands, whilst seeing less of the things God hates and forbids. What are our bodily eyes in this time of trial but the windows of sin through which we observe sins and sinners, or, worse still, behold and desire them and so fall into sin?

Farewell, my lord, and pray for me in Christ.

(Tangl, 63)

31

POPE ZACHARIAS TO BONIFACE CONCERNING CASES OF REBAPTISM IN BAVARIA

(July 746)

Zacharias, servant of the servants of God, to his very reverend and holy brother and fellow-bishop, Boniface.

We have heard from Virgilius[1] and Sedonius, men of religious life in Bavaria, that you have ordered them to confer Baptism for a second time on certain Christians. This report has caused us some anxiety and, if the facts are true, has greatly surprised us. They told us that there was a certain priest in that province who knew no Latin at all, and who at the ceremony of Baptism, through ignorance of Latin grammar, made the mistake of saying: "Baptizo te in nomine patria et filia et spiritus sancti ", and for this reason you considered a second Baptism to be necessary. But, very reverend brother, if the minister intended no error or heresy, but simply through ignorance made a slip in Latin, we cannot agree to a repetition of the baptismal rite. For, as you are well aware, even a person who has been baptized by a heretic in the name of the Father, Son and Holy Ghost, does not need to be baptized over again, but is merely absolved by the laying on of hands. If, then, the case is really such as the report makes out, you must no longer

---

[1] Probably the Irish Bishop of Salzburg (745–84), whose cosmological theories about the existence of another world, with sun and moon, below the earth, caused much controversy.

issue instructions to this effect. You must endeavour to conform
to the teaching and preaching of the Fathers of the Church.

May God keep you safe, most reverend brother.

Given on the kalends of July in the twenty-sixth year of our
pious and august emperor, Lord Constantine, crowned by God, in
the fourth year of his consulship, the fourteenth indiction.

(Tangl, 68)

32

BONIFACE WRITES A LETTER OF ADMONITION TO KING AETHELBALD
OF MERCIA
(746–7)

To my most dear lord Aethelbald, King of the English, beloved
in Christ above all other kings, Boniface, the archbishop, Legate
in Germany of the Roman Church, with Wera, Burchard,
Werberht, Abel, Willibald, Hwita and Leofwine, his fellow-
bishops,[1] lasting and loving greetings in Christ.

We confess before God and His holy angels that whenever
reliable messengers have brought us news of your prosperity,
your faith and good deeds in the sight of God and men, we have
been glad and given thanks to God in our prayers. We have also
prayed and entreated the Saviour of the world to keep you for
many years to come firm in faith, constant in good works and just
in your government of a Christian people. But whenever it has
come to our ears that you have suffered a setback either in the state
of your realm, the outcome of war or, what is more dangerous, in
the salvation of your soul, then we have been cast down with grief
and sadness, because we share in your joys and suffer with you in
your troubles.

We have heard that you are generous in the giving of alms. On
this we congratulate you, because they who give alms to the least

---

[1] These seven bishops, all Anglo-Saxons, were Boniface's coadjutors. There
are good reasons for thinking that Wera was Bishop of Utrecht between 741
and 753. Burchard was Bishop of Wurzburg, Willibald was Bishop of Eichstatt
(whose travels are described later in this volume), Abel was Archbishop of
Rheims and Hwita is usually supposed to be the Bishop of Buraburg; to
the others, Werberht, Leofwine, it is not possible to ascribe sees, but it is
unlikely that Leofwine is to be identified with Lebuin, whose biography occurs
later in this book.

of their needy brethren will hear on the day of judgment, as the Gospel says, a favourable sentence from the Lord: " As long as ye did it to one of these, my least brethren, ye did it to me. Come, ye blessed of my Father, receive the kingdom which has been prepared for you from the beginning of the world."

We have heard, also, that you vigorously suppress robbery and crime, perjury and plundering, and that you are known to be a protector of the widows and the poor: hence peace is established in your kingdom. For this we rejoice and praise God, because Christ, who is our peace and truth, has said: " Blessed are the peaceable, for they shall be called the children of God."

But with these good tidings one grave accusation against your otherwise good conduct, and one which we would prefer to think was false, has reached our hearing and caused us sorrow. We have learned from several sources that you have never taken a lawful wife. Marriage was instituted by the Lord our God from the beginning of the world and has been ordained and reaffirmed in his preaching by the Apostle Paul, saying: " Beware of fornication. Let each man have his own wife and let each woman have her own husband." For if you wished to act in this manner for the sake of practising chastity and continence and had refrained from taking a wife out of fear and love of God, and then had truly fulfilled your purpose, we should have been glad, because it is a laudable and not a reprehensible course to take. But if, as many say (which God forbid), you have not taken a lawful wife nor professed chastity for God's sake but have been driven by lust into the sins of fornication and adultery and have lost your good name before God and men, then we are deeply grieved.

And what is much worse, those who told us add that you have committed these sins, to your greater shame, in various monasteries with holy nuns and virgins vowed to God. Let us put the matter this way. If a slave is guilty of a heinous crime against his master, if he commits adultery with his lord's wife, how much greater is the crime of the man who besmirches with his lust the spouse of Christ, Creator of heaven and earth? Saint Paul says: " Do you not know that your bodies are the temples of the Holy Ghost? " And in another place: " Do you not know that you are the temple of God and that the spirit of God dwells in you? If any man defiles the temple of God, him shall God destroy: for the temple of God is holy, which you are." And again, he counts fornicators and adulterers, together with idolators, among the number of sinners, saying: "Know ye not that sinners will not inherit the kingdom of God. Be not deceived: neither fornicators nor idolators nor adulterers nor the effeminate, nor thieves nor drunkards nor revilers, nor extortioners shall possess the kingdom of God."

Among the Greeks and Romans a candidate for Holy Orders is closely questioned before his ordination about this sin, implying that anyone found guilty of it has committed a blasphemy against God, and if found guilty of having had intercourse with a nun veiled and consecrated to God he is debarred from entering the ranks of the clergy. For this reason one should carefully consider how grievous a sin this is in the eyes of the Eternal Judge. He who is guilty of it is classed as an idolator, and even though he has been reconciled to God by penance he is banished from the service of the altar. Our bodies, consecrated to God through the offering of our vows and the words of the priest, are said by the Holy Ghost to be the temple of God. Those, then, who violate them are to be regarded, according to the Apostle, as the sons of perdition. Peter, Prince of the Apostles, warned the lustful against the sin of fornication, saying: " The time past suffices,"[1] etc. And then: " A harlot's pay is but the price of a meal; the adulteress costs dearer, her price is a man's whole life."[2] Small blame to the thief when he steals to fill his hungry belly, and if he be caught, why, he can pay sevenfold or yield up all that he has; the adulterer, in the hunger of his heart, must risk losing life itself.[3]

It would be tedious to enumerate how many teachers have denounced the dread poison of this sin and forbidden it with terrible threats. Fornication is more grave and repellent than almost any other sin and may truly be called the snare of death, an abyss of hell and a whirlpool of perdition.

Wherefore, if you are still living in a state of sin, we beseech and entreat Your Grace through Christ, the Son of God, and through His coming, to amend your life by penance and cleanse

[1] Pet. iv.3–5.   [2] Prov. vi. 26.   [3] Prov. vi. 30–32.

it by purification. Bear in mind how vile a thing it is to change the image of God which has been created in you into the likeness of the devil through lust. Remember that you have been set as a king and ruler over many, not for your own deserts but through the overwhelming goodness of God, and that now by your lust you are making yourself the slave of the devil. The Apostle says: " Whatsoever sin a man commits, of that he becomes a slave." Not only by Christians, but even by pagans is this sin reckoned a shame and a disgrace. For even pagans, who know not the true God, observe in this matter, as if by instinct, the essence of the law and the ordinance of God, inasmuch as they respect the bonds of matrimony and punish fornicators and adulterers. In Old Saxony, if a virgin defiles her father's house by adultery or if a married woman breaks the marriage tie and commits adultery, they sometimes compel her to hang herself by her own hand, and then over the pyre on which she has been burned and cremated they hang the seducer. Sometimes a band of women get together and flog her through the villages, beating her with rods, and, stripping her to the waist, they cut and pierce her whole body with knives and send her from house to house bloody and torn. Always new scourgers, zealous for the purity of marriage, are found to join in until they leave her dead, or half dead, that others may fear adultery and wantonness. The Wends, who are a most degraded and depraved race, have such a high regard for the bonds of matrimony that when the husband is dead the wife refuses to live. A wife is considered deserving of praise if she dies by her own hand and is burned with her husband on the same funeral pyre.

If, then, the heathen who, as the Apostle says, know not God and have not the law carry out by instinct the injunctions of the law and show the works of the law written on their hearts, it is time now that you who are called a Christian and a worshipper of the true God should, if you have been defiled with lust in your youth, wallowed in the mire of adultery or drowned in the sea of lust as in the abyss of hell, call to mind your Lord, should escape from the snares of the devil and cleanse your soul from its foul iniquities. Now is the time for you to fear your Creator and to desist from defiling yourself by committing such crimes. Now is the time to spare the many people who, through following the example of a vicious prince, perish and fall into the pit of death. For it is certain that we shall be rewarded or punished by the eternal Judge according to the number of people we have led to heaven by our good example or swept into hell by our evil courses.

If the English race, as people in the provinces say and as the French, Italians and even the heathens insultingly proclaim, are despising lawful marriage and living in open adultery like the people of Sodom, then we must expect that from such intercourse with harlots, a people degenerate, degraded and mad with lust will be begotten. In the end the whole race, turning to base and ignoble ways, will cease to be strong in war, steadfast in faith, honoured by men or pleasing in the sight of God. So has it befallen other peoples of Spain, Provence and Burgundy. They turned away from God and yielded to lust until Almighty God allowed the penalties of such crimes to destroy them, first by letting them lose the knowledge of God and then by loosing the attacks of the Saracens upon them.

It should be noted that in this crime another and much greater crime is involved, because when these harlots, whether nuns or not, bring forth their children conceived in sin they generally kill them and so, instead of enlarging the Church by bringing in adoptive sons of Christ, they fill graves with corpses and hell with unhappy souls.

We have also been informed that you have violated the privileges of churches and monasteries and filched away their revenues. If this is true, it must be regarded as a grievous sin on the testimony of the Holy Ghost, which says: " Shall he who robs father or mother make light of it? He is next door to a murderer." It cannot be doubted that God, who created us, is our Father and the Church who regenerated us spiritually is our Mother. Therefore he who robs or plunders the money of Christ and the Church will be regarded as a murderer in the sight of the just Judge. Of him a certain wise man said: " He who steals from his neighbour is a robber; he who robs the Church of her possessions is guilty of sacrilege."

It is said that your governors and earls use greater violence and oppression towards monks and priests than any other Christian kings have ever done before. Ever since St. Gregory sent missionaries to convert the English people to the Catholic faith the privileges of the Church remained inviolate and sacrosanct until the days of Ceolred, King of Mercia and Osred, King of Deira and Bernicia. At the evil suggestion of the devil these two kings showed, by their accursed example, how these two deadly sins could be committed publicly against the commands of the Gospel and the teachings of our Saviour. They persisted in their crimes, namely, in the violation and seduction of nuns and the destruction of monasteries, until they were condemned by the just judgment of God and cast down from their royal state, overtaken by sudden and terrible death, deprived of eternal light and plunged into the depths of hell. For while Ceolred, Your Highness's predecessor, as those who were present testify, sat feasting amidst his nobles, an evil spirit which had seduced him into defying the law of God suddenly struck him with madness, so that still in his sins, without repentance or confession, raving mad, gibbering with demons and cursing the priests of God, he departed from this life and went certainly to the torments of hell. Osred, also, maddened and spurred on by his lust, outraged consecrated virgins in their convents until a shameful and ignominious death deprived him of his glorious kingdom, his young life and his impure soul.

Wherefore, beloved son, beware of the pit into which you have seen others fall before you. Beware the darts of the old foe with which you have seen your relatives fall wounded. Be on your guard against him who lays the snares that have entrapped your friends and companions, and by which you have seen them lose this life and the life to come. Follow not the example of such to your ruin. Such are they who, according to Holy Writ, have oppressed the good and taken away their works. On the day of judgment they will say: " Far, it seems, did our thoughts wander from the true path; never did any ray of justice enlighten them, never the true sun shone."

The riches of this world are of no avail on the day of judgment if a man comes to the end of his life still making evil use of them, for after the death of the body he shall fall into eternal punishment of the soul. Take these warnings to heart, my dear son; I pray you yield to the prudent words of God's law and reform your life. Turn away from your vices, make an effort to acquire holy virtues. So shall you prosper in this world and receive eternal reward in the world to come.

May Almighty God so turn your life to better things that you may be worthy of the grace of our Lord Himself for evermore.

(Tangl, 73)

33

BONIFACE TO ARCHBISHOP EGBERT OF YORK[1] ABOUT THE LETTER TO AETHELBALD AND ABOUT BOOKS

To his dear and reverend brother, Archbishop Egbert, Boniface, a servant of the servants of God, Legate of the Apostolic See in Germany, sincere greetings of spiritual brotherhood in Christ.

When I received your gifts and books I gave thanks to God for having found me such a friend in my journeys in these distant parts, one who helps me with material things and supports me spiritually with his prayers and the divine consolation of his friendship. From the depths of my heart I beg you to receive me, and those who work with me, into your fellowship, and to give me your advice and help in matters relating to ecclesiastical laws and decrees. Be assured that I am not trifling, but asking in all seriousness, without pride, arrogance or self-complacency. For when the Catholic, Apostolic and Roman Church sent me, an unworthy and lowly preacher, to the misguided pagan peoples of Germany, it laid an obligation upon me to use the authority of the Roman Pontiff and to strive with all my strength to recall to the way of salvation all those who were in error, or perverting the

---

[1] Egbert was cousin of Ceolwulf, King of Northumbria. With his brother Ecgred he went to Rome and was ordained deacon there. He was appointed to the See of York probably in 732. Bede wrote to him a letter of advice about the life, doctrine and administration of a bishop, urging him to fulfil the scheme of Pope Gregory the Great for the erection of dioceses. He received the pallium from Gregory III in Rome in 735 and thus became the second Archbishop of York. The famous school, from which later Alcuin was to come, was founded by him. He died in 766 and was buried in a porch or chapel of the cathedral.

church laws by evil practices or led away from the Catholic faith.

In fulfilment of this obligation, and supported by the counsel and consent of the bishops who are working with me, I sent a letter of admonition and reproof to Aethelbald, King of Mercia. This letter was, by my orders, to be shown to you, so that you could correct what was ill-expressed or emphasize and confirm by your authority what was well said. Also, if you were aware that the same evils objected in the letter against the king were rife amongst your own people you could check them immediately and root them out before they bore fruit and became like Sodom and Gomorrah, and their wine became the poison of dragons and the cruel venom of asps. It is an evil unheard-of in times past, and, as my colleagues here who are versed in Scripture say, three or four times worse than the corruption of Sodom, when a Christian people, flouting the custom of the whole world, nay more, the command of God, turns against lawful marriage and abandons itself to incest, lust, adultery and the seduction of veiled and consecrated women.

Have copied and sent to me, I pray you, some of the treatises of Bede, whom, we are told, God endowed with spiritual understanding and allowed to shine in your midst. We also would like to enjoy the light that God bestowed on you.

Meanwhile, I am sending to you as a token of affection a copy of the letters of St. Gregory, which I have received from the Roman archives, and which, so far as I know, have not yet reached Britain. If you wish, I will send more, for I have many from the same source.

I am sending also a cloak, and a towel to dry the feet of the brethren after you have washed them.

I pray that your Grace may enjoy good health and make progress in virtue.

(Tangl, 75)

34

BONIFACE ASKS ABBOT HUETBERT[1] OF WEARMOUTH TO SEND HIM THE WORKS OF BEDE

(746–7)

To his very dear and revered brother Abbot Huetbert, and to all the brethren of his holy community, Boniface, a humble servant of the servants of God, sends greeting of brotherly love in Christ.

We earnestly beseech you, kind brother, to assist us with your holy prayers in our labours among the rude and savage people of Germany, where we are sowing the seed of the Gospel. Pray that we may not be scorched by the fiery furnace of the Babylonians, but rather that the seed strewn in the furrows may germinate and grow an abundant harvest. For, in the words of the Apostle, " neither he that planteth nor he that watereth is of any account, but only God who giveth the increase".

Meanwhile, I beg you to be so kind as to copy and send me the treatises of the monk Bede, that profound student of the Scriptures, who, as we have heard, lately shone in your midst like a light of the Church.

If it would not give you too much trouble, pray send me also a cloak—it would be of great comfort to me in my journeys.

As a token of my deep affection for you I am sending you a coverlet, as they call them here, made of goat's hair. I beg you to accept it, trifling though it is, as a reminder of me.

May the Blessed Trinity, one God, guard you and prosper you in health and every holy virtue in this life, and glorify and reward you in future blessedness among the shining cohorts of the angels.

(Tangl, 76)

---

[1] Huetbert was brought up at Jarrow from childhood and later pursued his studies in Rome during the time of Pope Sergius (687–701). He became Abbot of the twin monasteries of Wearmouth and Jarrow about 716.

35

BONIFACE TO ARCHBISHOP CUTHBERT OF CANTERBURY[1] REPORTING
THE ESTABLISHMENT OF FRANKISH SYNODS AND THE OBSTACLES
TO HIS WORK

(747)

To his brother and fellow-bishop, Cuthbert [of Canterbury],
raised to the dignity of the archiepiscopate, and united to him by
the bond of spiritual kinship, Boniface, Legate for Germany and
the Catholic and Apostolic Church of Rome, sends greetings of
intimate love in Christ.

It is written in the book of Solomon: " Happy is the man who
has found a friend with whom he can speak as with himself."[2]
We have received by the hand of your son, the deacon Cynebert,
together with your generous gifts, a delightful and affectionate
letter. You have also sent me by him verbally a welcome discourse
concerning our fraternal relations. I hope that as long as life shall
last this exchange of spiritual counsel may go on, if God wills,
from whom alone " all holy desires, all good counsel, and all just
works do proceed ". May you and I be bound together in the
golden bonds of heavenly love which cannot be broken, you
better and more fully because God has endowed you with greater
gifts of knowledge and power, I striving to be instructed as your
devoted vassal, " faithful in many things ".

The work of our ministry is in one and the same cause: an equal
supervision over Churches and people is entrusted to us, whether
in teaching or in reproving or in admonition or in protecting all
classes of clergy and laity. Wherefore I humbly request that if at

---

[1] Cuthbert of Canterbury, said to have been of noble lineage, first appears
as Abbot of Liminge in Kent. In 736 he was consecrated Bishop of Hereford
and translated to Canterbury four years later. He went to Rome for the pallium
and received it from Gregory III some time before 29 November 741. He
presided at the Council of Cloveshoe, where every priest was ordered to learn
and explain to the people in their own tongue the Creed, the Lord's Prayer and
the Offices of Mass and Baptism. He sent the proceedings of this council to
Boniface by his deacon Cynebert and thus encouraged him to follow his
example.
[2] Ecclus. xxv. 12.

any time God shall inspire you or your synods with wholesome counsel you will not hesitate to share it with me. And I likewise, if God will impart to me in my weakness anything useful or profitable to you, will do the same by you. Our responsibility towards Churches and peoples is greater than that of other bishops on account of the pallium entrusted to us and accepted by us, while they have the care of their own dioceses only. And hence, dear friend (not that you, who are so wise, need to hear or read the decisions of us simple folk), we feel that on account of your holy and humble good will towards us you would like to be informed about the decisions we have taken here and so submit them to you for correction and improvement.

We decided in our synod that we will maintain the Catholic faith and unity and our subjection to the Roman Church as long as we live: that we will be loyal subjects of St. Peter and his vicar; that we will hold a synod every year; that our metropolitan bishops shall ask for their palliums from that see; and that in all things we shall obey the orders of St. Peter according to the canons, so that we may be numbered among the flock entrusted to his care. To these declarations we have all agreed and subscribed, and we have forwarded them to the shrine of St. Peter, prince of the Apostles. The Roman clergy and Pontiff have gratefully accepted them. We have decided that every year the canonical decrees, the laws of the Church, the rule of regular life, shall be read and renewed at the synod. We have decreed that the metropolitan, having received his pallium, shall exhort the other bishops and admonish them and make enquiry as to who among them is watchful over the people's welfare and who is negligent. We have forbidden the clergy to hunt, to go about in the woods with dogs and to keep falcons or hawks.

We have ordered every priest annually during Lent to render to his bishop an account of his ministry, the state of the Catholic faith, Baptism and every detail of his administration. We have decreed that every bishop shall make an annual visitation of his diocese confirming and instructing the people, seeking out and forbidding pagan rites, divination, fortune-telling, soothsaying, charms, incantations and all Gentile vileness. We have forbidden the servants of God to wear showy or martial dress or to carry arms.

We have decreed that it shall be the special duty of the metropolitan to enquire into the conduct of the bishops under him and their care for the people. He shall require them, on their return from the synod, each to hold a meeting in his own diocese with his priests and abbots and urge them to carry out the synodal decrees. And every bishop finding himself unable to reform or correct some fault in his own diocese shall lay the case openly in the synod before the archbishop for correction, just as the Roman Church at my ordination bound me by oath that if I found priests or people wandering from the law of God and could not correct them I would always faithfully report the case to the Apostolic See and the vicar of St. Peter for settlement. Thus, if I am not mistaken, should every bishop do to his metropolitan and to the Roman Pontiff if the case cannot be settled among themselves. So shall they be guiltless of the blood of lost souls.

Furthermore, dear brother, our labour is the same but our responsibility greater than that of other priests. The ancient canons prescribe, as everyone knows, that the metropolitan is to have charge of a whole province, and I fear that we have, so to speak, undertaken to steer a ship through the waves of an angry sea and can neither control it nor without sin abandon it, for as a certain wise man says:[1] " If it is dangerous to be negligent in steering a ship in the midst of the sea, how much more perilous to abandon it to the storm with the waves running high; and even so, the Church which makes its way through the ocean of this world like a great ship, buffeted in this life by diverse waves of temptation, is yet not to be abandoned but controlled."

As examples we have the early Fathers, Clement and Cornelius and many others in Rome, Cyprian in Carthage, Athanasius in Alexandria, who under pagan emperors guided the ship of Christ, nay his dearest spouse the Church, teaching, defending, labouring and suffering even to the shedding of blood. Of myself I can surely say, in the words of the Song of Songs: " The sons of my mother have fought against me. They made me keeper of the

[1] Julianus Pomerius, *De Vita Contemplativa*, P.L. 59, col. 431.

vineyards, but my own vineyard I have not kept". According to Nahum, the prophet, the vineyard is the house of Israel: but at the present time it is the Catholic Church.

By command of the Roman Pontiff and with the sanction of the princes of the Franks and Gauls, I have undertaken to bring together and address a synod in the hope of renewing the law of Christ. In that Church I have dug the ground round about, I have enriched it with manure, but I have not guarded it. While I waited for it to bear grapes it brought forth wild grapes, and according to another prophet: "The labour of the slave shall fail and the fields yield no harvest."[1] But, alas, my labour seems like the barking of a dog that sees thieves and robbers break in and plunder his master's house, but, because he has none to help him in his defence, can only whine and complain.

But now, finding myself in this position and asking your wholesome advice as to what seems right and prudent, I suggest that it is time to speak freely. I say like the Apostle Paul in the Acts of the Apostles[2]: "I testify unto you this day that I am pure from the blood of all men", etc. He says: "I have walked among you preaching the kingdom of God that I might keep myself guiltless of the destruction of all." The Apostle calls the priest "bishop", and the prophet calls him "watchman", the Saviour of the world calls him "shepherd of the Church". All agree that the teacher and guide who conceals the sins of the people in silence becomes thereby guilty of the blood of lost souls.

For this reason a dread necessity compels us to present ourselves as an example to the faithful according to the word of the Apostle; that is, if I am not mistaken, the teacher is to live so well that his deeds shall not contradict his words, and that while he himself may live prudently, he shall not be silently condemned for the sins of others. He is set over the Church to this end that he may set not only an example of right living to others but through his dutiful preaching may bring every man's sins before his eyes and show him what punishment awaits the hard of heart and what reward the obedient. For, according to the word of God to Ezechiel, when a man is entrusted with the preaching of the Gospel,

[1] Hab. iii. 17.   [2] Acts xx. 26–8.

even though he live a holy life, nevertheless if he is afraid or ashamed to rebuke those who live wickedly, he shall perish together with all those who perish by his silence. And what shall it profit him to escape the penalty of his own sins if he is to be punished for those of others.[1]

Finally, I will not conceal from Your Grace that all the servants of God here who are especially versed in Scripture and strong in the fear of God are agreed that it would be well and favourable for the honour and purity of your Church and a sure protection against vice if your synod and your princes would forbid matrons and nuns to make their frequent journeys back and forth to Rome. A great part of them perish and few keep their virtue. There are many towns in Lombardy and Gaul where there is not a courtesan or a harlot but is of English stock. It is a scandal and a disgrace to your whole Church.

As to the point that any layman, be he emperor or king, official or courtier, relying upon secular force, may wrest a monastery from the power of a bishop, abbot or an abbess and begin to rule there in place of the abbot, have monks under him and hold property bought by the blood of Christ, the ancient Fathers called such a man a robber, sacrilegious, a murderer of the poor, a satanic wolf entering the sheepfold of Christ, to be condemned with the extreme anathema before the judgment seat of God. Remember the words of St. Paul, the Apostle, about such men, when he said to Timothy: " Charge them that are rich in this present world that they be not high-minded nor have their hope set on the uncertainty of riches, but on God who giveth all things." If such men receive not the correction of the Church they are heathens and publicans and the Church of God refuses all communion to them alive or dead. Against such men let us sound the trumpet of God that we may not be condemned for our silence.

Strive with all your might against foolish superstitions in dress, a thing hateful to God. These ornaments, as they call them, but which others call foulness, with their wide embroidered purple stripes, are sent by Antichrist to herald his coming. Through his

---

[1] I have omitted here a long passage from Scripture on the responsibilities of bishops (Ed.).

craftiness he introduces into monasteries his own servants, fornication and lust, sinful friendships of youths in purple garments,
distaste for study and prayer, and the ruin of souls. Such attire
shows the wickedness of their souls, giving proof of arrogance and
pride, luxury, vanity, of which Wisdom says: " Pride and
arrogance and the evil way of the froward mouth I hate."

It is said also that the vice of drunkenness is far too common in
your parishes and that some bishops not only do not prohibit it
but themselves drink to the point of intoxication, and by offering
large drinks to others force them into drunkenness. There can be
no doubt that this is a grave offence in any servant of God, for the
canons of the Church Fathers order a drunken bishop or priest to
reform or be degraded. And the Truth Itself says: " Take heed
to yourselves lest at any time your hearts be overcharged with
surfeiting and drunkenness."[1]   And St. Paul[2] and the prophet
Isaiah.[3]   This is an evil peculiar to the heathen and to our race, for
neither the Franks nor the Gauls, nor the Lombards, nor the
Romans, nor the Greeks practise it. Let us, if possible, put a
check upon it by synodal action and the commands of Scripture.
At all events by avoiding it ourselves and prohibiting it we shall
declare our souls free from the blood of the damned.

As to the forced labour of monks upon royal buildings and
other works, a thing unheard-of anywhere except in England, let
not the priests of God keep silence or consent thereto. It is an
evil unknown in times gone by.

May God's hand preserve you safe, reverend and beloved
brother, against all adversity to make intercession for us.

(Tangl, 78)

36

BONIFACE REPORTS TO THE POPE THE FOUNDATION OF FULDA

(751)

To the most reverend and beloved lord and master to be revered
in fear and honour, Zacharias, invested with the privilege of the
apostolic office and raised to the dignity of the Apostolic See,

_____
[1] Luke xxi. 34.   [2] Eph. v. 18   [3] v. 22.

Boniface, your humble and most unworthy servant, but your devoted legate in Germany, sends greetings of unfailing love.

I beseech Your Gracious Highness with earnest prayer to receive with kindness and favour a priest of mine, Lull, and bearer of my letter. He brings certain confidential messages for your gracious hearing only, partly by word of mouth, partly in writing. He will also make certain enquiries of importance to me and bring me for the comfort of my old age your answers and fatherly advice given with all the authority of St. Peter, Prince of the Apostles. When you have heard and considered all these matters, if they meet with your approval, I shall strive with God's help to enlarge upon them, but if, as I fear, they may not altogether please you, I shall follow your apostolic precept and either crave your indulgence or do penance as is fitting.

When your predecessor once removed, Gregory II, of revered memory, consecrated me bishop, unworthy as I was, and sent me to preach the word of faith to the Germans, he bound me by oath to support by word and deed all those bishops and priests who were canonically elected and of blameless life. This by divine grace I have tried to do. False priests, however, and hypocrites misleading the people, I was either to convert to the way of salvation or to reject and refrain from associating with them. This I have in part accomplished, but in part have not been able to maintain. In spirit I have kept my oath, because I have not agreed with them nor taken part in their counsels; but in the letter I could not avoid contact with them because when I went to the Frankish court on urgent ecclesiastical matters there were men there whom I would rather not have met.

The Pontiff also told me to make reports to the Apostolic See on the life and customs of the races I visited. And this I hope that I have done. But on the matter which I made known to you about the archbishops making their pleas for pallia from Rome, as the Franks promised they would, I crave the indulgence of the Apostolic See, because they are slow to carry out their promises. They are still discussing the matter and putting it off, and it is uncertain what they intend to do. But had it been left to me, the promise would have been kept.

There is a wooded place in the midst of a vast wilderness situated among the peoples to whom I am preaching.[1] There I have placed a group of monks living under the rule of St. Benedict who are building a monastery. They are men of ascetic habits, who abstain from meat and wine and spirits, keeping no servants, but are content with the labour of their own hands. This place I have acquired by honourable effort through the help of pious and God-fearing men, especially of Carloman, formerly King of the Franks, and have dedicated it in honour of the Holy Saviour.

Here I propose with your kind permission to rest my aged and worn body for a little time and after my death to be buried here. The four peoples to whom we have preached the Word of God by the grace of God dwell, as all know, round about this place, and as long as I live and retain my faculties I can with your support be useful to them. It is my desire, sustained by your prayers and led by God's grace, to continue my close relations with you and to remain in your service among the German people to whom I was sent, and to follow your directions as it is written:[2] " Hear the judgment of your father, O my children, and so act that you may be saved. He that giveth glory to his father shall have length of days. In deed and word honour thy father that a blessing may come to thee from him, for a blessing of the father establisheth the houses of children."

(Tangl, 86)

37

PAPAL CHARTER FOR THE MONASTERY OF FULDA

(November 751)

Pope Zacharias to Bishop Boniface and through him to the abbots of the monastery built by him, in succession for ever.

Since reasonable requests ought always to be granted, it is right that the devotion of the founder of a house of prayer should not be denied the grant of privileges. Wherefore, since you have asked for the monastery, which you have built in a place called

---

[1] A fuller account of the foundation of the Abbey of Fulda will be found in the Life of St. Sturm, its first abbot.
[2] Ecclus. iii. 2.

Bochonia on the bank of the river Fulda, to be honoured by a privilege from the Apostolic See, so that being under the jurisdiction of our holy Church, of which, by God's will, we are servants, it may be withdrawn from the jurisdiction of any other Church, we grant your pious wish and by our authority fulfil your request.

Therefore, by this our authority, we forbid any priest of any Church except that of the Apostolic See to exercise any rights whatsoever over the said monastery. No one shall presume, except on the invitation of the abbot, even to celebrate Mass there, and the monastery shall remain for ever in the enjoyment of the rights implied in the apostolic privilege.

By this our decree we absolutely forbid all prelates of whatsoever Church they may be, of any rank or power, under penalty of excommunication, ever to dare to violate in any way the privilege granted by us to the said monastery.

Farewell.

(Tangl, 89)

38

BONIFACE BEGS EGBERT TO SEND HIM THE WORKS OF BEDE

(747–51)

To his friend in loving embrace, to his brother in the bonds of the Spirit, to Archbishop Egbert, invested with the insignia of the highest office, many greetings and unfailing love in Christ, from Boniface, a lowly bishop, legate in Germany of the Roman Catholic and Apostolic Church.

The gifts and books you have sent us have been received with a joyful and grateful heart. With hands upraised to heaven we beseech the Supreme Majesty to repay you with an ample reward amongst the angels in heaven. But now we beg Your Holiness with earnest prayer that in your kindness and affection you would deign to pray for us in our struggles and trials. The great burden that weighs upon us compels us to seek the help of good men, as it is written: " The earnest prayer of the just man availeth much." The brevity of this letter, however, prevents us from telling you all the ills we suffer both within and without.

For the present, we beg you from the bottom of our hearts to comfort us in our sorrow, as you have done before, by sending us a spark from that light of the Church which the Holy Spirit has kindled in your land; in other words, be so kind as to send us some of the works which Bede, the inspired priest and student of Sacred Scripture, has composed—in particular, if it can be done, his book of homilies for the year (because it would be a very handy and useful manual for us in our preaching), and the Proverbs of Solomon. We hear that he has written commentaries on this book.

In the meantime, we are greatly in need of your advice and counsel. When I find a priest who in the past has fallen into sin and has been restored to his office by the Franks after due penance, and now lives in a district where there are no other priests and continues to administer Baptism and celebrate Mass for a population which, though Christian, is prone to error, what should I do? If I relieve him of his post, acting on the established canons, then owing to the scarcity of priests, children will die without the sacred water of rebirth until I can find some better man to replace him.

Judge therefore between me and the living people. Is it better, or at least a lesser evil, to allow such a man to perform his sacred functions at the altar, or to leave the bulk of the people to die as pagans, seeing that they have no way of securing a better minister? Where there is no lack of priests, and I find one who has fallen into that same sin and, after doing penance, has been reinstated in his former rank, so that the whole body of priests and people have confidence in his good character, should I remove him? If at this stage he were to be degraded his secret sin would be revealed, the people would be shocked, many souls would be lost through scandal, and there would be great hatred of priests and distrust of the ministers of the Church, so that they would all be despised as faithless and unbelieving.

For this reason we have boldly ventured to tolerate the man under discussion and allow him to remain in the sacred ministry, thinking the danger from the offence of one man a lesser evil than the loss of the souls of almost the entire people. On this whole subject I earnestly desire to have your holy advice in writing. Tell me how far I must exercise forbearance in order to avoid scandal, and how much I must repress.

Finally, we are sending you by the bearer of this letter two small casks of wine, asking you in token of our mutual affection to use it for a merry day with the brethren. We beg you so to treat our requests that your reward may shine forth in the heavens.

(Tangl, 91)

39

BONIFACE PROVIDES FOR HIS ASSOCIATES AND THE APPOINTMENT OF LULL AS HIS SUCCESSOR

(752?)

Boniface, servant of the servants of God and bishop by the grace of Christ, to his beloved fellow-ecclesiastic Fulrad, priest,[1] affectionate greetings without end in Christ.

I know not how to return such thanks as you deserve for the spiritual friendship which, for Christ's sake, you have so often shown me in my trials; but I pray Almighty God to reward you for ever in heaven and in the joy of the angels. I beg you now to carry through to the end the good work you have begun so well: salute our glorious and gracious King Pippin from me and convey to him my deepest gratitude for all the kindness he has shown me. Report to him what my friends and I feel regarding the future.

It seems to me, considering my ill-health, that this mortal life of mine and the daily course of my activities must soon come to an end. Therefore I pray His Royal Highness, in the name of Christ, the Son of God, to indicate whilst I am still alive what future provision he is willing to make for my disciples. They are nearly all foreigners. Some are priests spending their lives in lonely places in the service of the Church and the people. Some are monks in cloisters or children learning to read. Others are men

---

[1] Fulrad was the Abbot of Saint-Denys and chaplain to the king. He had much influence, and his intervention was more likely to move the king than a direct appeal from Boniface, who, as a foreigner, was not *persona grata* in court circles.

of mature age who have been my companions and helpers for many years. My chief anxiety about all of them is that after my death they may have to disperse and be scattered abroad like sheep without a shepherd, unless they have the support and patronage of Your Highness. I am afraid also lest those people who are near the pagan border may lose their faith in Christ.

For this reason I earnestly beg Your Gracious Highness to have my son, the auxiliary bishop Lull,[1] appointed in my place as preacher and teacher to the priests and people, that is if it so please God and Your Grace. I hope, God willing, that in him the priests may find a master, the monks a teacher according to the spirit of the Rule, and the Christian people a faithful teacher and pastor.

I have a particular reason in making this request, because my priests living near the border of the heathens lead a very bare existence. They can get enough to eat, but they cannot procure clothing without help and support from elsewhere. Until now the assistance to maintain themselves in those districts for the service of the people has come from me.

If the grace of God shall move you to grant my requests, kindly send me word, either by these present messengers or in writing, so that in the secure knowledge of your care for them I may the more happily live or die.

(Tangl, 93)

40

BONIFACE COMMENDS A MESSENGER TO COUNT REGINBERT
(732–54)

To his dear son, Count Reginbert, Boniface, servant of the servants of God, greetings in the Lord for evermore.

May I beg a favour from Your Highness? Please allow this messenger, who is on his way to Rome with some letters of mine dealing with Church affairs, a safe conduct through your territory, so that he may pray at the shrines and bring back replies to me.

[1] Lull governed the bishopric of Mainz from 754 to 785.

Help him when he is in need as you have helped my previous messengers, for so they have told me on their return.

Pray comply with this request, that your reward with God may be greatly increased.

Farewell in Christ.

(Tangl, 95)

41

BONIFACE TO LEOBA, ABBESS OF BISCHOFSHEIM

(735-54)

To the reverend handmaid in Christ, Leoba, held ever in sincere affection, Boniface, a servant of the servants of God, sends heartfelt greetings in Christ.

Be it known to you, dear sister, that our brother and fellow priest Torhthat has reported to us that in response to his request you are willing to permit a certain maiden to receive instruction for a time if we give our consent.

Be assured, therefore, that whatever you may see fit to do in this matter for the increase of her merits shall have our consent and approval. Farewell in Christ.

(Tangl, 96)

42

BONIFACE COMMENDS A SERF

(732-54)

Boniface, servant of the servants of God, to the priest Denehard, greeting in Christ.

I commend to you, dear friend, this serf Athalere, begging you to aid him in case of need as if he were a free man and to pledge yourself to his friends for him as such and not as a serf. Since he is proposing to take a wife, I am thus eager to commend him that he may have no fears on account of his servile condition. Farewell in Christ.

(Tangl, 99)

43

THE PRIEST WIGBERT[1] WRITES TO THE MONKS OF GLASTONBURY ABOUT HIS ARRIVAL IN GERMANY

(732–54)

. . . I would like you to know that as soon as Archbishop Boniface heard of our arrival he had the kindness to journey a long distance to meet us and gave us a warm welcome. Believe me, our work here is not useless but will redound to your gain. For Almighty God in His great mercy and through your merits has crowned our labours with success, though there are many difficulties and dangers and we are constantly beset by hunger, thirst, cold and the hostility of the heathens. I beg you, therefore, to pray for us, that we may be given words to speak our mind boldly in making known the Gospel revelation, so that the results of our work may be permanent.

Farewell in the Lord. Give our greetings to the brethren in the neighbourhood, first to Abbot Ingold[2] and then to our own community. Give the news of our successful journey to Mother Tetta[3] and her nuns. Repay our constant prayers, I beg you all, and may the mercy of God keep you ever praying on our behalf.

(Tangl, 101)

44

KING ETHELBERT ASKS FOR FALCONS

(748–54)

To the most holy archbishop Wynfrith, called Boniface, and worthily invested with the pontifical insignia, Ethelbert, King of Kent, sends greeting in the Lord of lords.

[1] There are several persons with the name Wigbert who appear in connection with Boniface. It is unlikely that this writer is to be identified with Wigbert, the Abbot of Fritzlar, who died in 738.

[2] Ingold or Ingeld was abbot of a monastery not far from Glastonbury. In another letter the community of an abbot called Aldhun with two abbesses Cuenburg and Coenburga addresses Abbot Coengils, Ingeld and Wichbert, a priest. Coengils was Abbot of Glastonbury, Cuenberga was Abbess of Wimborne and sister to Ingeld: but nothing more can be said about him.

[3] Tetta was sister of the King of Wessex and Abbess of Wimborne. Under her St. Leoba and St. Agatha received instruction: see the Life of Leoba.

Some years ago the venerable abbess Bugga,[1] after a visit to the holy places of Rome for the purpose of offering prayer, returned thence to her native land and to the convent of holy women which she had formerly governed wisely under the law of the Church. At her invitation I had a conference with her, in which among other matters of importance she reminded me that while you were both in Rome and eagerly engaged in visiting the shrines of the Apostles you had given her permission to speak in familiar terms with Your Grace about her affairs. She told me further that because of our blood relationship she had asked and elicited from you a promise that you would give me, though I was absent and personally unknown to you, the same wise counsel and help of your prayers as she had received in your presence. When she told me that you had made this promise I cannot easily express the joy and comfort it gave me.

By the bearer of this letter I am sending Your Grace with my devoted affection a few gifts: a silver drinking-cup lined with gold, weighing three and a half pounds, and two woollen cloaks. I am not sending these gifts in the hope of receiving any earthly gift in return, but rather on bended knee begging from you what is far more necessary, namely, that in these days of manifold and sudden perils and in this world of scandals you would deign to help me with your prayers. And with this same purpose may Your Grace have in mind to urge others by command or persuasion to do the same, not only as long as I live, but after my death, should you survive me.

Having thus briefly mentioned these matters, there is one other favour I have to ask, which, from what I hear, will not be difficult for you to grant, namely, to send me a pair of falcons, quick and spirited enough to attack crows without hesitation and bring them back to earth after catching them. We ask you to procure these birds and send them to us, since there are few hawks of this kind over here in Kent, which produce good offspring, quick-witted, mettlesome and capable of being tamed, trained and taught for the purpose I have mentioned.

[1] St. Eadburga, Abbess of Minster in the Isle of Thanet.

Finally, I pray you to reply to my letter and be so kind as to let me know whether the things I am sending have duly arrived.

May divine grace give Your Grace long life to pray for us.

(Tangl, 105)

45

BONIFACE TO KING PIPPIN [1]

(753)

To the most noble lord Pippin, King of the Franks, Bishop Boniface sends greetings.

I give sincere thanks to Your Gracious Highness and pray our Lord Jesus Christ to grant you everlasting bliss in the kingdom of heaven because you have deigned to listen to my prayers and to give me comfort in my frail old age. And now, noble son, let me say that I believe, by the grace of God, that I can once more enter into your service. I ask you, therefore, to let me know whether I may attend the assembly to carry out your wishes.

A certain servant of my Church, named Ansfrid, who is an accomplished liar, ran away by stealth from me and now returns to me bearing an order from you demanding that I should do him justice. I am sending him back to you together with the letter and my messenger: you will then see how much he has lied to you. I beg you in your own interest to defend me against such liars and to give no ear to their falsehoods.

(Tangl, 107)

---

[1] Pippin the Short, son of Charles Martel. After the retirement of his brother Carloman from public life and his entrance into a monastery Pippin was in sole control of the Frankish kingdom. He was anointed king by Boniface probably in 752, the first-known instance in the West of such a ceremony.

46

BONIFACE GREETS THE NEW POPE

(752)

To the most noble lord Pope Stephen,[1] exalted and beloved above all pontiffs, endowed with the privilege of the apostolate, Boniface, a humble bishop and disciple of the Roman Church, sends affectionate greeting of love in Christ.

I pray for Your Holiness from the depths of my heart that I may be worthy to claim and possess that intimate union with the Apostolic See under your gentle sway and to remain your faithful and devoted servant and disciple in the same way as I have already served the Apostolic See under three of your predecessors, the two Gregories and Zacharias, of venerable memory, who always helped me and strengthened me with their letters of exhortation and with their authority. I pray Your Grace so to act that I may still more efficiently carry out and fulfil your fatherly intentions. For if I have accomplished anything of value in this Roman mission, in which I have been engaged now these six-and-thirty years, I desire to increase and fulfil it. Or if it be found that I have said or done anything wrong or unwise I pledge myself to correct it humbly and willingly and at once according to the judgment of the Roman Church.

Meanwhile I beg my gracious lord not to be offended by my tardiness in sending letters and a personal message to you. This delay was owing to my great preoccupation with the restoration of the churches burned by the heathen within our parishes and cloisters. They have pillaged and burned more than thirty churches. It was this, not careless negligence, which delayed my letters and address to Your Paternity.

(Tangl, 108)

---

[1] On the death of Pope Zacharias a certain Stephen was elected (23 March 752) but died three days later before his consecration could take place. Early writers did not include him in the list of Popes and this has caused confusion in the numbering of the Popes Stephen. The Pope who is addressed here is Stephen III, consecrated 26 March or 3 April 752, died 26 April 757.

47

BONIFACE ON THE DISPUTE WITH COLOGNE ABOUT UTRECHT
(753)

To his venerable and beloved apostolic lord and Pope Stephen, Boniface, a humble legate or messenger in Germany of the Catholic and Apostolic Church, sends greetings of love in Christ.

In the time of Sergius [687–701], Pontiff of the Apostolic See, there came to the shrine of the Apostles a Saxon priest of great holiness and self-denial, by name Willibrord, called also Clement. The aforementioned Pope consecrated him bishop and sent him to preach to the heathen Frisians by the shores of the western sea. For fifty years he preached to the Frisian people, converted a great part of them to the faith of Christ, destroyed their temples, and holy places, and built churches, establishing an episcopal see with a church in honour of the Holy Saviour in a fortified place called Utrecht. In that see and in the church which he had built he continued preaching up to his feeble old age. He also appointed an auxiliary bishop as his substitute to carry on his ministry and at the close of his long life entered into the peace of God.

Then Carloman, King of the Franks, entrusted the see to me to appoint a bishop and consecrate him. This I did.

But now the Bishop of Cologne claims the see of Bishop Clement consecrated by Pope Sergius, for himself, and declares that it belongs to him on account of the ruins of a certain little church destroyed by the heathen. This Willibrord discovered razed to the ground within the fortress of Utrecht, rebuilt it from the foundations with his own labour, and consecrated it in honour of St. Martin. He insists that the Castle of Utrecht, together with the ruined church, was given by Dagobert, formerly King of the Franks, to the diocese of Cologne on condition that the Bishop of Cologne should convert the Frisians to the Christian faith and be their pastor. But this he did not do. He did not preach to the Frisians nor convert them to Christianity. The Frisian people remained pagans until Sergius, Pontiff of the Roman See, sent

Willibrord as bishop and teacher to them. He it was who converted them to the faith of Christ.

Now the Bishop of Cologne wishes to annex this see of the missionary Willibrord so that there shall be no episcopal see under the Roman Pontiff for the Frisian mission. I answered him according to my conviction that the order of the Apostolic See, the consecration by Pope Sergius, and the mission of Willibrord ought to be far stronger reasons for the establishment of an episcopal see under the Roman Pontiff for the Frisian mission, a great part of them being still pagans, than the broken foundations of a little ruined church which had been trampled on by pagans and abandoned by the neglect of the bishops. He, however, does not agree with this.

May it please Your Paternity to give judgment for me. If my answer to the Bishop of Cologne is right and acceptable to you, confirm it by your authority so that the authority of Sergius and the see itself may be permanently established. It would be a great help to us if you would be willing to send me from the archives of your Church a copy of the instructions [written] by Sergius to Bishop Willibrord, who was consecrated by him, so that by the authority of Your Holiness I may be able to convince and overcome my opponents. If, however, some wiser course presents itself to Your Holiness, please send me your advice so that I may act accordingly.

(Tangl, 109)

48

Bishop Milret[1] of Worcester to Lull on the Death of Boniface

To the kindly and beloved master in Christ, Bishop Lull, Milret, a servant of those who serve God.

After I had been obliged to leave your company and the presence of the holy father Boniface and returned by the aid of

[1] Milret was probably coadjutor to Bishop Wilfrith, who ruled over what is now Worcester and Gloucester. In 754 or 755 he visited Boniface and Lull in Germany and had not long returned home when he heard of the news of Boniface's martyrdom. He died in 775.

your prayers to my native land through divers accidents and many adventures, hardly a year had passed when the sad news was brought to us that our blessed father had passed from the prison of the flesh to the world above. We may well call this sad tidings. And yet when we have been permitted to send before us such an advocate to heaven we have every confidence that we are supported by God's help and by his holy intercession. Though we lament with bitter tears the comfort we have lost in this life, yet he who is now consecrated a martyr to Christ by the shedding of his blood, the glory and crown of all those whom this country has sent forth, soothes and relieves our saddened hearts by his blessed life, by the fulfilment of his noble work and his glorious end. We mourn our fate, hungering in this vale of tears, in this life filled with temptations. He, his pilgrimage accomplished with mighty effort, attained to a glorious death as martyr of Christ and now sits in glory in the heavenly Jerusalem to be, as I believe, a faithful intercessor for our sins, if God's grace together with Christ and the holy citizens of heaven permit. So much I write of our loving father. I beg you earnestly to send me an account of his venerable life and his glorious end.

One other thing occurs to me to say, seeing that we are close friends. I humbly beg of you, as if I were kneeling at your feet, to cherish in your heart not only as a passing memory but permanently that fraternal love which our common father Boniface, of blessed memory, impressed upon us with his words in the love of Christ, uniting us in his gracious utterances. I am sure that it will, beyond all doubt, profit both you and me if we strive to carry out the precepts of so eminent a teacher.

Do not hesitate, loving master, to instruct me, the least deserving of your brethren, in brotherly love; fortify me by your precepts and assist me with your prayers. I pledge myself to follow faithfully and willingly all your directions in all things as far as I am able, and I promise, as God is my witness, to maintain that firm friendship as long as the spirit governs these limbs and the breath of life dwells in these mortal members. I pray with all my strength that with Christ's help the Scripture may be fulfilled: " They had all things in common."

What I have briefly set down I am sending to you verbally and more fully by the bearers of this letter, should Almighty God prosper their journey.

I have sent you some trifling gifts which I beg you to accept in the same affectionate spirit in which they are given.

May Christ protect you in your loving intercession for my sons.

The book I cannot send, because Bishop Cuthbert [of Canterbury] has not yet returned it.

God be with us.

(Tangl, 112)

THE *HODOEPORICON* OF ST. WILLIBALD
BY HUNEBERC OF HEIDENHEIM

The authoress of the following life remained anonymous for a long time until B. Bischoff discovered the interpretation of a cryptogram inserted in an early manuscript between the biographies of the two brothers Willibald and Wynnebald. It then appeared that her name was Huneberc, an Anglo-Saxon nun of Heidenheim. She had evidently taken down the description of Willibald's travels from his own mouth, when, as Bishop of Eichstatt, he related his experiences to his brethren. The changes in the narrative from " he " to " we " seem to point to interruptions in the story, as if the bell for Compline or some other monastic duty had intervened to break the continuity. The style is unpolished, full of digressions and marred by the piling up of adjectives to emphasize her meaning, but between the lines one can sense her intense curiosity to discover all about the places Willibald had visited. The repetitions and amplifications are obviously due to the questions put to him whilst the narrative was being told.

Willibald was first and foremost a pilgrim, and we must not expect to find in his narrative the notes of a scientific observer. He tells us little about a great number of things we should like to know, such for instance as the character of the people, the conditions of the country and the state of the towns he passed through. The value of the *Hodoeporicon* lies in its being the only narrative extant of a pilgrimage to the Holy Land in the eighth century, thus forming a bridge between the works of Arculfus (670) and Bernardus Monachus (865). His notices of the Holy Places at Jerusalem, however, are of the highest interest, and some of them are of great archaeological value. Among these, special attention may be called to his references to the Church of Calvary with its three memorial crosses outside its eastern wall; his statement that the stone in front of the sepulchre was only a copy of the one which the angel rolled away; his allusion to the column that marked the spot where, tradition said, the Jews had tried to carry off the body of our Lady; and his placing of the Church of Sion in the middle of Jerusalem.

THE *HODOEPORICON* OF ST. WILLIBALD
BY HUNEBERC OF HEIDENHEIM

PREFACE

TO THE venerable priests, deacons, abbots and brethren beloved in Christ, whom our holy bishop, as a good leader and tender father, has appointed throughout his diocese to be priests, chaste levites, monks and novices, to all these who live under religious observance, I, an unworthy sister of Saxon origin, last and least in life and manners, venture to write for the sake of posterity and present to you who are religious and preachers of the Gospel a brief account of the early life of the venerable Willibald. Although I lack the necessary experience and knowledge because I am but a weak woman, yet I would like, as far as lies in my power, to gather together a kind of nosegay of his virtues and give you something by which you may remember them. And here I repeat that I am not urged on through presumption to attempt a task for which I am so ill fitted. It is your authority and kindness and God's grace which has prompted me to describe the scenes where the marvels of the Incarnate Word were enacted, for Willibald visited and saw these places with his own eyes and trod with his feet in the footsteps of Him who was born into this world, suffered and rose again for our sake. Of all these places Willibald has given us a faithful description. For this reason, it did not seem right to allow these things to pass into oblivion, nor to be silent about the things God has shown to His servant in these our days. We heard them from his own lips in the presence of two deacons who will vouch for their truth: it was on the 20th of June, the day before the summer solstice.

I know that it may seem very bold on my part to write this book when there are so many holy priests capable of doing better, but as a humble relative I would like to record something of their deeds and travels for future ages.

In the hope, then, that you will excuse me and kindly grant me your indulgence, relying also on the grace of God, I present to you this narrative, traced in letters of ink and dedicated to the glory of God, the Giver of all good.

*   *   *

First of all, I will tell of the early life of the venerable high priest of God, Willibald: how he submitted to the discipline of monastic life, how he followed the examples of the saints and how he imitated and observed their way of life. Then I will speak of his early manhood, the time of his maturity and of his old age, even till he became decrepit, combining and putting into order the few facts that there are and weaving them into a continuous narrative.

When he was a baby in the cradle, a lovable little creature, he was cherished fondly by those who nursed him, especially by his parents, who lavished their affection on him and brought him up with great solicitude until he reached the age of three. At that age, when his limbs were still weak and delicate, he was suddenly attacked by a severe illness: the contraction of his limbs made it impossible for him to breathe and threatened to end his life. When his father and mother saw that he was at the doors of death they were full of fear and grief, and their suspense grew as they saw him, gripped by the disease, hovering between life and death. It seemed that the child, whom they had hoped would be their survivor and heir, would soon be carried to an untimely grave. But God Almighty, Creator of heaven and earth, did not intend that His servant should be released from the prison of his body and depart unknown to the rest of the world, for he was destined to preach the Gospel to the ends of the earth and to bring a multitude of neophytes to the faith of Christ.

But let us return to the early infancy of the blessed man. When his parents, in great anxiety of mind, were still uncertain about the fate of their son, they took him and offered him up before the holy Cross of our Lord and Saviour. And this they did, not in the church but at the foot of the Cross, for on the estates of the nobles and good men of the Saxon race it is a custom to have a cross, which is dedicated to our Lord and held in great reverence, erected on some prominent spot for the convenience of those who wish to pray daily before it. There before the cross they laid him. Then they began earnestly to implore God, the Maker of all things, to bring them consolation and to save their son's life. And in their prayers they made a solemn promise that in return for the health of their child they would at once have him tonsured as the first step to Sacred Orders and would dedicate him to the service of Christ under the discipline of monastic life.

No sooner had they made these vows than they put their words into deeds. They enlisted their son in the service of the heavenly King; their favour was granted by the Lord, and the former health of the child was restored.

When this remarkable boy had reached the age of five he began to show the first signs of spiritual understanding. His parents hastened to carry out the promises they had made, and as soon as they had taken council with their noble friends and kinsfolk they lost no time in instructing him in the sacred obligations of monastic life. Without delay they entrusted him to the care of Theodred, a man both venerable and trustworthy, and begged him to be responsible for taking the child to the monastery, where he should make suitable arrangements and dispositions on his behalf. So they set out and took him to the monastery which is called Waldheim [Bishops Waltham]. There they handed him over to the venerable Abbot Egwald, offering him as a novice, because of his age, to be obedient in all things. In accordance with the rules of monastic life the abbot immediately laid the case before the community and asked them if they would advise and allow this to be done. The response of the monks was immediate, and by their unanimous consent he was accepted and received by them into the community to share in their life.

Afterwards this boy of unassuming manners was initiated and perfectly trained in sacred studies. He gave careful and assiduous attention to the learning of the psalms and applied his mind to the examination of the other books of Holy Writ. Young though he was in age, he was advanced in wisdom, so that in him through the divine mercy the words of the prophet were fulfilled: " Out of the mouths of babes and sucklings thou hast perfected praise." Then, as his age increased and his mental powers developed, and more so as the growth of divine grace kept pace with his increasing strength and stature, he devoted his energies to the pursuit of divine love. Long and earnest meditation filled his days. Night and day he pondered anxiously on the means of monastic perfection and the importance of community life, wondering how he might become a member of that chaste fellowship and share in the joys of their common discipline.

Next he began to inquire how he could put these ideas into effect so that he could despise and renounce the fleeting pleasures of this world and forsake not merely the temporal riches of his earthly inheritance but also his country, parents and relatives. He began also to devise means of setting out on pilgrimage and travelling to foreign countries that were unknown to him. After some time had elapsed, when he had outgrown the foolish pranks of childhood, the unsteadiness of youth and the disturbing period of adolescence, through the ineffable dispensation of divine grace he came to manhood. By that time he was greatly beloved by the community because of his obedience and his meekness. All held him in the deepest affection and respect. By assiduous application to his daily duties and continual attention to his studies he disciplined his mind with such vigour and firmness that he made unbroken progress in the way of monastic perfection.

The young servant of Christ, as we have already mentioned, was eager to go on pilgrimage and travel to distant foreign lands and find out all about them. When he had decided to brave the perils of the pathless sea he went immediately to his father and opened his heart to him, telling him the secrets he had concealed from others. He begged him earnestly to advise him on the project and to give his permission; but not content with that, he asked his father to go with him. He invited him to share in this hazardous enterprise and to undertake this difficult mode of life, eager to detach him from the pleasures of the world, from the delights of earth and from the false prosperity of wealth. He asked him to enter, with the help of God, into the divine service and to enroll in the heavenly army, to abandon his native country and to accompany him as a pilgrim to foreign parts. Using all his powers of persuasion, he coaxed him to join his sons on a visit to the sacred shrine of St. Peter, Prince of the Apostles. At first his father declined, excusing himself from the journey on the plea that he could not leave his wife and small children. It would be cruel, and unchristian, he said, to deprive them of his protection and to leave them at the mercy of others. Then the soldier of Christ repeated his solemn exhortations and his long and urgent entreaties, beseeching him, now with fearful threats of damnation, now with bland promises of eternal life, to consent, softening his heart by describing the beauty of paradise and the sweetness of the love of Christ. In this way, employing every means of persuasion and speaking to him heart to heart, he strove to extort from him his agreement to the plan. At last, by the help of Almighty God, his insistence prevailed. His father and his brother Wynnebald gave their promise that they would embark on the enterprise he had in mind and in which he had persuaded them to join.

Following this discussion, a certain time elapsed. At the change of the seasons, towards the end of summer, his father and unmarried brother set out on the journey to which they had agreed. At a suitable time in the summer they were ready and prepared. Taking with them the necessary money for the journey and accompanied by a band of friends, they came to a place, which was known by the ancient name of Hamblemouth, near the port of Hamwih. Shortly afterwards they embarked on a ship. When the captain of the swift-sailing ship had taken their fares, they sailed, with the west wind blowing and a high sea running, amidst the shouting of sailors and the creaking of oars. When they had braved the dangers at sea and the perils of the mountainous waves, a swift course brought them with full sails and following winds safely to dry land. At once they gave thanks and disembarked, and, pitching their tents on the banks of the river Seine, they encamped near the city which is called Rouen, where there is a market.

For some days they rested there and then continued their journey, visiting the shrines of the saints that were on their way and praying there. And so going by degrees from place to place they came to Gorthonicum.[1] Pursuing their journey, they came to Lucca. Hitherto Willibald and Wynnebald had taken their father along with them on their journey. But at Lucca he was struck down almost at once by a severe bodily sickness and after a few days it seemed that his end was near. As the sickness increased, his weary limbs grew cold and stiff, and in this way he breathed his last. As soon as the two brothers saw that their father was dead they wrapped his body in a fine shroud and with filial piety buried it in the Church of Saint Frigidian at Lucca, where it still rests.[2] Immediately afterwards they set out on their way, going steadily on foot through the vast land of Italy, through the deep valleys, over the craggy mountains, across the level plains, climbing upwards towards the peaks of the Apennines. And after they had gazed on the peaks covered with snow and wreathed in banks of cloud, with the help of God and the support of His saints they passed safely through the ambushes of the fierce and arrogant soldiery[3] and came with all their relatives and company to the shrine of St. Peter, Prince of the Apostles. There they besought his protection and gave many thanks to God, because they had escaped unscathed from the grievous perils of the sea and the manifold difficulties of travel in a foreign land, and been accounted worthy to climb the Scala Santa and reach the famous basilica of St. Peter.

The two brothers remained there from the feast of St. Martin until Easter of the following year. During that time, whilst the cold and bare winter was passing and spring with its flowers was beginning to appear and Eastertide was shedding its sunny

---

[1] Possibly Dertonicum or the neighbourhood of the chief town in Liguria, called Chortina in the ancient Life of Charlemagne.

[2] On the legend created by Reginald of Eichstatt about St. Richard, the father of Willibald, see M. Coens, "Légende et Miracles du Roi S. Richard", *Analecta Bollandiana*, xlix, 1231, pp. 353–97.

[3] In 721 the Saracen conquerors of Spain had been defeated by Duke Eudes beneath the walls of Toulouse. Liudprand, King of the Lombards, held armed possession of the greater part of Italy, while the Exarchs of Ravenna represented the tyranny of the Eastern Empire, ruled at that time by Leo, the Isaurian. The reigning Pope was Gregory II.

radiance over the whole earth, the two brothers had been leading
a life of monastic discipline under the prescriptions of the Holy
Rule. Then with the passing of the days and the increasing heat
of the summer, which is usually a sign of future fever, they were
struck down with sickness. They found it difficult to breathe,
fever set in, and at one moment they were shivering with cold,
the next burning with heat. They had caught the black plague.
So great a hold had it got on them that, scarcely able to move,
worn out with fever and almost at the point of death, the breath
of life had practically left their bodies. But God in His never-
failing providence and fatherly love deigned to listen to their
prayers and come to their aid, so that each of them rested in turn
for one week whilst they attended to each other's needs. In spite
of this, they never failed to observe the normal monastic Rule as
far as their bodily weakness would allow; they persevered all the
more zealously in their study and sacred reading, following the
words of Truth, who said: " He who perseveres unto the end shall
be saved."

After this celebrated bearer of Christ's Cross had continued to
pursue the life of perfection with great steadfastness of mind and
inward contemplation, he grew more eager to follow a stricter
mode of life. A more austere and rigorous observance of the
monastic Rule, not an easier one, was what he most desired.
He longed to go on pilgrimage to a more remote and less well-
known place than the one in which he was now staying. So,
energetic as ever, he sought the advice of his friends and asked
permission from his kinsmen to go. He begged them to follow
him on his wanderings with their prayers, so that throughout the
course of his journey their prayers would keep him from harm
and enable him reach the city of Jerusalem and gaze upon its
pleasant and hallowed walls.

So after the solemnities of Easter Sunday were over this restless
battler set off on his journey with two companions. On their way
they came to a town east of Terracina [Fondi] and stayed there
two days. Then, leaving it behind, they reached Gaeta, which
stands at the edge of the sea. At this point they went on board a
ship and crossed over the sea to Naples, where they left the ship

in which they had sailed and stayed for two weeks. These cities belong to the Romans: they are in the territory of Benevento, but owe allegiance to the Romans. And at once, as is usual when the mercy of God is at work, their fondest hopes were fulfilled, for they chanced upon a ship that had come from Egypt, so they embarked on it and set sail for a town called Reggio in Calabria. At this place they stayed two days; then they departed and betook themselves to the island of Sicily, that is to say, to Catania, where the body of St. Agatha, the virgin, rests. Mount Etna is there. Whenever the volcanic fire erupts there and begins to spread and threaten the whole region the people of the city take the body of St. Agatha and place it in front of the oncoming flames and they stop immediately.[1] They stayed there three weeks. Thence they sailed for Syracuse, a city in the same country. Sailing from Syracuse, they crossed the Adriatic and reached the city of Monembasia,[2] in the land of Slavinia, and from there they sailed to Chios, leaving Corinth on the port side. Sailing on from there, they passed Samos and sped on towards Asia, to the city of Ephesus, which stands about a mile from the sea. Then they went on foot to the spot where the Seven Sleepers lie at rest.[3] From there they walked to the tomb of St. John, the Evangelist, which is situated in a beautiful spot near Ephesus, and thence two miles farther on along the sea coast to a great city called Phygela, where they stayed a day. At this place they begged some bread and went to a fountain in the middle of the city, and, sitting on the edge of it, they dipped their bread in the water and so ate. They pursued their journey on foot along the sea shore to the town of Hierapolis, which stands on a high mountain; and thence they went to a place called Patara, where they remained until the bitter and icy winter had passed. Afterwards they sailed from

---

[1] This is reported in her *Acta* to have taken place for the first time in A.D. 252, when the pagans took her veil. See *Acta Sanctorum* for 5 February.

[2] Monembasia is a small town near the south of Morea. The Slavonic Bulgarians were all-powerful at Constantinople, where they had placed Leo III on the imperial throne. It is not surprising, then, that Morea should have been occupied by them.

[3] See Bollandists, *Acta Sanctorum*, 27 July. These seven martyrs suffered under the Emperor Decius about A.D. 250. He stopped up the mouth of the cave where they had taken refuge and so starved them to death. The names are: John, Constantine, Maximinian, Malchus, Martinian, Denys and Serapion.

there and reached a city called Miletus,[1] which was formerly threatened with destruction from the waters. At this place there were two solitaries living on " stylites ", that is, columns built up and strengthened by a great stone wall of immense height, to protect them from the water. Thence they crossed over by sea to Mount Chelidonium and traversed the whole of it. At this point they suffered very much from hunger, because the country was wild and desolate, and they grew so weak through lack of food that they feared their last day had come. But the Almighty Shepherd of His people deigned to provide food for His poor servants.

Sailing from there, they reached the island of Cyprus, which lies between the Greeks and the Saracens, and went to the city of Pamphos, where they stayed three weeks. It was then Easter-time, a year after their setting out. Thence they went to Constantia,[2] where the body of St. Epiphanius rests, and they remained there until after the feast of St. John the Baptist.

Once more they set sail and reached the town of Antarados,[3] which lies near the sea in the territory of the Saracens. Then they went on foot for about nine or twelve miles to a fort called Arche,[4] where they had a Greek bishop. There they sang a litany according to the Greek rite.[5] Leaving this place, they set out on foot for the town named Emesa,[6] about twelve miles distant, where there is a large church built by St. Helena in honour of St. John the Baptist[7] and where his head was for a long time preserved. This is in Syria now.

[1] If Miletus is meant, the pilgrims must have landed there before reaching Patara. The only place between Patara and Chelidonia is a town, now a village, called Myra, mentioned in the Acts of the Apostles xxvii. 27 in the Greek version. The Vulgate calls it Lystra.

[2] Costanza near Famagosta, anciently called Salamis. St. Epiphanius was Bishop of Salamis for thirty-six years and died in A.D. 403.

[3] Called Antaradus by the Greeks and Tortosa in the Middle Ages. The ruins of a magnificent Gothic cathedral can still be seen. The modern name is Tartus.

[4] Akkar on Jebel Akkar? It has a ruined Saracenic castle, but is quite off the road. The place corresponding to Willibald's description may be Husn el-Akrad, or the Kurds' castle, which is fifteen miles from Antaradus.

[5] The Greek liturgy with its constant repetition of the Kyrie would naturally strike the pilgrims as a litany, and this is the word they use here.

[6] The modern name is Hums, with extensive ruins dating from the first century. It was captured by the Saracens in A.D. 636.

[7] The church which is mentioned by Eusebius as among those built by the Empress Helena; but he says (Vita Constantini, iii, 47) that at the same time that Helena was building churches in Jerusalem and Bethlehem Constantine was building them " in all the other provinces ".

At that time there were seven companions with Willibald and he made the eighth. Almost at once they were arrested by the pagan Saracens, and because they were strangers and came without credentials they were taken prisoner and held as captives. They knew not to which nation they belonged, and, thinking they were spies, they took them bound to a certain rich old man to find out where they came from. The old man put questions to them asking where they were from and on what errand they were employed. Then they told him everything from the beginning and acquainted him with the reason for their journey. And the old man said: " I have often seen men coming from those parts of the world, fellow-countrymen of theirs; they cause no mischief and are merely anxious to fulfil their law." Then they left him and went to the court, to ask permission to pass over to Jerusalem. But when they arrived there, the governor said at once that they were spies and ordered them to be thrust into prison until such time as he should hear from the king what was to be done with them. Whilst they were in prison they had an unexpected experience of the wonderful dispensation of Almighty God, who mercifully deigns to protect his servants everywhere, amidst weapons of war and tortures, barbarians, and soldiers, prisons and bands of aggressors, preserving and shielding them from all harm. A man was there, a merchant, who wished to redeem them and release them from captivity, so that they should be free to continue their journey as they wished. He did this by way of alms and for the salvation of his own soul. But he was unable to release them. Every day, therefore, he sent them dinner and supper, and on Wednesday and Saturday he sent his son to the prison and took them out for a bath and then took them back again. Every Sunday he took them to church through the market place, so that if they saw anything on sale for which they had a mind he could buy it for them and so give them pleasure. The citizens of the town, who are inquisitive people, used to come regularly to look at them, because they were young and handsome and clothed in beautiful garments. Then whilst they were still languishing in prison a man from Spain came and spoke with them inside the prison itself and made careful inquiries about their nationality and homeland. And they told him everything about their journey from first to last. This Spaniard had a brother at the king's court, who was the chamberlain of the King of the Saracens. And when the governor who had sent them to prison came to court, both the Spaniard who had spoken to them in prison and the captain of the ship in which they had sailed from Cyprus came together in the presence of the Saracens' king, whose name was Emir-al-Mummenin. And when the conversation turned on their case, the Spaniard told his brother all that he had learned about them whilst speaking to them in the prison, and he asked his brother to pass this information on to the king and to help them. So when, afterwards, all these three came to the king and mentioned their case, telling him all the details from first to last, the king asked whence they came; and they answered: " These men come from the West where the sun sets; we know nothing of their country except that beyond it lies nothing but water." Then the king asked them, saying: " Why should we punish them? They have done us no harm. Allow them to depart and go on their way." The other prisoners who were in captivity had to pay a fine of three measures of corn, but they were let off scot-free.

With this permission they at once set out and travelled a hundred miles to Damascus, in Syria, where the body of St. Ananias rests. They staycd there a week. About two miles distant stands a church on the spot where St. Paul was first converted and where our Lord said to him: " Saul, Saul, why persecutest thou me ", etc. After praying in the church, they went on foot to Galilee, to the place where Gabriel first came to our Lady and said: " Hail Mary." There is a church there now, and the village where the church is is called Nazareth. The Christians have often had to come to terms with the pagan Saracens about this church, because they wished to destroy it. After commending themselves to the Lord there, they set out on foot and came to the town of Chana, where our Lord changed water into wine. A vast church stands there, and in the church one of the altars has on it one of the six waterpots which our Lord ordered to be filled with water and then changed into wine; from it they drank some wine. They stayed for one day there. Departing thence, they reached Mount Thabor, where our Lord was transfigured. At the moment there is a monastery of monks there, and the church is dedicated to our Lord, Moses and Elias, and the place is called by those who live there Holy Mount. There they prayed.

Then they made for the town called Tiberias. It stands at the edge of the sea on which our Lord walked dry-shod and where Peter sank when walking on the waters towards Him. Many churches and synagogues of the Jews are built there, and great honour is paid to our Lord. They remained there for several days. At that point the Jordan flows into the lake. Thence they set off round the lake and went to the village of Magdalene and came to the village of Capharnaum, where our Lord raised to life the ruler's daughter. Here there was a house and a great wall, and the people said that Zebedee used to live there with his sons John and James. Then they went to Bethsaida, the native place of Peter and Andrew. A church now occupies the site where their home once stood. They passed the night there, and on the following morning set off for Corazain, where our Lord cured the man possessed of the devil and drove the demons into a herd of swine. A church stands there now.

After praying there, they departed and came to the spot where two fountains, Jor and Dan, spring from the earth and then pour down the mountainside to form the river Jordan. There, between the two fountains, they passed the night and the shepherds gave us[1] sour milk to drink. At this spot there are wonderful herds of cattle, long in the back and short in the leg, bearing enormous horns; they are all of one colour, dark red. Deep marshes lie there, and in the summer-time, when the great heat of the sun scorches the earth, the herds betake themselves to the marshes and, plunging themselves up to their necks in the water, leave only their heads showing.

Departing thence, they came to Caesarea, where there was a church and a great number of Christians. They rested there for a short time and set out for the monastery of St. John the Baptist, where about twenty monks were living. They stayed the night

---

[1] It will be noticed that the writer seems to be reporting the very words of Willibald as she introduces the pronoun *us*.

and then went forward about a mile to the Jordan, where our Lord was baptized. At this spot there is now a church built high up on columns of stone; beneath the church, however, the ground is dry. On the very place where Christ was baptized and where they now baptize there stands a little wooden cross: a little stream of water is led off and a rope is stretched over the Jordan and tied at each end. Then on the Feast of the Epiphany the sick and infirm come there and, holding on to the rope, plunge themselves in the water. Barren women also come there. Our Bishop Willibald bathed himself there in the Jordan. They passed the day there and then departed.

Thence they came to Galgala, which is about five miles away. In the church there, which is small and made of wood, there are twelve stones. These are the twelve stones which the children of Israel took from the Jordan and carried more than five miles to Galgala and set up as witnesses of their passage. After saying prayers there, they went on towards Jericho, which is more than seven miles distant from the Jordan. The fountain which bubbled up there on the brow of the hill was barren and quite useless to man before the prophet Eliseus came and blessed it and made it flow. Afterwards the people of the city drew it off into their fields and gardens and other places that needed it, and now wherever this fountain flows, the crops increase and promote health, all by reason of the blessing given by Eliseus the prophet. They went on from there to the monastery of St. Eustochium, which stands in the middle of the plain between Jericho and Jerusalem.

Then they came to Jerusalem, to the very spot where the holy cross of our Lord was found. On the site of the place called Calvary now stands a church. Formerly this was outside Jerusalem, but when Helena discovered the cross she placed the spot within the walls of Jerusalem. There now stand three crosses outside the church near the wall of the eastern end, as a memorial to the cross of our Lord and those who were crucified with Him. At present they are not inside the church, but outside beneath a pent roof. Nearby is the garden in which the tomb of our Saviour was placed. This tomb was cut from the rock and the rock stands above ground: it is squared at the bottom and tapers towards a point at the top.

On the highest point of it stands a cross, and a wonderful house has been constructed over it. At the eastern end a door has been cut in the rock of the sepulchre, through which people can enter into the tomb to pray. Inside there is the slab on which the body of our Lord lay, and on this slab fifteen lamps of gold burn day and night; it is situated on the north side of the interior of the tomb and lies at one's right hand as one enters the tomb to pray. In front of the door of the sepulchre lies a great square stone, a replica of that first stone which the angel rolled away from the mouth of the sepulchre.

On the Feast of St. Martin our bishop came there, and as soon as he reached the spot he began to feel sick and was confined to his bed until a week before Christmas. Then when he recovered and began to feel a little better he got up and went to the church called Holy Sion, which stands in the centre of Jerusalem. He prayed there and then went to Solomon's Porch, where there is a pool at which the sick used to lie waiting for the angel to move the waters, after which the first who went down into them was cured: this is where our Lord said to the paralytic: " Arise, take up thy bed and walk."

Willibald himself said that in front of the gate of the city stood a tall pillar, on top of which rose a cross, as a sign and memorial of the place where the Jews attempted to take away the body of our Lady. For when the eleven Apostles were bearing the body of Holy Mary away from Jerusalem the Jews tried to snatch it away as soon as they reached the gate of the city. But as soon as they stretched out their hands towards the bier and endeavoured to take her their arms became fixed, stuck as it were to the bier, and they were unable to move until, by the grace of God and the prayers of the Apostles, they were released, and then they let them go. Our Lady passed from this world in that very spot in the centre of Jerusalem which is called Holy Sion. And then the eleven Apostles bore her, as I have already said, and finally the angels came and took her away from the hands of the Apostles and carried her to paradise.

Bishop Willibald came down from the mount and went to the valley of Josaphat: it is situated to the east of the city of Jerusalem.

In the valley there is a church of our Lady and in the church is her tomb (not that her body lies at rest there, but as a memorial to her). After praying there, he climbed Mount Olivet, which is near to the valley at its eastern end—the valley lies between Jerusalem and Mount Olivet. On Mount Olivet there is now a church on the spot where our Lord prayed before His passion and said to his Disciples: " Watch and pray that ye enter not into temptation." Then he came to the very hill whence our Lord ascended into heaven. In the centre of the church is a beautiful candlestick sculptured in bronze: it is square and stands in the middle of the church where our Lord ascended into heaven. In the middle of the bronze candlestick is a square vessel of glass, and in the glass is a small lamp, and round about the lamp, closed on all sides, is the glass. The reason why it is closed on all sides is that the lamp may burn both in good weather and bad. The church has no roof and is open to the sky, and two pillars stand there inside the church, one against the northern wall, the other against the southern wall. They are placed there in remembrance of the two men who said: " Men of Galilee, why stand ye looking up into heaven? " Any man who can squeeze his body between the pillars and the wall is freed from his sins.

Then he came to the place where the angel appeared to the shepherds and said: " I announce to you tidings of great joy." Thence he came to Bethlehem, where our Lord was born, about six miles distant from Jerusalem. The place where our Lord was born was formerly a cave underneath the ground and is now a square chamber cut out of the rock; the earth has been dug away on all sides and thrown aside, and now the church has been built above it. There our Lord was born. An altar has been raised above it also, but another small [portable] altar has been made, so that when they wish to celebrate Mass within the cave they can take up the small altar whilst Mass is being said and afterwards can take it out again. The church which stands over the spot where our Lord was born is built in the form of a cross, a house of great beauty.

After praying there, they departed and came to a large town called Thecua: this is the place where the Holy Innocents were slaughtered by Herod. A church stands there now. In it rests the body of one of the prophets. Then they came to the Laura in the valley: it is a great monastery and there resides the abbot and the doorkeeper who keeps the keys of the church. Many are the monks who belong to that monastery, and they dwell scattered round the valley on the summits of the hills where they have little cells cut out for them from the stony rock of the hills. The mountain surrounds the valley in which the monastery is built: there lies the body of St. Saba.[1]

Thence they came to the spot where Philip baptized the eunuch. A small church stands there in the wide valley between Bethlehem and Gaza. From there they made towards Gaza,[2] where there is a holy place, and after praying there they went to St. Mathias, where there is a large temple to the Lord. And whilst solemn High Mass was being celebrated there, our Bishop Willibald, standing and listening, lost his sight and was blind for two months. Thence they went to St. Zacharias, the prophet, not the father of St. John the Baptist, but the other prophet. Thence they went to the town of Hebron, where lie the bodies of the three patriarchs Abraham, Isaac and Jacob with their wives.

Then he returned to Jerusalem, and, going into the church where the holy Cross of Christ was found, his eyes were opened and he received his sight. He stayed there for a little while and then set out for a place called Lydda, to the Church of St. George,[3] which lies about ten miles distant from Jerusalem. Thence he came to another village [Joppe], where stands a church to St. Peter, the Apostle: this was where St. Peter raised up the widow Dorcas to life. He prayed there and set out once more and came

[1] St. Saba founded the monastery in A.D. 483 and was made by the Patriarch of Jerusalem archimandrite over all the monasteries of Palestine.
[2] The pilgrims seem to have gone back on their tracks. The ruins of the church built by Constantine at Gaza may still be seen.
[3] The remains of the church of St. George, who was said to have been born there, are still to be seen: they have been restored as a Greek Church. Arculf gives the first account of St. George known to have been circulated in Britain. It is worthy of notice that the north of England, where his narrative was well known, had a great devotion to St. George, a place being assigned to him in the Anglo-Saxon ritual of Durham, which is probably of the early ninth century. A " Passion of St. George " was written by Aelfric, Archbishop of York, A.D. 1021–51. Arculf describes the marble column to which St. George was bound whilst being scourged.

to the Adriatic sea at a great distance from Jerusalem, to the cities of Tyre and Sidon. These two cities are six miles apart and stand on the edge of the sea. Thence he went to Tripoli on the sea-shore, and crossed over Mount Libanus to Damascus. From there he went to Caesarea and back once more, for the third time, to Jerusalem, where he spent the whole winter.

He then travelled over three hundred miles to the town of Emesa in Syria, and thence he came to Salamias[1] which is on the farther borders of Syria. He spent the whole season of Lent there because he was ill and unable to travel. His companions, who were in his party, went forward to the King of the Saracens, named Murmumni, to ask him to give them a letter of safe conduct, but they could not meet him because he himself had withdrawn from that region on account of the sickness and pestilence that infested the country. And when they could not find the king they returned and stayed together in Salamias until a week before Easter. Then they came again to Emesa and asked the governor there to give them a letter of safe conduct, and he gave them a letter for every two persons. They could not travel there in company but only two by two, because in this way it was easier for them to provide food for themselves. Then they came to Damascus.

From Damascus they came for the fourth time to Jerusalem, and after spending some time there they went to the town of Sebaste, which was formerly called Samaria; but after it was destroyed they built another town there and called it Sebaste. At the present time the bodies of St. John the Baptist, Abdias and Eliseus the prophet rest there. Near the town is the well where our Lord asked the Samaritan woman to give Him water to drink. Over that well there now stands a church, and there is the Mount on which the Samaritans worshipped and of which the woman said to our Lord: " Our forbears worshipped on this mount, but Thou sayest that Jerusalem is the place where men ought to worship." Then, after praying there, they passed through the country of the Samaritans to a large town on the far borders of their land and spent one night there.

[1] Now 'Salámeyeh.

Then they travelled across a wide plain covered with olive trees, and with them travelled an Ethiopian and his two camels, who led a woman on a mule through the woods. And as they went on their way, a lion with gaping jaws came out upon them, growling and roaring, ready to seize and devour them; it terrified them greatly. But the Ethiopian said: " Have no fear—let us go forward." So without hesitation they proceeded on their way and as they approached the lion it turned aside and, through the help of Almighty God, left the way open for them to continue their journey. And they said that a short time after they had left that place they heard the same lion roaring, as if in his fury he would devour many of the men who went there to gather olives. When they came to the town which is called Ptolomaeis, which stands by the edge of the sea, they continued their journey and reached the summit of Libanus, where that mountain juts out into the sea and forms a promontory. There stands the tower of Libanus. Anyone who lands there without having a safe conduct cannot pass through the place because it is guarded and closed; and if anyone comes without a pass the citizens arrest him immediately and send him back to Tyre. The mount is between Tyre and Ptolomaeis. Then the bishop came to Tyre for the second time.

When Bishop Willibald was in Jerusalem on the previous occasion he bought himself some balsam and filled a calabash with it; then he took a hollow reed which had a bottom to it and filled it with petroleum and put it inside the calabash. Afterwards he cut the reed equal in length to the calabash so that the surfaces of both were even and then closed the mouth of the calabash. When they reached the city of Tyre the citizens arrested them, put them in chains and examined all their baggage to find out if they had hidden any contraband. If they had found anything they would certainly have punished them and put them to death. But when they had thoroughly scrutinized everything and could find nothing but one calabash which Willibald had, they opened it and snuffed at it to find out what was inside. And when they smelt petroleum, which was inside the reed at the top, they did not find the balsam which was inside the calabash underneath the petroleum, and so let them go.

They were there for a long time waiting for a ship to get ready. Afterwards they sailed during the whole of the winter, from the feast of St. Andrew [30 November] until a week before Easter. Then they landed at the city of Constantinople, where the bodies of three saints, Andrew, Timothy and Luke the Evangelist, lie beneath one altar, whilst the body of St. John Chrysostom lies before another. His tomb is there where, as a priest, he stood to celebrate Mass. Our bishop stayed there for two years and had an alcove in the church so that every day he could sit and gaze upon the place where the saints lay at rest. Thence he went to Nicea, where formerly the Emperor Constantine held a council at which three hundred and eighteen bishops were present, all taking an active part. The church there resembles the one at Mount Olivet, where our Lord ascended into heaven; and in the church are all the portraits of the bishops who took part in the Council. Willibald went there from Constantinople to see how the church was built, and then returned by water to Constantinople.

After two years they set sail from there with the envoys of the Pope and the Emperor[1] and went to the city of Syracuse in the island of Sicily. Thence they came to Catania and then to Reggio, a city of Calabria. They embarked again for Volcano, where the Hell of Theodoric is.[2] When they arrived there they disembarked to see what this inferno was like. Willibald, who was inquisitive and eager to see without delay what this Hell was like inside, wanted to climb to the top of the mountain underneath which the crater lay: but he was unable to do so because the ashes of black tartar, which had risen to the edge of the crater, lay there in heaps: and like the snow which, when it drops from heaven with its falling masses of flakes, heaps them up into mounds, the ashes lay piled in heaps on the top of the mountain and prevented Willibald from going any farther. All the same, he saw the black and

---

[1] The return of the legates to Rome was occasioned by the excommunication of Leo the Isaurian in 728, who had threatened Pope Gregory II.

[2] See the *Dialogues* of Gregory the Great, iv. c. 30. Theodoric was supposed to have been cast into hell for having imprisoned and caused the death of Pope John V and for having killed Symmachus, the Senator. Arculf's narrative, written by Adamnan, also describes the volcano. This island, the ancient Hiera, known as *Volcani Insula* from its volcanic phenomena, is the southernmost of the Lipari islands. It lies twelve miles from Sicily.

terrible and fearful flame belching forth from the crater with a noise like rolling thunder: he gazed with awe on the enormous flames, and the mountainous clouds of smoke rising from below into the sky. And that pumice stone which writers speak of he saw issuing from the crater, thrown out with flames and cast into the sea, then washed up again on the seashore by the tide, where men were collecting it and carting it away. After they had satisfied their curiosity with the sight of the fearsome and terrible burning fire, its fumes, its stinking smoke and its shooting flames, they weighed anchor and sailed to the church of St. Bartholomew the Apostle [at Lipari], which stands on the seashore, and they came to the mountains which are called Didyme, and after praying there they spent one night. Embarking once more, they came to a city called Naples and remained there several days. It is the seat of an archbishop whose dignity is great there. Not far away is the small town of Lucullanum, where the body of St. Severinus is preserved. Then he came to the city of Capua, and the archbishop there sent him to the bishop of another town; that bishop sent him to the Bishop of Teano, and he in turn sent him to St. Benedict's [at Monte Cassino]. It was autumn when he reached Monte Cassino, and it was seven years since he first began his journey from Rome and ten years in all since he had left his native country.

And when the venerable man Willibald and Tidbercht, who had travelled everywhere with him, came to St. Benedict's, they found only a few monks there under Abbot Petronax. Without delay he joined the community, for which he was so well fitted both by his great self-discipline and his natural aptitude for obedience. He learned much from their careful teaching, but he in turn taught them more by his outward bearing; he showed them not so much by words as by the beauty of his character what was the real spirit of their institute; and by proving himself to be a model of monastic virtue he compelled the admiration, love and respect of all.

In the first year that he spent there he was sacristan of the church, in the second a dean of the monastery, and for eight years afterwards he was porter in two monasteries, four years as porter in the monastery which is perched on a very high hill, and four years more in the other monastery which stands lower down near the river Rapido, about two miles away. So for ten years the venerable man Willibald tried to observe, as far as possible, every detail of the monastic observance as laid down by the Rule of St. Benedict. And he not only observed it himself but led the others, whom he had brought over long distances by foot and by sea, to follow him in the traditional path of regular life.

After this, a priest who came from Spain to St. Benedict's and stayed there asked permission of Abbot Petronax to go to Rome. When the permission was asked Petronax without hesitation begged Willibald to accompany him and take him to St. Peter's. He gave his consent at once and promised to fulfil the mission. So they set out, and when they came to Rome and entered the basilica of St. Peter they asked the protection of the heavenly keeper of the keys and commended themselves to his kindly patronage. Then the sacred Pontiff of the Apostolic See, Gregory III, hearing that the venerable man Willibald was there, sent for him to come into his presence. And when he came to the Supreme Pontiff he fell down at once on his face to the ground and greeted him. And immediately that pious Shepherd of the People began to question him about the details of his journey and asked him earnestly how he had spent seven years travelling to the ends of the earth and how he had contrived to escape for so long a time the wickedness of the pagans.

Then the active servant of Christ humbly recounted to the glorious Ruler of the People all the details of his travels as they occurred. He told him how he had passed from place to place, how he had visited Bethlehem and prayed in the birthplace of his heavenly Creator, how he had seen where Christ was baptized in the river Jordan and had himself bathed there. He described his four visits to Jerusalem and Holy Sion, where our Holy Saviour had hung on the cross, was killed and buried and then ascended into heaven from Mount Olivet. All these things he told him and described.

After they had discussed these matters during a pleasant and intimate conversation, the sacred and holy Pontiff intimated to Willibald in a serious and unmistakable tone that St. Boniface had asked him to arrange for Willibald to leave St. Benedict's and come to him without delay in the country of the Franks. And after the Apostolic Lord, Pope Gregory III, had made known to him the desires of St. Boniface, he tried to persuade him, now with peaceable words of exhortation, now pleading, now commanding, to go to St. Boniface. Then the illustrious athlete of God, Willibald, promised that he would carry into immediate effect the request and command of the Pontiff provided he could ask permission, according to the prescriptions of the Rule, from his abbot. The Supreme Pontiff, in whom is vested the highest authority, at once replied that his command was sufficient permission, and he ordered him to set out obediently without any qualm of conscience, saying: " If I am free to transfer the abbot Petronax himself to any other place, then certainly he has no permission or power to oppose my wishes." And so Willibald replied on the spot that he would willingly carry out his wishes and commands, not only there but anywhere in the world, wherever he had a mind to send him. He then pledged himself to go in accordance with his wishes without any further delay. After this, the discussion being ended, Willibald departed at Easter-time, reaching his journey's end on the Feast of St. Andrew. Tidbercht, however, remained behind at St. Benedict's.

He went to Lucca, where his father was buried, and thence to the city of Pavia, from there to Brescia and thence to a place which is called Garda. Then he came to Duke Odilo and stayed a week with him, and thence to Suitgar, with whom he also stayed a week. Suitgar and Willibald left there for Linthard, where St. Boniface was, and St. Boniface sent them to Eichstatt to see how they liked the place. Suitgar handed over the territory there to St. Boniface for the redemption of his soul, and St. Boniface passed it on to our bishop Willibald. At that time it was all waste land—there was not a single house there and the only building was the church of St. Mary, which still stands, smaller than the other church which Willibald afterwards built on the site.

When Willibald and Suitgar had remained together at Eichstatt for some little time, they explored and surveyed the ground and eventually chose a site suitable for a house. After that they went to St. Boniface at Freising and stayed with him until all of them

returned once more to Eichstatt. There St. Boniface ordained
Willibald to the priestly dignity. The day on which Willibald was
ordained was 22 July, the Feast of St. Apollinaris and St. Mary
Magdalen.

After a whole year had passed, St. Boniface commanded him to
come to him at once in Thuringia. And the venerable man of God,
Willibald, set off at once for Thuringia and dwelt as a guest in the
house of his brother St. Wynnebald, who had not seen him for the
past eight and a half years since he had parted from him in Rome.
And they were glad to see each other and congratulated each other
on their meeting. It was then the season of autumn when Willibald came to Thuringia.

Soon after he came there, the archbishop St. Boniface, Burchard
and Wizo consecrated him and invested him with the sacred
authority of the episcopate. He remained there for a week after he
was consecrated bishop and then returned once more to the place
which had been allotted him. At the time of his consecration
Willibald was forty-one years old; he was consecrated at Salzburg
in the autumn, about three weeks before the Feast of St. Martin.

The long course of Willibald's travels and sightseeing on which
he had spent seven long years was now over and gone. We have
tried to set down and make known all the facts which have been
ascertained and thoroughly investigated. These facts were not
learned from anyone else but heard from Willibald himself; and
having received them from his own lips, we have taken them down
and written them in the Monastery of Heidenheim, as his deacons
and other subordinates can testify. I say this so that no one may
afterwards say that it was an idle tale.

At the time that he came to the province from Rome with three
of his fellow-countrymen he was forty-one years old, already
mature and middle-aged; then he was consecrated bishop. Afterwards he began to build a monastery in the place called Eichstatt,
and he shortly afterwards practised the monastic life there
according to the observance which he had seen at St. Benedict's
[Monte Cassino], and not merely there, but also in many other
monastic houses, which he had examined with his experienced eye
as he travelled through various lands. This observance he taught

to others by the example of his own life. With a few fellow-labourers he tilled the wide and spacious fields for the divine seed, sowing and cultivating them until harvest-time. And so like a busy bee that flits through the meadows, purple with violets, aromatic with scented herbs and through the tree branches yellow with blossom, drinking the sweet nectar but avoiding bitter poison, and returns to the hive bearing honey on its thighs and body, so the blessed man chose out the best from all that he had seen abroad with his own eyes, adopted it, and, having adopted it, submitted it to his disciples for acceptance, showing them good example by word and deed, in zeal for observance, avoidance of evil, piety, forbearance and temperance.

Soon after the energetic champion of our good God had begun to dwell in the monastery men flocked to him from all sides, not only from the neighbouring provinces but even from distant countries, to hear his salutary teaching and wisdom. Willibald and Mother Church, like a hen that cherishes her offspring beneath her wings, won over many adoptive sons to the Lord, protecting them continually with the shield of his kindliness. These he trained with gentleness and sympathy, detaching them from their imperfections until they reached perfect maturity. These, having followed in the steps of their master and absorbed his teaching, have now become famous for the training they give to others.

This, then, was Willibald, who at first began to practise a holy life with the support of but a few helpers, but who at last, after struggling in many ways against the opposition of numerous chieftains and courtiers, gained possession of a people worthy of the Lord. Far and wide through the vast province of Bavaria he drove his plough, sowing the seed and reaping the harvest with the help of many fellow-labourers. And all though the land of Bavaria, now dotted about with churches, priests' houses and the relics of the saints, he amassed treasures worthy of our Lord. From these places antiphons now resound, sacred lessons are chanted, a noble throng of believers shout aloud the miracles of Christ and with joyful hearts echo from mouth to mouth triumphant praises of their Creator.

What shall I now say of Willibald, my master and your devoted brother? Who was more outstanding than he in piety, more perfect in humility? Who more forbearing in patience, more strict in temperance, greater in meekness? When was he ever backward in consoling the downcast? Who was more eager to assist the poor or more anxious to clothe the naked? These things are said not for the sake of boasting but for the sake of recounting what I have seen and heard, things done not by the power of man but by the grace of God, in order that, according to the words of the Apostle: "He who glories may glory in the Lord." Amen.

THE LIFE OF ST. STURM
BY EIGIL, ABBOT OF FULDA

Though Eigil is called " Saint ", his name is not to be found in any martyrology. He was born in Norica of noble parents, and shortly after the martyrdom of St. Boniface he was sent to Fulda to be educated under the supervision of his relative Sturm, first abbot of the monastery. As he is careful to point out, he remained at his side for twenty years. After Sturm's death in 779 the abbey was ruled first by Bangulf, then by Ratgar, but the latter's mania for building impeded the progress of the school and brought on other troubles which led to his deposition and banishment. In his place Eigil was elected about the year 818, and he continued in office until his death in 822. There is reason to believe that Eigil shared in the movement which demanded the deposition of Ratgar and which placed a request before Charlemagne in 811 for the enforcement of stricter monastic discipline. But one of Eigil's first acts after his installation as abbot was to demand the return of Ratgar from Louis the Pious.

The Life of Sturm was written at the request of the virgin Angildruth. It contains interesting details about the foundation of the Abbey of Fulda and the various changes that took place there. Eigil's own biography was drawn up by his disciple Candidus and survives in two forms: one in prose, the other in verse.

THE LIFE OF ST. STURM
BY EIGIL, ABBOT OF FULDA

I HAVE always known, O Angildruth, that you were fired with divine love and filled with a desire for better things. And for this reason I comply with your request. For you ask me to recount the life of the holy and venerable Abbot Sturm and to put into writing the early beginnings of the monastery of the Holy Saviour which he founded and which is known by the name of Fulda. You also ask me to describe the events connected with the monastery as I have heard or seen them. As far as my capabilities allow, I have carried out your request and I have compressed into this little book both the early days and life of Sturm as reliable witnesses have recounted them to me, and the foundation of the aforesaid monastery. I have also added some details about the changes effected in the course of time, such as I have heard from others or seen with my own eyes. For I, Eigil, was his disciple for more than twenty years, and I was brought up and trained in the observance of his monastery from childhood. Some of the events, therefore, which I describe can be vouched for from my own experience.

So here you have what you asked for, a slip of parchment inscribed with your name to be kept or laid aside as you choose. It rests with you to answer for me to the criticisms of my enemies: defend me as one moved more by goodwill than presumption, and sustain me by your holy prayers with Christ as your true Spouse.

At the time the venerable Archbishop Boniface set foot in Norica, imparting the faith to the priests and people of the Church, suppressing there the errors of the heretics and curbing with the true doctrine of Christ those people who, although already Christians, were infected with the evil teaching of the pagans, certain nobles came to him vying with each other to offer their sons to be brought up in the service of God. Among those whom he accepted at the instance of his parents was Sturm, a native of

Norica and a member of a noble Christian family. Leaving behind all his relatives and following the Father of our redemption, he set out joyfully on a journey with the bishop who had accepted him, much to the grief of his father and mother. After they had traversed several provinces they reached Frizlar in the land of the Hessians, where the bishop entrusted him to the care of a certain priest named Wigbert. This holy priest took great pains to instruct the boy Sturm in the service of God.

After he had learned the psalms by heart and mastered many books by repeatedly going over them in his mind, the boy began to understand the spiritual meaning of the Scriptures and set himself to learn the hidden secrets of the four Gospels of Christ, and, as far as he was able, to fix in his mind by continual reading the Old and New Testaments. His meditation was upon the law of God, as Scripture says, night and day. His understanding was profound, his thoughts full of wisdom, his words of prudence. Pleasant in countenance, modest in bearing, good-mannered, irreproachable in his conduct, charitable, humble, mild, ready to perform any service, he drew to himself everyone's affection. After a certain length of time he was, with common consent, ordained priest, and as opportunity presented itself he began to explain to the people the hidden words of Christ. Through the power of the Holy Ghost many miracles were wrought by him. Many times he drove out evil spirits by his prayers from sinful Christians. Many times he cured souls that had been infected with the poisonous doctrines of error. Those who were at enmity with one another were ordered by him to become reconciled before the setting of the sun; and to all he taught patience, mildness, humility, longanimity, faith, hope and charity.

When he had spent almost three years of his priesthood preaching and baptizing he was divinely inspired to undertake the rigorous life of a hermit. This idea haunted him at every moment of the day, until on a divine impulse he opened his heart to his spiritual master, the archbishop Boniface. On learning of his intention, the holy man quickly saw that the Lord had deigned to move him by His grace, and, seeing that the inspiration came from God, he encouraged him and became the chief supporter in his design. He therefore gave him two companions, carefully instructed them and, after praying and giving them his blessing, said: " Go to the solitude which is called Bochonia and see if the place is fit for servants of God to dwell in, for even in the desert God is able to prepare a place for His followers."

So the three of them set out to find a place for a hermitage; and when they reached a wild and uninhabited spot and could see nothing except earth and sky and enormous trees they devoutly prayed to God to guide their footsteps in the way of peace. After three days they came to a place which is nowadays called Hersfeld; and when they had explored all the district round about they asked Christ to bless it and make it fit for them to dwell in. This is the spot on which the monastery now stands. There they made small huts roofed over with the bark of trees, and there they stayed for a long time serving God in fasts, watching and prayer.

Some time later, when Sturm had settled down to the hermitical life, he left the solitude and went to the holy archbishop Boniface, to whom he described in detail the situation, the quality of the soil, the running water, the fountains and valleys and everything else connected with his foundation. Boniface listened intently to all he had to say, and after turning it over in his mind ordered him to remain at his side for a time. They discussed together, among other things, the abundant consolation to be found in Holy Scripture, and then the archbishop said: " You have indeed found a place to live in, but I am afraid to leave you there on account of the savage people who are close by, for, as you are aware, there are Saxons not far from that place and they are a ferocious race. Look for a spot farther away, deeper in the woods, where you can serve God without danger to yourselves."

Thereupon blessed Sturm meekly accepted the suggestion of the archbishop and, being anxious to discover another site, set out eagerly for the hermitage. When he reached his companions he found them in their huts anxiously awaiting his return. As soon as he saw them he gave them greetings from the archbishop and brought them comfort by telling them all about his journey, about the archbishop, and described in detail all that the archbishop had said to him. Then he took the two brothers with him and set off upstream in a boat. As they glided along the river Fulda they kept a sharp look-out for streams and fountains. They then disembarked and traversed the country on all sides, looking at the soil, the mountains, the hills, the heights and the valleys to see if the Lord would show them a place in the wilderness fit for them to live in.

At last, on the third day, they came to a spot where the river Luodera flows into the Fulda. But finding nothing that suited their purpose, they turned downstream from there and began to row back to their own hermitage, stopping for a short time on the way at a place called Ruohenbach, where it seemed possible that servants of God might be able to live. On the whole they thought that the archbishop might not approve of it. Then, sailing back along the same river, after a short time they arrived at their own poor huts. There they continued to pray to God to find them a suitable site for a hermitage where they might be able to serve Him in accordance with the requirements of the archbishop Boniface. Day and night they persevered in fasting, watching and prayer, always keeping the memory of God before their eyes and saying in their hearts: " I have set the Lord always before me: because He is at my right hand I shall not be moved." The praise of God was also ever on their lips and in their hearts, and they fulfilled the saying of the psalmist: " I will bless God at all times: His praise is ever on my lips."

Then the holy bishop Boniface, mindful of his hermit Sturm and pleased at what he had done to find another site, sent for him and asked him to come quickly to his presence. The messenger lost no time in coming and found him dwelling in the above-mentioned huts and greeted him, saying: " Our revered bishop has great desire to see you. You should come because he has many matters to discuss." At these words the holy man Sturm gave this humble reply: " I give thanks to God that so great a bishop should be mindful of my lowly self and should deign to send his messenger to me in this wilderness." Then calling his brethren to him, he commanded them to show all kindness to the messenger. Carefully carrying out his behest, they set a table before him and offered him such food as they had; and when he had eaten, the brethren asked his leave to withdraw. Then the man of God summoned the messenger, thanked him for his labour and said: " Greet the holy bishop Boniface in the name of his servants and say that I will hasten to him as quickly as I can." Then he blessed him and allowed him to return.

On the following day the man of God asked the blessing of his brethren and set out at once and, taking the road to Seleheim [near Amoeneburg], hastened to meet the bishop. On the second day after he had set out he met him in the place we have already mentioned, called Frizlar. When it was told the bishop that the hermit Sturm had arrived he gave orders that he should be brought into his presence. When this had been done Sturm fell prostrate at his feet and, greeting the bishop, asked for his blessing. The bishop returned his greetings, blessed him and ordered him to approach and, after kissing him, commanded him to sit at his side. He rejoiced at his coming and asked him for the sake of the love he bore him to relax somewhat his usual fast. The man of God, acting with great discretion and out of reverence for his master the bishop, complied. " Anything that you may command," said he, " I believe to be holy."

Presently the table was set in the presence of the bishop, and Sturm ate the food which he had commanded him to take. When he had eaten and the table was removed the bishop rose, took him aside into a quiet place where they could be alone, and there they talked for a long time about spiritual matters and about the Christian life. For, as afterwards appeared, the bishop was very eager to establish monastic life in the wilderness, and for this reason he enquired, among other things, what had transpired in the hermit's search for a site. Sturm answered: " We travelled upstream along the river Fulda for several days, but we found no place which we could recommend to you." The holy bishop understood from this that the place predestined by God had not yet been revealed, and an interior prophetic voice told him: " A place has indeed been prepared in the wilderness, and when Christ wills He will show it to His servants. For this reason continue the search, knowing and believing that you will certainly find it." And so, assuring Sturm that a site would eventually be found, and, encouraging him in his love of the monastic life and fortifying him against the attacks of the devil, he allowed him to return to his hermitage. Coming to his cell, which had been built at Hersfeld, already mentioned, he greeted his brethren and related to them the commands and the promise of the bishop.

When he had rested with them for a short time and recovered from his fatigue he saddled his ass and, taking provisions, set out alone, commending his journey to Christ, who is the Way, the Truth and the Life. Alone on his ass, he began his wanderings through the pathless wilderness.

Then the insatiable explorer, scrutinizing with his experienced gaze the hills and the plains, the mountains and valleys, the fountains and streams and rivers, went on his way. Singing psalms with his mouth, he raised his mind to God in prayer, staying in no place except where night compelled him to stop. And wherever he spent the night he cut down trees with a tool which he carried in his hand and made a circular fence for the protection of his ass, so that it would not be devoured by the wild beasts which were numerous there. He himself, making a sign of the cross on his forehead, lay down to rest without fear. And thus the man of God, accoutred with weapons of the spirit, covering his body with the breastplate of justice, guarding his breast with the shield of faith, protecting his head with the helmet of salvation, girded with the sword of the Word of God, went forth to the fray against the devil. One day, whilst he was ambling along, he came to a road leading from Thuringia to Mainz which the merchants use, and in the street which goes over the river Fulda he came upon a great number of Slavs swimming in the river and washing themselves. When the ass on which he was riding saw their naked bodies he began to quiver with fear, and even the man of God could not bear the stench of them. They, on their side, like all heathens, began to jeer at him, and when they tried to do him harm they were held back by divine power and prevented from carrying out their intention. One of them, who acted as their interpreter, asked him where he was going. He replied that he was on his way to a hermitage higher up.

So the man of God continued his journey through the frightful

wilderness, seeing nothing but wild beasts, of which there was a
great number, birds flying, enormous trees and the rough thickets
of the forests, until on the fourth day he passed the spot where the
monastery now stands, and, climbing up a hill, reached the
confluence where the river Gysilaha flows into the Fulda. Con-
tinuing a little farther, he came at sunset to the path which was
called by the old name Ortessveca. There he passed the night after
providing protection for his ass against attacks. Whilst he was
busy there putting up the fence he heard afar off the sound of
water trickling, but he could not make up his mind whether the
noise was caused by man or beast. He stood stock still listening
intently, and again he heard the trickle of water. Then because
the man of God did not wish to shout, and knowing instinctively
that a man was astir, he struck a hollow tree with the weapon he
was carrying in his hand. The other, hearing the sound of the
beaten tree trunk, came running towards him, crying out. When
he came near they saw and greeted each other. The man of God
asked him who he was and where he came from. The other replied
that he was on his way from Wetteran and that the horse he was
leading by the halter belonged to his lord Ortis. And so, talking,
they passed the night together in that place, for the other man
knew the district very well; and when the man of God told him
what he had in mind and what he wished to do the other gave him
the names of the various places and explained where the streams
and fountains were to be found. The place in which they were
resting was called Eihloh. The next morning when they rose they
blessed each other and immediately the layman set out on his
journey to Grapfelt.

But Sturm, the servant of God, taking another direction and
placing his trust in God, began to pick his way through the wilderness alone. After he had made a circuit of Eihloh and found it
unsuitable for his purpose he went towards the torrent which
even now is called Grezzibach and spent some time there examin-
ing the site and the quality of the soil. Then he turned back a
short distance and came to the blessed spot foreordained by God
on which the present monastery is built. At the sight of it Sturm
was filled with great joy and continued his journey in high spirits,

for he was convinced that through the merits and prayers of St. Boniface the place had been revealed to him by God. As he walked over the ground and saw all the advantages the place possessed, he gave thanks to God; and the more he looked at it from every angle, the more pleased with it he became. So charmed was he with the beauty of the spot that he spent practically a whole day wandering over it, exploring its possibilities. Finally, he blessed it and turned his face towards home.

After two days' journey the man of God arrived at Hersfeld, where he found his brethren engaged in prayer. He told them of the new site and ordered them to set out with him at once. Without further delay he asked the prayers of the brethren for himself and set off to see the bishop. The journey took several days, but when he came into his presence and was kindly received by him he began to describe the place he had found and to enlarge upon its advantages. " I think," he said, " that I have found a site of which you will approve ", and when he had acquainted him with the lie of the land, the fertility of the soil and of the supply of running water, which satisfies the needs of the monastery even at the present time, the bishop was filled with enthusiasm. Both of them congratulated each other and gave thanks to God: and then they embarked upon a long discussion on the monastic life and its observances.

For a few days the bishop entertained the hermit in his house, and after some pleasant talks together he took pains to speak to him on spiritual matters, stimulating him to a love of the monastic life by examples taken from Sacred Scriptures. And so, instructed and confirmed by sound doctrine and the teaching of Holy Writ, Sturm was allowed by the bishop to return to his cell. Boniface on his part set out for the king's court to seek confirmation for the appropriation of the land for the monastery. Eventually Sturm returned to his brethren, who were dwelling in the hermitage. But when he was on the point of taking them with him to the place he had discovered, which was nine years after he first began to live the solitary life, and of returning from Hersfeld, the devil, who is envious of good designs, fearing the effect of their good lives in the wilderness, stirred up the passions of wicked men to prevent the servants of God from taking possession of the site. Being unable to withstand their stubborn opposition, the servants of God withdrew and settled in another place called Dryhlar.

St. Boniface, as we have mentioned, went to Carloman, the King of the Franks, and addressed him with these wise and humble words: " I believe that it would redound to your everlasting reward if, God willing, and with your help, monastic life could be established and a monastery could be founded in the eastern part of your kingdom, a thing that has not been attempted before our time. For this reason I beg your kind help in this project, so that in future and for ever a never-fading reward may be laid up for you before Christ, the High King. We have found a site suitable for monastic life in the wilderness which is called Bochon, near the river Fulda, but this property belongs to you. I now beg Your Highness to give us this place, so that under your protection we may serve Christ there."

On hearing these words the king was glad and called together the nobles of his court. He spoke to them with approbation of the bishop's request and in their presence handed over to him the property for which he had asked. " The place you seek and which, as you say, is called Eihloh on the banks of the river Fulda, and any other property I am supposed to possess there at this date, is granted whole and entire to God, and all the land that lies north, south, east and west of that point for a distance of four miles shall be included." A charter of this gift was ordered to be drawn up, signed by the king's own hand, and all the nobles in the vicinity of Grapfelt were summoned by messengers and asked to follow the king's example, if by any chance they possessed any property in that quarter. On the day appointed, when they had gathered together, the messengers of the king addressed them. " All of you," they said, " have come here in obedience to the king's command; he asks, or, more correctly, he requires each one of you who has any claim to land in the place called Eihloh to give it to the servants of God for the use of their monastery." On hearing this, they eagerly abandoned in favour of Sturm whatever rights to property they had in that place, and thus was God's will fulfilled.

The donation was accordingly confirmed by all and passed from the possession of men into the possession of God. Blessed Sturm departed to his brethren at Dryhlar and after a few days took seven of the brethren with him to the spot where the monastery now stands. On the twelfth day of January in the year of the Incarnation seven hundred and forty-four, during the reign of the two brothers Carloman and Pippin, the twelfth indiction, the brethren set foot for the first time on this holy spot preordained for this purpose by God. They prayed to the Lord to watch over and protect it at all times by His invincible power, and then, serving Him day and night in fasting, watching and prayer, they set to work, as far as they were able, to cut down the trees and to clear the site with their own hands.

At the end of two months, the venerable archbishop Boniface, accompanied by a great throng of men, came to see them, and after inspecting all the ground and being made aware of all its advantages and usefulness, he rejoiced in the Holy Ghost and gave thanks to God for having granted to His servants so suitable a place to dwell in. The bishop and the monks then agreed that a church should be built, and so he ordered all the men who had accompanied him to the spot to cut down the woods and clear the undergrowth, whilst he himself climbed the brow of a hill, which is now called *Mons Episcopi*, and spent his time praying to God and meditating on Sacred Scripture. This is the reason why the hill bears its name.

After a week of felling trees and clearing away the brushwood the turf was piled up ready to make lime: then the bishop gave the brethren his blessing, commended the place to God and returned home with the workmen he had brought with him. The following year the bishop came again to visit his new monastery, which by that time was called Fulda, taking its name from the river which flowed close by; and after greeting them remained with them for several days, during which time he gave the newly recruited monks instruction and established the observances of monastic life according to the principles laid down in the Holy Rule. Whilst he was explaining the Holy Rule to the brethren he read out the passage which states that the drinking of wine does not befit the vocation of a monk, and so they decided by common consent not to take any strong drink that might lead to drunkenness but only to drink weak beer. Much later this rule was relaxed at a council held in the time of King Pippin, when, owing to the increasing numbers in the community, there were many sick and ailing among them. Only a handful of the brethren abstained from wine and strong drink until the end of their lives.

Shortly afterwards the bishop had a confidential talk with Sturm and gave him advice about the way to govern others, and then, after addressing the brethren on the need for obedience and submission, he commended them to Christ, bade them farewell and departed. Every year he came to visit them in this way, and whenever he was free from his episcopal duties, which were exacting, he came to stay with them and worked with his own hands. And often he spent long hours on his beloved hill, of which we have already spoken, meditating on the hidden truths of the Scriptures.

When the brethren had conceived a burning desire to follow the rule of the holy father St. Benedict, and had striven to conform their ideas and actions to the discipline of the monastic life, they formed a plan of sending some of their members to well-established monasteries in other places so that they could become perfectly acquainted with the customs and observances of the brethren. When this prudent plan was submitted to the bishop he heartily approved of it and commanded Sturm to undertake the experiment himself. All necessary preparations were made for the journey, two other brethren were chosen to accompany him, and so, four years after the foundation of the monastery, he set out for Rome. There he visited all the monasteries and spent a whole year enquiring into the customs, observances and traditions of the brethren who lived in them. In the following year, much edified by the holiness he had met, he returned home. When he reached his own country he was seized with sickness, and by divine providence was compelled to remain in bed for four weeks at the monastery of Kitzingen. But he recovered from his illness and set out to visit Bishop Boniface, who at that time was in Thuringia. On seeing him, the bishop was greatly pleased, and, giving thanks to God for his safe return, asked him many questions about the places he had seen. And when he noticed how shrewdly Sturm had observed the manners of the people and the observance of the monks there, he said: " Go back to the newly founded monastery at Fulda and as far as you are able establish monastic discipline on the pattern of the monks you have seen there." Blessed Sturm begged the bishop's blessing, and, setting off at once to his solitude, reached it after four days, full of joy at seeing his brethren once again. To them he described what he had seen in Italy and the things he had learned from the fathers of the monasteries in Tuscany, and by wise remarks and his personal example stimulated them to follow in his footsteps. For whenever he suggested the adoption of some point of monastic discipline he always took pains to do it first himself so that no one should say: " Why are your words not confirmed by deeds? "

At that time there was a great desire in the community to adapt their mode of life to the observances either described or shown to them or exemplified in the lives of the saints, and they carried out in every detail the Rule of St. Benedict which they had vowed to follow. So for many years they lived in fervour and holiness. Through the coming of recruits the monastery increased, since many came to serve God there and offered both themselves and their possessions. With this growth in the community and the enlarging of their estates the reputation of Fulda spread throughout the countryside, so that its good name reached the ears of brethren in monasteries situated at great distances from it. And since a great number of monks led there a strict life under the discipline of the Holy Rule, the bishop was eager to visit them often; and as he was moved to pity at the sight of their poverty, he gave them small properties in order to provide them with necessary food.

Ten years after his first visit to the holy place the archbishop Boniface took counsel with the king and the other Christians and went into the distant parts of Frisia, which were steeped in paganism. There by teaching and baptizing he gained a great number of people to the faith of Christ. Some years later he departed from them and returned unharmed to the Church in

Germany. But the following year he went once more to the swampy homesteads of the Frisians, hoping to complete the missionary work he had begun. On a certain day after his arrival, when he had called the people together to listen to his teaching, they came, not humbly to hear the Word of God, but stirred by an evil spirit. They rushed in during the sermon brandishing weapons, slew the holy Christian bishop with the sword and slaughtered all his companions. After the martyrdom of the bishop and of many who were with him the brethren from the monastery of Trech in upper Frisia came and took the bodies of the martyrs, placing some in tombs, bringing others with them, among them being the bodies of Bishop Boniface, the deacons and priests who suffered with him, and a certain bishop named Eoban, whose head, which was cut off by the attackers, could not be found. When they came [to Trech] they placed the body of St. Boniface together with the bier, on which it had been brought by boat, in a small church, which was near by. The rest of the martyrs' remains they buried. Then all the inhabitants of that place decided that the remains of St. Boniface should always rest among them, for they thought that it would be a great help to them to remain under the protection of so great a martyr. Fasting and prayer was enjoined and they prayed to God that the holy martyr would deign to remain in their midst. But the holy martyr wished his body to be taken to the place of solitude which by the will of God he had chosen for himself. This soon became clear, for, whilst they were trying to bear him to the other church and place him in a tomb there, they put their hands to the bier but were unable to move it. Many others joined forces with them, but even so they were unable to raise the bier on which the holy body lay.

They understood, therefore, that he did not wish to stay in that place, so they said that he should be taken to the city of Mainz. Straightway they raised it without difficulty, and, taking it to the river and placing it on board a boat, they began to draw the boat along the Rhine and make upstream. When Sturm heard of this he made haste from his Abbey of Fulda in the wilderness to meet them and went along with them until they came after a quiet and uneventful journey to Mainz. Forthwith the priests, clergy and people with one voice declared that it was not right to remove the holy martyr of God to another place but that his body should rest where during his life he had held his episcopal see. A messenger also came from the king's court bringing orders that the martyr's body should remain in the city if he so wished.

But Sturm and those who had gathered together from the monastery repeatedly declared that on many occasions whilst the bishop was staying with them he had pointed out the place where they should lay his body to rest and they had no doubts that he would wish to remain at the monastery. But whilst they were arguing in this way, and Lull, the bishop of the city, strongly forbade the body to be taken to the solitude, the holy bishop appeared one night in a dream to a certain deacon and said: " Why do you delay to take me to my place at Fulda? Arise and bear me into the wilderness where God has foreordained a place for me." And the deacon rose and recounted what had been told him in the dream, first to Sturm and then to all the nobles. At this all were struck with fear and did not dare to oppose any further the removal of the holy martyr from that place. Lull, however, who was bishop there, did not wish to believe in the revelation until the man who had seen the vision had placed his hand upon the altar and taken an oath on the veracity of what he had seen. Then, according to the power of God, whose will cannot be withstood, the body of the blessed martyr was raised with great honour, borne to the river to the accompaniment of hymns, placed on board a ship and rowed as far as Hohleim, a village standing on the banks of the Moyn. From there, after a few days—that is, thirty days after his death—the sacred remains of the bishop were carried to the Abbey of Fulda and placed in a new tomb. On the following day Bishop Lull departed together with the clerics and the throng of people who had come with him. Then the venerable abbot Sturm and his brethren gave thanks to God because they had been granted the presence of so powerful a patron as the holy martyr St. Boniface in their midst.

After the coming of the martyr the spot chosen by God began to increase, its reputation was enhanced and the monastery grew in numbers, because many nobles vied with each other in going there and offered themselves and their goods to the Lord. So, day by day, the number of monks grew apace, and under the protection of the Lord the brethren who served God there preserved the strict observance of their holy life with unabated and unflagging fervour. How many miracles were performed there and are still performed to this day I leave to writers better than myself to describe.

But Sturm, who was beloved by all the community and revered by all the people, dutifully fulfilled his ministry, setting himself as an example to the others, for he exhibited in his conduct what he taught by his words. Lull, however, who was bishop there, grew envious of his good reputation and allowed his jealousy to influence his conduct towards him. Since Sturm preached the Word of God everywhere and at all times and was listened to by all with rapt attention, the bitter enemy of the human race, not enduring so great usefulness to remain among the people, began to sow discord among the brethren and stirred up three false brethren to make false accusations against Sturm in the presence of the king, Pippin. These men, led astray by the persuasion of the devil, entered into a conspiracy and, relying on the support of Bishop Lull, went to the king and accused the blessed man of a trumped-up crime, saying that he was an enemy of the king. And when the man of God presented himself at the court he patiently bore their untruths and made no attempt to exculpate himself. " My witness," said he, " is in heaven and He that voucheth for me is on high, and therefore I am not put to confusion."

The will of the wicked, however, prevailed, and King Pippin ordered the blessed man to be taken away and sent with some of his monks and clerics into exile at the great Abbey of Jumièges, where he was welcomed with kindness and honour by the abbot who governed that monastery. For two years he lived in exile there, beloved by all. When the monks at the Abbey of Fulda heard this and it was told them that their abbot had been taken away from them they were greatly troubled and grieved more than one can say. Then there arose a great disturbance in the house of God: some wished to leave the monastery, others to go to court, others implored God with fasting and prayer to show His mercy and come to their aid. At that time it was widely believed and rumoured that the blessed abbot Sturm had been removed from the Abbey of Fulda at the instance of Bishop Lull: all men without exception took this very ill and there was no Church in the eastern region which did not bewail his exile.

In the meantime Lull, by giving bribes, obtained from King Pippin permission to place the Abbey of Fulda under his jurisdiction, and when this power was granted he installed there as abbot a certain priest of his named Marcus who would obey him in everything; but since the feelings of the brethren were turned against him because of the love they bore to his predecessor, he remained a stranger to them, and their manners did not agree. And because of this disagreement in outlook, though they dwelt together in body, they were separated in mind. Living in this state of disharmony, the brethren were always thinking how, through the grace of God, they could recall their abbot Sturm, and at length, being unable to endure the friction any longer, they hit on the plan of expelling Marcus, whom they had unwillingly accepted as their abbot after Lull had appointed him. Therefore they unanimously agreed to consider him no longer as their superior. When he was removed, all the brethren wished to leave the monastery and go to the court of King Pippin to demand the return of their abbot Sturm. When Lull heard of this, he tried to calm them by persuasive words, promising them the power to appoint as abbot any member of the community of their own choosing. As this proposal was acceptable, the brethren elected a monk named Prezzold, a true servant of God, possessed of every good quality, whom blessed Sturm had trained and loved since he was a small boy. They appointed him as their abbot but with the sole purpose in view of discussing together as the days went by how, with the help of the holy martyr St. Boniface and the grace of Almighty God, they could induce King Pippin to restore to them their former master Sturm. Prezzold governed the brethren for no little time, uniting them together in charity and co-operating with them on the method of persuading King Pippin to recall their abbot to them.

At length, when Prezzold had given long consideration to the matter and the brethren were stricken with grief at Sturm's absence, they implored God in unceasing prayer to use His invincible power to bring their master back to them. And when they had done this for a long time and all the churches, monasteries and convents in the eastern parts had joined in continual prayer with them, God, the Comforter of the lowly, heard the prayers of His suppliants. And He put it into the heart of King Pippin to think about blessed Sturm. And he commanded him to be brought with honour from his place of exile to the court. When he had come in haste to the court he waited in the king's chapel for several days, praying to God and waiting on the king's pleasure. It happened one day that as the king was going out to hunt and, as was his custom, came at dawn to pray, the rest of the king's servants were taking their rest after Matins. Sturm was praying in the chapel alone, and, seeing the king about to enter, opened the doors for him and led him to the altar with a lighted candle. When the king had humbly prayed to God at the sacred altars, he rose and, gazing on Sturm, he said with a smile: " God has brought us together at this moment. What the accusation was which your monks made against you in my presence I cannot remember, and why I was enraged against you I cannot recall." Then without hesitation Sturm answered: " Although I am not free from sin, never, O King, have I committed any crime against you." Then the king said: " Whether or not you have ever conceived an evil design against me or have done me any wrong, may God forgive you as I do from my heart. For the future, enjoy my favour and friendship all the days of my life." And taking a thread from his cloak, he let it fall to the ground and said: " Lo, as witness of perfect forgiveness, I cast this thread from my cloak on the ground that all may see that my former enmity against you is annulled." And so, reconciled and firmly united in friendship, the king set out on the expedition he had prepared.

After a short time, when Prezzold and the rest of the brethren learned that their beloved master Sturm had been received back into the king's favour and friendship, they thought of going to the court and asking for their master. They sent deputies to the court humbly asking the king to send their abbot back to them. As everything that God wills is done, they easily obtained their request. The king kindly acceded to their wishes and promised to send Abbot Sturm to them—a result, we are convinced, due to the many prayers of the servants and handmaids of God. After a short time the king summoned Sturm to his presence and commended to him the government of the Abbey of Fulda, which he had held before. He released him from the jurisdiction of Bishop Lull and commanded him to return with all honour to Fulda, there to govern the monastery with the privileges which blessed Pope Zacharias, the Supreme Pontiff, had formerly granted to Boniface. The privilege just mentioned is preserved to this day in the monastery. He also ordered him to consider the king as the abbey's sole protector. On receiving this power from the king, Sturm returned to the monastery, bearing with him the privilege which he accepted from the hands of the king.

The news spread at once throughout all the provinces that Sturm would shortly return, and wherever the monks and nuns heard of it they gave thanks to Christ. When the brethren were told of his approach to the monastery they took up a golden cross and the relics of the saints and went out in procession to meet him at some distance from the abbey. Then they greeted him and those who had accompanied him, and brought him to the monastery, rejoicing and singing hymns. And they praised God who had restored to them the abbot they had long desired. So there was great joy on all sides.

Sturm himself, having given much thought to the question of how to make a new start, began by correcting the faults of the brethren and restoring discipline. He put the administration of the abbey on a better footing, embellished the church which they had at that time, and repaired the monastic buildings by adding new columns, great wooden beams and new roofs. Shortly afterwards he began to wonder how he could carry out the prescription of the Holy Rule which says that divers crafts should be exercised within the monastery in order to obviate the necessity of the brethren's wandering abroad. So he collected together as many workmen as he could. Then with his usual ingenuity, having surveyed the course of the river Fulda, he drew off a stream from it at some distance from the monastery and made it flow through large canals underneath the abbey workshops, so that the stream of waters made glad the city of God. What great profit this enterprise conferred on the brethren and how great are the advantages it brings to us even at the present time is obvious both to those who see it and those who use it.

Over the tomb of the blessed martyr Boniface he built a ciborium wrought of silver and gold, which we call a *requiem*, and which, as the custom then was, was a work of remarkable craftsmanship. It can be seen to this day, together with the altar of gold, over the tomb of the martyr of Christ.

Because this upright and perfect man of God was held in high esteem by all, and particularly by King Pippin, he asked the king, as a token of the intimate friendship that existed between them, to assign him the revenues and the royal possessions in Onamstat as an alms for the monastery. He also begged him to confirm the gift by charter according to the usual custom. On the death of Pippin in the year of the Incarnation seven hundred and sixty-eight, in the twenty-third year of his reign, Charles, his son, succeeded to the kingdom. Since the young king wished to gain the favour of all those who had been honoured by his father, he bestowed large presents upon them. With the same end in view he summoned Sturm, renewed ties of friendship with him and loaded him with honours and princely gifts. At a certain time he was inspired by God to consider his eternal welfare, and, calling Sturm to his side, he decided to transfer to the Abbey of Fulda the vill of Hammelburg with all the revenues that pertained to it. This gift was gratefully accepted by the brethren, who even now pray to the Lord for his salvation. Thenceforward St. Sturm enjoyed the favour of King Charles as long as he lived. It was at this time that Sturm went on an embassy from King Charles to Thasilo, the head of the province of Norica, and established friendly relations between them for several years.

After King Charles had reigned prosperously for four years he began to consider how he might gain the Saxon people to Christ, for they still remained savage and hostile to all their neighbours and were deeply attached to their pagan rites. He took counsel with the servants of God and asked them to pray that the Lord would grant his desire. Then he gathered together a mighty army, placed it under the patronage of Christ, and, accompanied by bishops, abbots and priests and all true believers, set out for Saxony. His purpose was to bring this people, which had been fettered from the beginning with the devil's bonds, to accept the faith and to submit to the mild and sweet yoke of Christ. When the king reached Saxony he converted the majority of the people partly by conquest, partly by persuasion, partly even by bribes, and not long afterwards he divided the whole of the province into episcopal sees and handed it over to the servants of God to evangelize and baptize. The greater part of that territory with its people was entrusted to Sturm. He accordingly undertook the labour of preaching, employed every means in his power and so gained a great harvest for the Lord. He seized every opportunity to impress on them in his preaching that they should forsake idols and images, accept the Christian faith, destroy the temples of the gods, cut down the groves and build sacred churches in their stead. After he and his priests had spent much time in instructing them and had built churches in each of the districts, the Saxons, who are a depraved and perverse race, lapsed from the Christian faith and reverted once more to their former errors. Then, when they had mustered an army, they streamed across the borders and came as far as the Rhine, laying everything waste and slaughtering all the inhabitants. On their return march they put to the sword everyone they met with savage ferocity. Then they encamped near Lahngau at a short distance from the monastery and planned to send a picked band of warriors from the army to attack the abbey, to burn it to the ground with all its contents and to slaughter all the servants of God. When this news came to the ears of Sturm he summoned the brethren, acquainted them with their imminent danger and advised them to take the body of the holy martyr [St. Boniface] and hasten to Hammelburg. Sturm himself set off for Wedereib to see if he could possibly prevent the soldiers from putting their plan into effect. We, his disciples, took the body of the martyr from its tomb in which it had lain for twenty-four years and began to leave the monastery with all the servants of God. On the first night we rested at the next cell, where the waters of the Fulda and the Fleden meet. Then early next day we reached Sinner on the far side and there we pitched a tent in which we placed the sacred body of the martyr of Christ, whilst the monks encamped around it. After spending three days in tents, messengers came to us on the fourth day telling us that some of our people in the district had banded themselves together and attacked the Saxons, and that the Saxons had been beaten and put to flight. At this news, we took up the bones of the blessed martyr and returned with joy to the monastery, where we interred them once more in the place they had formerly occupied. Then we gave thanks to the Lord Christ for restoring the peace and allowing us to dwell once more in our monastery.

Then King Charles set out a second time for that country to establish by force of arms the Christian faith which had taken root there. He ordered Sturm, now weak and weary with age, to remain with his companions at Heresburg and to keep guard over the city. When everything had been arranged according to his desire, the king, on his return, commanded the holy man to remain for some days in the city already mentioned. After this number of days had elapsed, the man of God returned to the monastery accompanied by the royal physician, named Wintanus, who was to attend him in his illness. One day he gave him some kind of potion as a remedy for his sickness, but instead of diminishing it rather increased it, so that the painful disease grew stronger and more virulent. Sturm began to say with some anxiety that the physician whose duty it was to cure him had inflicted great harm upon him. He therefore gave orders to his attendants to bear him quickly to the church, to summon all the brethren and to tell them that his death was imminent; then he asked them to pray earnestly for him. When the community had gathered together, he had them brought into the chamber where he was lying and addressed the assembled brethren with these words: " My brethren, you are well aware of my last wishes. You know how I have laboured, even till the present day, for your profit and peace, particularly for the continuance of this monastery after my death, so that you may be able to serve God here with sincerity and charity according to the will of Christ. Persevere, then, all the days of your life in the ideal you have set before you. Pray to God for me; and if I have committed any fault among you through human frailty or wronged anyone unjustly, forgive me as I also forgive all those who have offended or wronged me, including Lull, who always took sides against me."

After these and some other good words, he bade farewell to the brethren and sent them away. After the brethren had departed, the holy man began rapidly to lose strength and to hasten above. All were filled with grief; great sorrow afflicted the hearts of the brethren, who implored God with tears to have mercy on him, and they commended the death of their holy and revered abbot to the Lord. The next day, which was the seventeenth of December, his weakness increased and his end rapidly approached. Whilst we stood around his bed and saw how quickly his end would be, one of us said: " Father, we have no doubt that you are going to God and that you will enjoy eternal life. Therefore, we beg Your Paternity to be mindful of us there and to pray for us, your disciples; for our confidence is great that it will be to our profit to have sent on before us so powerful a patron." And he, gazing upon us, said at once: " Show yourselves worthy and so conduct yourselves that I shall be justified in praying for you. Then I will do what you ask." After these words his holy soul was released from the flesh and freed from the prison of the body. Full of good merits, it passed to Christ, whose kingdom endures for ever and ever, Amen.

THE LIFE OF ST. LEOBA
BY RUDOLF, MONK OF FULDA

The author of the following Life was Rudolf, a monk of Fulda and a pupil of Rhabanus Maurus, probably the most learned man of his age. We do not know the exact year of his birth, but by 821 he was a sub-deacon. After his ordination to the priesthood he was placed in charge of the school at Fulda in succession to Rhabanus and carried on the traditions for which the school had become so famous. One of his pupils, Ermenric, Abbot of Elwangen, tells us, in the preface to a work which he dedicated to Rudolf, that his scholarship was of a high order and that he was no less talented than Rhabanus. Louis, King of Germany, impressed by his attainments, took him from Fulda to become his chaplain, preacher and confessor, and in recognition of his services gave him certain revenues which Rudolf left after his death for the benefit of his school.

The life of Leoba, Abbess of Bischofsheim in the diocese of Mainz, was composed by him on the orders of Rhabanus Maurus, and was probably finished by the year 836. He tells us that Mago, one of the priests from whom he had obtained some of his details, had been dead five years; and as Mago is recorded as having died in 831, this enables us to fix the date of the composition fairly accurately. It was certainly written before 837, for in that year was made the translation of the relics of Leoba, a fact which Rudolf passes over in silence. As Leoba died in 779, Rudolf could not write from first-hand knowledge, and therefore he gives us the sources of his information, the memoirs of four nuns of Bischofsheim and the written notes of Mago, the monk of Fulda.

In his life of Rhabanus Maurus, who died in 856, Rudolf recalls this biography of Leoba.

THE LIFE OF SAINT LEOBA
BY RUDOLF, MONK OF FULDA

THE SMALL book which I have written about the life and virtues of the holy and revered virgin Leoba has been dedicated to you, O Hadamout, virgin of Christ, in order that you may have something to read with pleasure and imitate with profit. Thus by the help of Christ's grace you may eventually enjoy the blissful reward of him whose spouse you now are. Most earnestly do I beg you and all the nuns who unceasingly invoke the name of the Lord to pray for me, so that I, Rudolf, a monk of Fulda and a wretched sinner, in spite of my unworthiness to share the fellowship of the elect of God, may through the merits of those who are pleasing to Him receive pardon of my sins and escape the penalties due to them.

PROLOGUE

Before I begin to write the life of the blessed and venerable virgin Leoba, I invoke her spouse, Christ, our Lord and Saviour, who gave her the courage to overcome the powers of evil, to inspire me with eloquence sufficient to describe her outstanding merits. I have been unable to discover all the facts of her life. I shall therefore recount the few that I have learned from the writings of others, venerable men who heard them from four of her disciples, Agatha, Thecla, Nana and Eoloba. Each one copied them down according to his ability and left them as a memorial to posterity.

One of these, a holy priest and monk named Mago, who died about five years ago, was on friendly terms with these women and during his frequent visits to them used to speak with them about things profitable to the soul. In this way he was able to learn a great deal about her life. He was careful to make short notes of everything he heard, but, unfortunately, what he left was almost unintelligible, because, whilst he was trying to be brief and succinct, he expressed things in such a way as to leave the facts open to misunderstanding and provide no basis for certainty. This happened, in my opinion, because in his eagerness to take down every detail before it escaped his memory he wrote the facts down in a kind of shorthand and hoped that during his leisure he could put them in order and make the book more easy for readers to understand. The reason why he left everything in such disorder, jotted down on odd pieces of parchment, was that he died quite suddenly and had no time to carry out his purpose.

Therefore it is not from presumption but in obedience to the command of my venerable father and master, Abbot Rhabanus, that I have tried to collect together all the scattered notes and papers left by the men I have mentioned. The sequence of events, which I have attempted to reconstruct for those who are interested in knowing them, is based on the information found in their notes and on the evidence I have gathered from others by word of mouth. For there are several religious men still living who can vouch for the facts mentioned in the documents, since they heard them from their predecessors, and who can add some others worthy of remembrance. These latter appeared to me suitable for inclusion in the book and therefore I have combined them with material from the written notes. You will see, then, that I have not only reorganized and completed the work set on foot by others but have written something on my own account. For it seems to me that there should be no doubt in the minds of the faithful about the veracity of the statements made in this book, since they are shown to be true both by the blameless character of those who relate them and by the miracles which are frequently performed at the shrine of the saint.

But before I begin the narration of her remarkable life and virtues, it may not be out of place if I mention a few of the many things I have heard about her spiritual mistress and mother, who first introduced her to the spiritual life and fostered in her a desire for heaven. In this way the reader who is made aware of the qualities of this great woman may give credence to the achievements of the disciple more easily the more clearly he sees that she learned the elements of the spiritual life from so noble a mistress.

In the island of Britain, which is inhabited by the English nation, there is a place called Wimbourne, an ancient name which may be translated " Winestream ". It received this name from the clearness and sweetness of the water there, which was better than any other in that land. In olden times the kings of that nation had built two monasteries in the place, one for men, the other for women, both surrounded by strong and lofty walls and provided with all the necessities that prudence could devise. From the beginning of the foundation the rule firmly laid down for both was that no entrance should be allowed to a person of the other sex. No woman was permitted to go into the men's community, nor was any man allowed into the women's, except in the case of priests who had to celebrate Mass in their churches; even so, immediately after the function was ended the priest had to withdraw. Any woman who wished to renounce the world and enter the cloister did so on the understanding that she would never leave it. She could only come out if there was a reasonable cause and some great advantage accrued to the monastery. Furthermore, when it was necessary to conduct the business of the monastery and to send for something outside, the superior of the community spoke through a window and only from there did she make decisions and arrange what was needed.

It was over this monastery, in succession to several other abbesses and spiritual mistresses, that a holy virgin named Tetta was placed in authority, a woman of noble family (for she was a sister of the king), but more noble in her conduct and good qualities. Over both the monasteries she ruled with consummate prudence and discretion. She gave instruction by deed rather than by words, and whenever she said that a certain course of action was harmful to the salvation of souls she showed by her own conduct that it was to be shunned. She maintained discipline with such circumspection (and the discipline there was much stricter than anywhere else) that she would never allow her nuns to approach clerics. She was so anxious that the nuns, in whose company she always remained, should be cut off from the company of men that she denied entrance into the community not merely to laymen and clerics but even to bishops. There are many instances of the virtues of this woman which the virgin Leoba, her disciple, used to recall with pleasure when she told her reminiscences. Of these I will mention but two examples, so that from these the rest may be conjectured.

In that convent there was a certain nun who, because of her zeal for discipline and strict observance, in which she surpassed the others, was often appointed prioress and frequently made one of the mistresses. But as she was too incautious and indiscreet in enforcing discipline over those under her care, she aroused their resentment, particularly among the younger members of the community. Though she could easily have mollified them and met their criticisms, she hardened her heart against taking such a course of action and went so far in her inflexibility that even at the end of her life she would not trouble to soften their hearts by asking their pardon. So in this stubborn frame of mind she died and was buried; and when the earth had been heaped over her, as the custom is, a tomb was raised over her grave. But this did not appease the feelings of the young nuns who hated her, and as soon as they saw the place where she was buried they reviled her cruelty and even climbed on to her tomb, as if to stamp upon her corpse, uttering bitter curses over her dead body to assuage their outraged feelings. Now when this came to the ears of the venerable abbess of the community she reprehended the young nuns for their presumption and vigorously corrected them. She went to the grave and noticed that in some extraordinary way the earth which had been heaped over the corpse had subsided and lay about six inches below the surface of the surrounding ground. This sight struck her with great fear. She understood from the subsidence of the ground how the dead woman had been punished, and judged the severity of God's sentence upon her from the sinking of the grave. She therefore called all the sisters together and began to reproach them for their cruelty and hardness of heart. She upbraided them for failing to forgive the wrongs they had suffered and for harbouring ill feelings on account of the momentary bitterness caused by harsh discipline. She told them that one of the fundamental principles of Christian perfection is to be peaceable with those who dislike peace, whereas they, far from loving their enemies as God had commanded, not only hated their sister whilst she was alive but even pursued her with their curses now that she was dead. She counselled them to lay aside their resentment, to accept the ill-treatment they had received and to show without delay their forgiveness: if they wished their own sins to be forgiven by God they should forgive others from the bottom of their hearts. She begged them to forget any wrongs inflicted by the dead woman before her death and to join with her in prayer that God, in His mercy, would absolve her from her sins. When they had all agreed to follow her advice, she ordered them to fast for three days and to give themselves earnestly to watching, prayer and the recitation of psalms for the repose of her soul.

At the end of the fast on the third day she went with all the nuns into the church, singing litanies and invoking the Lord and His saints; and after she had prostrated herself before the altar she prayed for the soul of the deceased sister. And as she persevered in prayer, the hole in the grave, which previously had appeared to be empty, suddenly began to fill in and the ground rose, so that the moment she got up from her knees the grave became level with the surface of the ground. By this it was made clear that when the grave returned to its normal state the soul of the deceased sister, through the prayers of Tetta, had been absolved by divine power.

On another occasion it happened that when the sister who looked after the chapel went to close the door of the church before going to bed after Compline she lost all the keys in the darkness. There were very many of them belonging to various things locked away in the treasury of the church, some of silver, others of bronze or iron, all fastened together with a metal clasp. When she rose at the sound of the bell for Matins and could not find the keys for opening the doors of the church, she lit a candle and carefully searched all the places in which there was any hope of finding them; and as if one search was not enough, she went over the same ground again and again looking for them. When she had done this several times without success, she went to the abbess, who as usual had anticipated the hour for the night office and was deep in prayer, whilst the others were still at rest. Trembling with fear, the nun threw herself at the feet of the abbess and humbly confessed the negligence of which she was guilty. As soon as the abbess heard it she felt convinced that it was the work of the devil, and, calling the sisters together, she recited Matins and Lauds in another building. When this was ended, they all gave themselves to prayer. At once the wickedness of the old enemy was brought to light, for, whilst they were still at prayer, a little dead fox was suddenly seen at the doors of the chapel holding the keys in his mouth, so that what had been given up as lost was found. Then the venerable mother took the keys and ordered the doors to be opened; and going into the church accompanied by the nuns, who at that time were about fifty in number, she gave thanks to God in hymns and praise for mercifully hearing His servants who had trusted in Him and for putting the wicked spirit to confusion. For he who had said " I will set my throne higher than God's stars " was transformed for his pride into a beast, and he who would not humbly submit to God was unmasked as a fox through the prayers of the nuns and made to look foolish.

Let these instances of the virtues of the venerable mother Tetta suffice. We will now pursue our purpose of describing the life of her spiritual daughter, Leoba the virgin.

*

As we have already said, her parents were English, of noble family and full of zeal for religion and the observance of God's commandments. Her father was called Dynno, her mother Aebba. But as they were barren, they remained together for a long time without children. After many years had passed and the onset of old age had deprived them of all hope of offspring, her mother had a dream in which she saw herself bearing in her bosom a church bell, which on being drawn out with her hand rang merrily. When she woke up she called her old nurse to her and told her what she had dreamt. The nurse said to her: " We shall yet see a daughter from your womb and it is your duty to consecrate her straightway to God. And as Anna offered Samuel to serve God all the days of his life in the temple, so you must offer her, when she has been taught the Scripture from her infancy, to serve Him in holy virginity as long as she shall live." Shortly after the woman had made this vow she conceived and bore a daughter, whom she called Thrutgeba, surnamed Leoba because she was beloved, for this is what Leoba means. And when the child had grown up her mother consecrated her and handed her over to Mother Tetta to be taught the sacred sciences. And because the nurse had foretold that she should have such happiness, she gave her her freedom.

The girl, therefore, grew up and was taught with such care by the abbess and all the nuns that she had no interests other than the monastery and the pursuit of sacred knowledge. She took no pleasure in aimless jests and wasted no time on girlish romances, but, fired by the love of Christ, fixed her mind always on reading or hearing the Word of God. Whatever she heard or read she committed to memory, and put all that she learned into practice. She exercised such moderation in her use of food and drink that she eschewed dainty dishes and the allurements of sumptuous fare, and was satisfied with whatever was placed before her. She prayed continually, knowing that in the Epistles the faithful are counselled to pray without ceasing. When she was not praying she worked with her hands at whatever was commanded her, for she had learned that he who will not work should not eat. However, she spent more time in reading and listening to Sacred Scripture than she gave to manual labour. She took great care not to forget what she had heard or read, observing the commandments of the Lord and putting into practice what she remembered of them. In this way she so arranged her conduct that she was loved by all the sisters. She learned from all and obeyed them all, and by imitating the good qualities of each one she modelled herself on the continence of one, the cheerfulness of another, copying here a sister's mildness, there a sister's patience. One she tried to equal in attention to prayer, another in devotion to reading. Above all, she was intent on practising charity, without which, as she knew, all other virtues are void.

When she had succeeded in fixing her attention on heavenly things by these and other practices in the pursuit of virtue she had a dream in which one night she saw a purple thread issuing from her mouth. It seemed to her that when she took hold of it with her hand and tried to draw it out there was no end to it; and as if it were coming from her very bowels, it extended little by little until it was of enormous length. When her hand was full of thread and it still issued from her mouth she rolled it round and round and made a ball of it. The labour of doing this was so tiresome that eventually, through sheer fatigue, she woke from her sleep and began to wonder what the meaning of the dream might be. She understood quite clearly that there was some reason for the dream, and it seemed that there was some mystery hidden in it. Now there was in the same monastery an aged nun who was known to possess the spirit of prophecy, because other things that she had foretold had always been fulfilled. As Leoba was diffident about revealing the dream to her, she told it to one of her disciples just as it had occurred and asked her to go to the old nun and describe it to her as a personal experience and learn from her the meaning of it. When the sister had repeated the details of the dream as if it had happened to her, the nun, who could foresee the future, angrily replied: " This is indeed a true vision and presages that good will come. But why do you lie to me in saying that such things happened to you? These matters are no concern of yours: they apply to the beloved chosen by God." In giving this name, she referred to the virgin Leoba. " These things," she went on, " were revealed to the person whose holiness and wisdom make her a worthy recipient, because by her teaching and good example she will confer benefits on many people. The thread which came from her bowels and issued from her mouth, signifies the wise counsels that she will speak from the heart. The fact that it filled her hand means that she will carry out in her actions whatever she expresses in her words. Furthermore, the ball which she made by rolling it round and round signifies the mystery of the divine teaching, which is set in motion by the words and deeds of those who give instruction and which turns earthwards through active works and heavenwards through contemplation, at one time swinging downwards through compassion for one's neighbour, again swinging upwards through the love of God. By these signs God shows that your mistress will profit many by her words and example, and the effect of them will be felt in other lands afar off whither she will go." That this interpretation of the dream was true later events were to prove.

At the time when the blessed virgin Leoba was pursuing her quest for perfection in the monastery the holy martyr Boniface was being ordained by Gregory, Bishop of Rome and successor to Constantine, in the Apostolic See. His mission was to preach the Word of God to the people in Germany. When Boniface found that the people were ready to receive the faith and that, though the harvest was great, the labourers who worked with him were few, he sent messengers and letters to England, his native land, summoning from different ranks of the clergy many who were learned in the divine law and fitted both by their character and good works to preach the Word of God. With their assistance he zealously carried out the mission with which he was charged, and by sound doctrine and miracles converted a large part of Germany to the faith. As the days went by, multitudes of people were instructed in the mysteries of the faith and the Gospel was preached not only in the churches but also in the towns and villages. Thus the Catholics were strengthened in their belief by constant exhortation, the wicked submitted to corrrection, and the heathen, enlightened by the Gospel, flocked to receive the grace of Baptism. When the blessed man saw that the Church of God was increasing and that the desire of perfection was firmly rooted he established two means by which religious progress should be ensured. He began to build monasteries, so that the people would be attracted to the church not only by the beauty of its religion but also by the communities of monks and nuns. And as he wished the observance in both cases to be kept according to the Holy Rule, he endeavoured to obtain suitable superiors for both houses. For this purpose he sent his disciple Sturm, a man of noble family and sterling character, to Monte Cassino, so that he could study the regular discipline, the observance and the monastic customs which had been established there by St.

Benedict. As the future superior, he wished him to become a novice and in this way learn in humble submission how to rule over others. Likewise, he sent messengers with letters to the abbess Tetta, of whom we have already spoken, asking her to send Leoba to accompany him on this journey and to take part in this embassy: for Leoba's reputation for learning and holiness had spread far and wide and her praise was on everyone's lips. The abbess Tetta was exceedingly displeased at her departure, but because she could not gainsay the dispositions of divine providence she agreed to his request and sent Leoba to the blessed man. Thus it was that the interpretation of the dream which she had previously received was fulfilled. When she came, the man of God received her with the deepest reverence, holding her in great affection, not so much because she was related to him on his mother's side as because he knew that by her holiness and wisdom she would confer many benefits by her word and example.

In furtherance of his aims he appointed persons in authority over the monasteries and established the observance of the Rule: he placed Sturm as abbot over the monks and Leoba as abbess over the nuns. He gave her the monastery at a place called Bischofsheim, where there was a large community of nuns. These were trained according to her principles in the discipline of monastic life and made such progress in her teaching that many of them afterwards became superiors of others, so that there was hardly a convent of nuns in that part which had not one of her disciples as abbess. She was a woman of great virtue and was so strongly attached to the way of life she had vowed that she never gave thought to her native country or her relatives. She expended all her energies on the work she had undertaken in order to appear blameless before God and to become a pattern of perfection to those who obeyed her in word and action. She was ever on her guard not to teach others what she did not carry out herself. In her conduct there was no arrogance or pride; she was no distinguisher of persons, but showed herself affable and kindly to all. In appearance she was angelic, in word pleasant, clear in mind, great in prudence, Catholic in faith, most patient in hope, universal in her charity. But though she was always cheerful, she never broke out into laughter through excessive hilarity. No one ever heard a bad word from her lips; the sun never went down upon her anger. In the matter of food and drink she always showed the utmost understanding for others but was most sparing in her own use of them. She had a small cup from which she used to drink and which, because of the meagre quantity it would hold, was called by the sisters " the Beloved's little one ". So great was her zeal for reading that she discontinued it only for prayer or for the refreshment of her body with food or sleep: the Scriptures were never out of her hands. For, since she had been trained from infancy in the rudiments of grammar and the study of the other liberal arts, she tried by constant reflection to attain a perfect knowledge of divine things so that through the combination of her reading with her quick intelligence, by natural gifts and hard work, she became extremely learned. She read with attention all the books of the Old and New Testaments and learned by heart all the commandments of God. To these she added by way of completion the writings of the church Fathers, the decrees of the Councils and the whole of ecclesiastical law. She observed great moderation in all her acts and arrangements and always kept the practical end in view, so that she would never have to repent of her actions through having been guided by impulse. She was deeply aware of the necessity for concentration of mind in prayer and study, and for this reason took care not to go to excess either in watching or in other spiritual exercises. Throughout the summer both she and all the sisters under her rule went to rest after the midday meal, and she would never give permission to any of them to stay up late, for she said that lack of sleep dulled the mind, especially for study. When she lay down to rest, whether at night or in the afternoon, she used to have the Sacred Scriptures read out at her bedside, a duty which the younger nuns carried out in turn without grumbling. It seems difficult to believe, but even when she seemed to be asleep they could not skip over any word or syllable whilst they were reading without her immediately correcting them. Those on whom this duty fell used afterwards to confess that often when they saw her becoming drowsy they made a mistake on purpose to see if she noticed it, but they were never able to escape undetected. Yet it is not surprising that she could not be deceived even in her sleep, since He who keeps watch over Israel and neither slumbers nor sleeps possessed her heart, and she was able to say with the spouse in the Song of Songs: " I sleep, but my heart watcheth."

She preserved the virtue of humility with such care that, though she had been appointed to govern others because of her holiness and wisdom, she believed in her heart that she was the least of all. This she showed both in her speech and behaviour. She was extremely hospitable. She kept open house for all without exception, and even when she was fasting gave banquets and washed the feet of the guests with her own hands, at once the guardian and the minister of the practice instituted by our Lord.

Whilst the virgin of Christ was acting in this way and attracting to herself everyone's affection, the devil, who is the foe of all Christians, viewed with impatience her own great virtue and the progress made by her disciples. He therefore attacked them constantly with evil thoughts and temptations of the flesh, trying to turn some of them aside from the path they had chosen. But when he saw that all his efforts were brought to nought by their prayers, fasting and chaste lives, the wily tempter turned his attention to other means, hoping at least to destroy their good reputation, even if he could not break down their integrity by his foul suggestions.

There was a certain poor little crippled girl, who sat near the gate of the monastery begging alms. Every day she received her food from the abbess's table, her clothing from the nuns and all other necessities from them; these were given to her from divine charity. It happened that after some time, deceived by the suggestions of the devil, she committed fornication, and when her appearance made it impossible for her to conceal that she had conceived a child she covered up her guilt by pretending to be ill. When her time came, she wrapped the child in swaddling clothes and cast it at night into a pool by the river which flowed through that place. In this way she added crime to crime, for she not only followed fleshly sin by murder, but also combined murder with the poisoning of the water. When day dawned, another woman came to draw water and, seeing the corpse of the child, was struck with horror. Burning with womanly rage, she filled the whole village with her uncontrollable cries and reproached the holy nuns with these indignant words: " Oh, what a chaste community! How admirable is the life of nuns, who beneath their veils give birth to children and exercise at one and the same time the function of mothers and priests, baptising those to whom they have given birth. For, fellow-citizens, you have drawn off this water to make a pool, not merely for the purpose of grinding corn, but unwittingly for a new and unheard-of kind of Baptism. Now go and ask those women, whom you compliment by calling them virgins, to remove this corpse from the river and make it fit for us to use again. Look for the one who is missing from the monastery and then you will find out who is responsible for this crime." At these words all the crowd was set in uproar and everybody, of whatever age or sex, ran in one great mass to see what had happened. As soon as they saw the corpse they denounced the crime and reviled the nuns. When the abbess heard the uproar and learned what was afoot she called the nuns together, told them the reason, and discovered that no one was absent except Agatha, who a few days before had been summoned to her parents' house on urgent business: but she had gone with full permission. A messenger was sent to her without delay to recall her to the monastery, as Leoba could not endure the accusation of so great a crime to hang over them. When Agatha returned and heard of the deed that was charged against her she fell on her knees and gazed up to heaven, crying: " Almighty God, who knowest all things before they come to pass, from whom nothing is hid and who hast delivered Susanna from false accusations when she trusted in Thee, show Thy mercy to this community gathered together in Thy name and let it not be besmirched by filthy rumours on account of my sins; but do Thou deign to unmask and make known for the praise and glory of Thy name the person who has committed this misdeed."

On hearing this, the venerable superior, being assured of her innocence, ordered them all to go to the chapel and to stand with their arms extended in the form of a cross until each one of them had sung through the whole psalter, then three times each day, at Tierce, Sext and None, to go round the monastic buildings in procession with the crucifix at their head, calling upon God to free them, in His mercy, from this accusation. When they had done this and they were going into the church at None, having completed two rounds, the blessed Leoba went straight to the altar and, standing before the cross, which was being prepared for the third procession, stretched out her hands towards heaven, and with tears and groans prayed, saying: " O Lord Jesus Christ, King of virgins, Lover of chastity, unconquerable God, manifest Thy power and deliver us from this charge, because the reproaches of those who reproached Thee have fallen upon us." Immediately after she had said this, that wretched little woman, the dupe and the tool of the devil, seemed to be surrounded by flames, and, calling out the name of the abbess, confessed to the crime she had committed. Then a great shout rose to heaven: the vast crowd was astounded at the miracle, the nuns began to weep with joy, and all of them with one voice gave expression to the merits of Leoba and of Christ our Saviour.

So it came about that the reputation of the nuns, which the devil had tried to ruin by his sinister rumour, was greatly enhanced, and praise was showered on them in every place. But the wretched woman did not deserve to escape scot-free and for the rest of her life she remained in the power of the devil. Even before this God had performed many miracles through Leoba, but they had been kept secret. This one was her first in Germany and, because it was done in public, it came to the ears of everyone.

On another occasion, when she sat down as usual to give spiritual instruction to her disciples, a fire broke out in a part of the village. As the houses have roofs of wood and thatch, they were soon consumed by the flames, and the conflagration spread with increasing rapidity towards the monastery, so that it threatened to destroy not only the buildings but also the men and beasts. Then could be heard the mingled shouts of the terrified villagers as they ran in a mob to the abbess and begged her to avert the danger which threatened them. Unruffled and with great self-control, she calmed their fears and, without being influenced by

their trust in her, ordered them to take a bucket and bring some
water from the upper part of the stream that flowed by the
monastery. As soon as they had brought it, she took some salt
which had been blessed by St. Boniface and which she always
kept by her, and sprinkled it in the water. Then she said: " Go
and pour back this water into the river and then let all the people
draw water lower down the stream and throw it on the fire."
After they had done this the violence of the conflagration died
down and the fire was extinguished just as if a flood had fallen
from the skies. So the buildings were saved. At this miracle the
whole crowd stood amazed and broke out into the praise of God,
who through the faith and prayers of his handmaid had delivered
them so extraordinarily from a terrible danger.

I think it should be counted amongst her virtues also that one
day, when a wild storm arose and the whole sky was obscured by
such dark clouds that day seemed turned into night, terrible
lightning and falling thunderbolts struck terror into the stoutest
hearts and everyone was shaking with fear. At first the people
drove their flocks into the houses for shelter so that they should not
perish; then, when the danger increased and threatened them all
with death, they took refuge with their wives and children in the
church, despairing of their lives. They locked all the doors and
waited there trembling, thinking that the last judgment was at
hand. In this state of panic they filled the air with the din of their
mingled cries. Then the holy virgin went out to them and urged
them all to have patience. She promised them that no harm would
come to them; and after exhorting them to join with her in prayer,
she fell prostrate at the foot of the altar. In the meantime the
storm raged, the roofs of the houses were torn off by the violence
of the wind, the ground shook with the repeated shocks of the
thunderbolts, and the thick darkness, intensified by the incessant
flicker of lightning which flashed through the windows, redoubled
their terror. Then the mob, unable to endure the suspense any
longer, rushed to the altar to rouse her from prayer and seek her
protection. Thecla, her kinswoman, spoke to her first, saying:
" Beloved, all the hopes of these people lie in you: you are their
only support. Arise, then, and pray to the Mother of God, your

mistress, for us, that by her intercession we may be delivered from this fearful storm." At these words Leoba rose up from prayer and, as if she had been challenged to a contest, flung off the cloak which she was wearing and boldly opened the doors of the church. Standing on the threshold, she made a sign of the cross, opposing to the fury of the storm the name of the High God. Then she stretched out her hands towards heaven and three times invoked the mercy of Christ, praying that through the intercession of Holy Mary, the Virgin, He would quickly come to the help of His people. Suddenly God came to their aid. The sound of thunder died away, the winds changed direction and dispersed the heavy clouds, the darkness rolled back and the sun shone, bringing calm and peace. Thus did divine power make manifest the merits of His handmaid. Unexpected peace came to His people and fear was banished.

There was also another of her deeds which everyone agrees was outstanding and memorable, and which I think it would be wrong to pass over in silence. One of the sisters of the monastery named Williswind, of excellent character and edifying conduct, was attacked by a grave illness; she suffered from what the doctors call haemorrhoids, and through loss of blood from her privy parts was racked by severe pains of the bowel. As the ailment continued and increased from day to day in severity, her strength ebbed away until she could neither turn over on her side nor get out of bed and walk without leaning on someone else. When she was no longer able to remain in the common dormitory of the monastery because of the stench, her parents who lived close by asked and obtained permission for her to be taken on a litter to their house across the river Tuberaha. Not long afterwards, as the sickness gained hold, she rapidly drew near her end. As the lower part of her body had lost all sense of feeling and she was barely able to breathe, the abbess was asked by her parents not to come and visit the sick nun but to pray to God for her happy decease. When Leoba came, she approached the bed, now surrounded by a weeping throng of neighbours, and ordered the covering to be removed, for the patient was already enveloped in a linen cloth, as corpses usually are. When it was taken away she placed her hand on her breast and said: " Cease your weeping, for her soul is still in her." Then she sent to the monastery and ordered them to bring the little spoon which she usually used at table; and when it was brought to her she blessed milk and poured it drop by drop down the throat of the sick nun. At its touch, her throat and vitals recovered; she moved her tongue to speak and began to look round. Next day she had made such progress that she was able to take food, and before the end of the week she walked on her own feet to the monastery, whence she had previously been carried on a litter. She lived for several years afterwards and remained in the service of God until the days of Lewis, King of the Franks, always strong and healthy, even after the death of Leoba.

The people's faith was stimulated by such tokens of holiness, and as religious feeling increased so did contempt of the world. Many nobles and influential men gave their daughters to God to live in the monastery in perpetual chastity; many widows also forsook their homes, made vows of chastity and took the veil in the cloister. To all of these the holy virgin pointed out both by word and example how to reach the heights of perfection.

In the meantime, blessed Boniface, the archbishop, was preparing to go to Frisia, having decided to preach the Gospel to this people riddled with superstition and unbelief. He summoned his disciple Lull to his presence (who was afterwards to succeed him as bishop) and entrusted everything to his care, particularly impressing on him a solicitude for the faithful, zeal for preaching the Gospel and the preservation of the churches, which he had built in various places. Above all, he ordered him to complete the building of the monastery of Fulda which he had begun to construct in the wilderness of Bochonia, a work undertaken on the authority of Pope Zacharias and with the support of Carloman, King of Austrasia. This he did because the monks who lived there were poor and had no revenues and were forced to live on the produce of their own manual labour. He commanded him also to remove his body thither after his death. After giving these and other instructions, he summoned Leoba to him and exhorted her not to abandon the country of her adoption and not to grow weary of the life she had undertaken, but rather to extend the scope of the good work she had begun. He said that no consideration should be paid to her weakness and that she must not count the long years that lay ahead of her; she must not count the spiritual life to be hard nor the end difficult to attain, for the years of this life are short compared to eternity, and the sufferings of this world are as nothing in comparison with the glory that will be made manifest in the saints. He commended her to Lull and to the senior monks of the monastery who were present, admonishing them to care for her with reverence and respect and reaffirming his wish that after his death her bones should be placed next to his in the tomb, so that they who had served God during their lifetime with equal sincerity and zeal should await together the day of resurrection.

After these words he gave her his cowl and begged and pleaded with her not to leave her adopted land. And so, when all necessary preparations had been made for the journey, he set out for Frisia, where he won over a multitude of people to the faith of Christ and ended his labours with a glorious martyrdom. His remains were transported to Fulda and there, according to his previous wishes, he was laid to rest with worthy tokens of respect.

The blessed virgin, however, persevered unwaveringly in the work of God. She had no desire to gain earthly possessions but only those of heaven, and she spent all her energies on fulfilling her vows. Her wonderful reputation spread abroad and the fragrance of her holiness and wisdom drew to her the affections of all. She was held in veneration by all who knew her, even by kings. Pippin, King of the Franks, and his sons Charles and Carloman treated her with profound respect, particularly Charles, who, after the death of his father and brother, with whom he had shared the throne for some years, took over the reins of government. He was a man of truly Christian life, worthy of the power he wielded and by far the bravest and wisest king that the Franks had produced. His love for the Catholic faith was so sincere that, though he governed all, he treated the servants and handmaids of God with touching humility. Many times he summoned the holy virgin to his court, received her with every mark of respect and loaded her with gifts suitable to her station. Queen Hiltigard also revered her with a chaste affection and loved her as her own soul. She would have liked her to remain continually at her side so that she might progress in the spiritual life and profit by her words and example. But Leoba detested the life at court like poison. The princes loved her, the nobles received her, the bishops welcomed her with joy. And because of her wide knowledge of the Scriptures and her prudence in counsel they often discussed spiritual matters and ecclesiastical discipline with her. But her deepest concern was the work she had set on foot. She visited the various convents of nuns and, like a mistress of novices, stimulated them to vie with one another in reaching perfection.

Sometimes she came to the Monastery of Fulda to say her prayers, a privilege never granted to any woman either before or since, because from the day that monks began to dwell there entrance was always forbidden to women. Permission was only granted to her, for the simple reason that the holy martyr St. Boniface had commended her to the seniors of the monastery and because he had ordered her remains to be buried there. The following regulations, however, were observed when she came there. Her disciples and companions were left behind in a nearby cell and she entered the monastery always in daylight, with one nun older than the rest; and after she had finished her prayers and held a conversation with the brethren, she returned towards nightfall to her disciples whom she had left behind in the cell. When she was an old woman and became decrepit through age she put all the convents under her care on a sound footing and then, on Bishop Lull's advice, went to a place called Scoranesheim, four miles south of Mainz. There she took up residence with some of her nuns and served God night and day in fasting and prayer.

In the meantime, whilst King Charles was staying in the palace at Aachen, Queen Hiltigard sent a message to her begging her to come and visit her, if it were not too difficult, because she longed to see her before she passed from this life. And although Leoba was not at all pleased, she agreed to go for the sake of their long-standing friendship. Accordingly she went and was received by the queen with her usual warm welcome. But as soon as Leoba heard the reason for the invitation she asked permission to return home. And when the queen importuned her to stay a few days longer she refused; but, embracing her friend rather more affectionately than usual, she kissed her on the mouth, the forehead and the eyes and took leave of her with these words: " Farewell for evermore, my dearly beloved lady and sister; farewell, most precious half of my soul. May Christ our Creator and Redeemer grant that we shall meet again without shame on the day of judgment. Never more on this earth shall we enjoy each other's presence."

So she returned to the convent, and after a few days she was stricken down by sickness and was confined to her bed. When she saw that her ailment was growing worse and that the hour of her death was near she sent for a saintly English priest named Torhthat, who had always been at her side and ministered to her with respect and love, and received from him the viaticum of the body and blood of Christ. Then she put off this earthly garment and gave back her soul joyfully to her Creator, clean and undefiled as she had received it from Him. She died in the month of September, the fourth of the kalends of October. Her body, followed by a long cortège of noble persons, was carried by the monks of Fulda to their monastery with every mark of respect. Thus the seniors there remembered what St. Boniface had said, namely, that it was his last wish that her remains should be placed next to his bones. But because they were afraid to open the tomb of the blessed martyr, they discussed the matter and decided to bury her on the north side of the altar which the martyr St. Boniface had himself erected and consecrated in honour of our Saviour and the twelve Apostles.

After some years, when the church had grown too small and was being prepared by its rectors for a future consecration, Abbot Eigil, with permission of Archbishop Heistulf, transferred her bones and placed them in the west porch near the shrine of St. Ignatius the martyr, where, encased in a tomb, they rest glorious with miracles. For many who have approached her tomb full of faith have many times received divine favours. Some of these which occur to me at the moment I will set down plainly and truthfully for my readers.

A certain man had his arms so tightly bound by iron rings that the iron was almost covered by the bare flesh that grew up around it on either side. One of these had already come off one arm and had left a deep scar that was plain to see. This man came to the church and went round the shrines of the saints, praying at each altar. When he reached the tomb of the holy virgin Leoba and began to pray some hidden force expanded the iron ring and, breaking the clamps, cast it from his arm, leaving it all bloody. With joy and gladness he gave thanks to God, because by the merits of the blessed nun he, who until that moment had been bound in fetters on account of his sins, was released.

There was another man from Spain, who for his sins was so afflicted that he twitched most horribly in all his limbs. According to his own account he contracted this infirmity through bathing in the river Ebro. And because he could not bear his deformity to be seen by his fellow-citizens he wandered about from shrine to shrine, wherever he had a mind to go. After travelling the length of France and Italy, he came to Germany. When he had visited several monasteries to pray there, he came to Fulda, where he was received into the pilgrim's hospice. He stayed three days there, going into the church and praying that God would be appeased and restore him to his former state of health. When he entered the chapel on the third day and had gone from altar to altar praying, he automatically came to the shrine of the holy virgin. He ended his prayer there and then went down to the western crypt above which the body of the holy martyr Boniface lies at rest. Prostrate in prayer, he lay like one asleep, but not twitching as he usually did when he slept. A saintly monk and priest named Firmandus, who used to sit there because he had an infirmity which prevented him from standing, noticed this and was struck with astonishment. He ordered those who wished to lift him not to touch him, but rather to wait to see what would happen. Suddenly the man got up and, because he was cured, he did not twitch. On being questioned by the priest, who, as an Italian, understood his language, he said that he had had an ecstasy in which he saw a venerable old man, vested in a bishop's stole, accompanied by a young woman in a nun's habit, who had taken him by the hand, lifted him up and presented him to the bishop for his blessing. When the bishop had made the sign of the cross on his breast an inky-black bird like a raven had flown out of his bosom and through the hood of his tunic; as soon as it alighted on the ground it changed into a hen and then transformed itself into the shape of a very ugly and horrible little man, who emerged from the crypt by the steps of the north entrance. No Christian man can doubt that he was restored to health through the prayers of the holy virgin and the merits of the blessed martyr. These two, though they do not share a tomb, yet lie in one place and never fail to look on those who seek their intercession with the same kindliness now they are in glory as they did when they lived on earth and showed pity and compassion on the wretched.

Many other marvels did God perform through the prayers of the holy virgin, but I will not mention them lest by prolonging my story I inflict tedium on the reader. But I recall these two, because several of the brethren who are still alive have borne witness in words that are not lightly to be disregarded that they saw them. I also was present when they occurred. I write this, then, for the praise and glory of the name of our Lord Jesus Christ, who glorifies those who glorify him and who grants to those who serve Him not only the kingdom of heaven but also in this world nobility and honour. To whom be glory with the Father and the Holy Spirit for ever and ever, Amen.

THE LIFE OF ST. LEBUIN

Though the life of St. Lebuin written by Hucbald of St. Amand is better known and was considered for a long time to be the first, M. J. A. Moltzer showed in 1909 that it was based on an older biography, which is here translated. Hucbald was born about A.D. 840 and became a monk of Elnone on the Scarpe. He went to Auxerre, where he followed the lectures of Heiric, a disciple of John Scotus Eriugena. Later he passed to St. Bertin, where he was placed in charge of the schools. The successor of Hincmar of Rheims, Fulques (881–900), invited him to reorganize the schools in the cathedral city, and after doing so he returned to St. Amand, where he died, 20 June, probably in the year 931. Among a number of other lives of Saints, he wrote a biography of St. Lebuin at the request of Baldric, the restorer of the diocese of Utrecht (918–76), but as he merely pads out the facts without making any original contribution it has seemed better to present the original and earlier text to the reader.

THE LIFE OF ST. LEBUIN

THE LAND of England which was converted to the faith of Christ by the intervention of the blessed Pope Gregory has always been most steadfast in its religion. And just as it is prolific in all kinds of animals, so also is it productive of holy men. There one finds laymen devoted to the service of God, virgins of exceptional virtue and monks of outstanding generosity spurning the world for the love of Christ. Very many of these have forsaken their country for the Lord's sake, either to expiate their sins or benefit pagans and Christians by their teaching.

The Lord Himself admonished St. Lebuin to forsake his country and to preach to the Saxons across the sea and told him to instruct the people who dwelt in the lands of the Franks and Saxons near the river Isel. After receiving this command, not once but a second and a third time, he embarked on a ship and came to the priest Gregory, who at that time was in charge of the church at Utrecht, which in olden times was called Wiltenburg. Though Gregory was only a priest, he was fulfilling the duties of a bishop. This man, who was the scion of a noble Frankish family, had been brought up in the service of St. Boniface since he was a boy and first joined him when at God's command he went to preach to the people of Hesse and Thuringia. Boniface had come from England at the time of Charles and became so renowned for his wisdom and holiness in the days of that king's two sons, Carloman and Pippin, that he was able to effect reforms both in religion and belief throughout the whole Frankish kingdoms. Though he set out as a poor pilgrim, such was his eloquence and prudence that he was chosen by the kings and the people to be Bishop of Mainz, and when he went to Rome to be consecrated archbishop by Pope Gregory the third his name was changed from Wynfrith to Boniface because of his good deeds [bona facta]. But after this blessed master was slain by the sword with fifty-two companions whilst he was preaching in Frisia, St. Gregory spent the rest of his life ministering to the young Christian community which St. Willibrord and other disciples of the Lord had baptized in Frisia and in the districts round about.

St. Lebuin, therefore, told St. Gregory what the Lord had commanded him and asked to be conducted to the spot in his diocese which the Lord had pointed out and commended to his care. After blessed Gregory had listened to him, congratulated him and welcomed this visitation from the Lord, he directed him to the place he had mentioned and gave him as a companion the servant of God, Marchelmus, who had been one of Willibrord's disciples. Then he was received into the house of a widow named Abarhilda and enjoyed her hospitality for some days.

When many had accepted his teaching, the Christians who lived there built an oratory for him near the western bank of the river Isel at a place called Wilp, and not long afterwards they built a church and a dwelling-place on the eastern bank of the same river, where the man of God remained intent on the work of God. From time to time he went into Saxony to see if he could gain souls to God, and he persuaded many to accept the faith of Christ. Among his friends and acquaintances were people of the nobility, one of whom was a rich man named Folcbert who lived in the village of Suderg.

But as it were not possible for him who bore the light of Christ to remain concealed for long, nor for the seed of Christ to grow without persecution, complaints arose among those who did not believe and they began to threaten the man of God because some of their number had abandoned the ancient worship and had turned to new ways. " Why do we not get hold of this fanatic," they said, " and give him what he deserves for gadding about the province and jabbering his incantations and sending people out of their minds?" And so they banded together in a mob, burned down his church and drove out the Christians from their midst.

In olden times the Saxons had no king but appointed rulers over each village; and their custom was to hold a general meeting once a year in the centre of Saxony near the river Yser at a place called Marklo. There all the leaders used to gather together and they were joined by twelve noblemen from each village with as many freedmen and serfs. There they confirmed the laws, gave judgment on outstanding cases and by common consent drew up plans for the coming year on which they could act either in peace or war.

Folcbert, whom we have already mentioned, had a son named Helco, who was to set out with the other youths for the meeting. One morning, whilst he was speaking to his son, he said, among other things: " I feel anxious about Wine "—for this is what he used to call Lebuin— " and I am afraid that if he meets with those who hate him they will either kill him or drag him to the meeting place and have him killed there." Whilst he was still speaking, the dogs began barking in the hall and growling at someone coming in. The young man Helco went to the door to see who it was and there he found Lebuin trying to ward off the dogs with his stick. He ran up to him and, driving the dogs away, brought him with joy to his father. After they had greeted each other and sat down, Folcbert said to the man of God: " You have just come at the right time, my dear Wine, for I was wanting to see you and have a few words with you. Where do you intend to go now? " The man of God said: " I am going to the meeting of the Saxons." Folcbert said: " You are on friendly terms with many of us, dear Wine, and what you say gives pleasure even to me. But I hear that there are many insolent young fellows who insult and threaten you. Listen to me and be on your guard against them. Do not go to the meeting, but return home to your friend Davo. For once the meeting is over you may go about with less danger and then you can come here in safety and we shall listen to your words with very great pleasure." The man of God replied: " I must not fail to be present at this meeting, for Christ himself has commanded me to make known his words to the Saxons." Folcbert said: " You will not get away." He answered: " I shall escape easily enough, for He who sent me will be my aid."

Since he could not persuade him, he sent him away.

When the day of the meeting came round, all the leaders were present, as were others whose duty it was to attend. Then, when they had gathered together, they first offered up prayers to their gods, as is their custom, asking them to protect their country and to guide them in making decrees both useful to themselves and pleasing to the gods. Then when a circle had been formed they began the discussions.

Suddenly Lebuin appeared in the middle of the circle, clothed in his priestly garments, bearing a cross in his hands and a copy of the Gospels in the crook of his arm. Raising his voice, he cried: " Listen to me, listen. I am the messenger of Almighty God and to you Saxons I bring his command." Astonished at his words and at his unusual appearance, a hush fell upon the assembly. The man of God then followed up his announcement with these words: " The God of heaven and Ruler of the world and His Son, Jesus Christ, commands me to tell you that if you are willing to be and to do what His servants tell you He will confer benefits upon you such as you have never heard of before." Then he added: " As you have never had a king over you before this time, so no king will prevail against you and subject you to his domination. But if you are unwilling to accept God's commands, a king has been prepared nearby who will invade your lands, spoil and lay them waste and sap away your strength in war; he will lead you into exile, deprive you of your inheritance, slay you with the sword, and hand over your possessions to whom he has a mind: and afterwards you will be slaves both to him and his successors."

At this they could no longer hold their tongue and cried out in a loud voice: " This is the wandering charlatan who goes about the country preaching wild, fantastic nonsense. Catch him and stone him to death." In spite of the efforts of the wiser among them to prevent it, the mob ran to the fence close by, wrenched stakes from it, pared and sharpened them and threw them, trying to transfix him. But suddenly he was no longer there. Then, all of them, both those who had been put to confusion and those who had tried to control them, condemned their action as unjust, and one of them in particular, a speaker named Buto, climbed on to the trunk of a tree and addressed them as follows: " All you who have any sense of justice, listen to what I have to say. When the Normans, Slavs and Frisians or any other people send messengers to us we receive them peacefully and listen with courtesy to what they have to say. But now, when a messenger of God comes to us, look at the insults we pour upon him! The ease with which he escaped from our hands ought to prove to you that he spoke the truth and that the threats he uttered will not be long in happening."

Moved by regret at what they had done, they decided that the messenger of God should go unharmed if he appeared again and that he should be allowed to travel wheresoever he pleased. Then, after this decision had been reached, they continued with the business they had in hand.

St. Lebuin, therefore, went about wherever the Spirit of God led him, persevering in the work of God until he gave back his soul to its Creator. He was buried after his death in the church which had formerly been burned down and rebuilt. But after his death the wicked Saxons laid waste that place and set the church on fire and for three days tried without success to find his body. At the same time Abbot Gregory also died and his diocese was taken over by his nephew Albricus, who loved Liutger[1] with a deep affection. He said to him: " Because you are now my dearest brother, I beg you to carry out my wishes. For the place in which St. Lebuin carried out his work until his death and where he is now buried has been laid waste. I want you to restore that place and to rebuild the church over his body."

---

[1] The St. Liutger mentioned in this biography was the first Bishop of Munster in Westphalia. Born at Zuilen near Utrecht about 774 (d. 26 March 809), he was sent to the school of Gregory at Utrecht and from there went to York with Alubert, who was consecrated bishop. At York Liutger studied under Alcuin and contracted a friendship with him that lasted throughout his life. It was in 775 that he was despatched to Deventer to restore the chapel destroyed by the Saxons and to find the relics of St. Lebuin, after which he spent some time teaching at the school of Utrecht. In 777 he was ordained at Cologne and put in charge of the Eastern part of Friesland, with Dokkum, the scene of St. Boniface's martyrdom, as his centre. After seven years he was driven out by the Frisians, instigated by Widukind, leader of the Saxons, and in 785 visited Rome, where he was received by Pope Adrian. For the next two years he stayed at Monte Cassino, and there, on the arrival of Charlemagne, was appointed missionary to the five districts at the mouth of the river Ems. In 793 Charlemagne wished to make him Bishop of Trier, but he declined the honour and proposed instead to evangelize the Saxons. He built a monastery in the place, later called Munster, and lived there under the Rule of St. Chrodegang of Metz, which a few years before had been imposed in all Frankish territories. Sometime between 802 and 803 he was consecrated Bishop of Munster and died on Passion Sunday 809. His body rests at Werden, the Benedictine monastery begun by him in 799 and completed in 804.

Therefore the servant of God Liutger, in obedience to the commands of his master, looked for the body of the saint in the place just mentioned but was unable to find it. He began to raise a church, however, in the part where he thought it ought to be. When he had laid the foundations and was trying to erect the walls St. Lebuin appeared to him in a dream and said: " Dearest brother Liutger, you have done well in restoring the church of God which the heathens destroyed so long ago: my body, which you were looking for, will be found buried under the south wall which you have built." On the following morning, after saying his prayers, Liutger found the body in the place described to him in the dream, and, gathering together a large band of men, he had the foundations moved to the south part of the building so that the tomb of the saint could be enclosed within the church. It is in this place that God works many miracles through his servant Lebuin even to the present day.